Praise for *Kubernetes Best Practices*, Second Edition

Written by luminaries in the cloud native space, *Kubernetes Best Practices* is a masterclass in managing container orchestration at scale. From setup to security, this book is a comprehensive resource that not only teaches but empowers. Cut your learning curve in half and build better applications faster with the proven strategies in this essential read.

—*Joseph Sandoval, Principal Product Manager, Adobe Inc.*

Just because we can do something, doesn't mean we should. Cloud native is a large topic so there are ample opportunities to go awry. These expert authors focus their deep knowledge on the key recipes to help keep your Kubernetes deliveries on the rails.

—*Jonathan Johnson, Cloud Native Architect, Presenter, Trainer*

Your roadmap to building successful applications with Kubernetes; laden with expert insights and real-world best practices.

—*Dr. Roland Huß,*
Senior Principal Software Developer, Red Hat

A trove of wisdom about container management from true mavens. Quote this book in meetings! It's not stealing ideas—they want you to read this book.

—*Jess Males, Devops Engineer, TriumphPay*

The Kubernetes ecosystem has expanded significantly over time. The specific, actionable recommendations detailed in this excellent guide make the current complexity approachable for the growing community.

—*Bridget Kromhout, Principal Product Manager, Microsoft*

Having written a book on Kubernetes and reviewed numerous others, I can attest to the uniqueness and depth of *Kubernetes Best Practices*. This book is a masterclass for those familiar with Kubernetes, designed specifically for teams operating and managing Kubernetes. It offers a systematic approach to understanding best practices, covering essential areas crucial for large-scale application deployment, from developer workflows to global application distribution, policy, governance, and the seamless integration of external services. Every page is infused with technical insights, presenting a comprehensive perspective that I haven't encountered in other Kubernetes literature. It not only serves as a blueprint for designing clusters but also provides a flexible guide, pinpointing the *what* and *why*, while allowing readers to adapt the intricate *how* to their specific organizational contexts.

—*Bilgin Ibryam, Coauthor of* Kubernetes Patterns,
Principal Product Manager, Diagrid

SECOND EDITION

Kubernetes Best Practices

*Blueprints for Building Successful
Applications on Kubernetes*

*Brendan Burns, Eddie Villalba,
Dave Strebel, and Lachlan Evenson*

Beijing · Boston · Farnham · Sebastopol · Tokyo

Kubernetes Best Practices

by Brendan Burns, Eddie Villalba, Dave Strebel, and Lachlan Evenson

Published by O'Reilly Media, Inc., 1005 Gravenstein Highway North, Sebastopol, CA 95472.

O'Reilly books may be purchased for educational, business, or sales promotional use. Online editions are also available for most titles (*http://oreilly.com*). For more information, contact our corporate/institutional sales department: 800-998-9938 or *corporate@oreilly.com*.

Acquisitions Editor: John Devins	**Indexer:** nSight, Inc.
Development Editor: Jill Leonard	**Interior Designer:** David Futato
Production Editor: Beth Kelly	**Cover Designer:** Karen Montgomery
Copyeditor: Piper Editorial Consulting, LLC	**Illustrator:** Kate Dullea
Proofreader: Piper Editorial Consulting, LLC	

November 2019:   First Edition
October 2023:   Second Edition

Revision History for the First Edition
2023-10-04:   First Release

See *https://www.oreilly.com/catalog/errata.csp?isbn=0636920805021* for release details.

978-1-098-14216-2

[LSI]

Table of Contents

Preface. xv

1. Setting Up a Basic Service. 1
   Application Overview   1
   Managing Configuration Files   2
   Creating a Replicated Service Using Deployments   3
       Best Practices for Image Management   4
       Creating a Replicated Application   4
   Setting Up an External Ingress for HTTP Traffic   6
   Configuring an Application with ConfigMaps   8
   Managing Authentication with Secrets   9
   Deploying a Simple Stateful Database   12
   Creating a TCP Load Balancer by Using Services   16
   Using Ingress to Route Traffic to a Static File Server   17
   Parameterizing Your Application by Using Helm   19
   Deploying Services Best Practices   21
   Summary   21

2. Developer Workflows. 23
   Goals   23
   Building a Development Cluster   24
   Setting Up a Shared Cluster for Multiple Developers   25
       Onboarding Users   26
       Creating and Securing a Namespace   29
       Managing Namespaces   30
       Cluster-Level Services   31
   Enabling Developer Workflows   31
       Initial Setup   32

　　　Enabling Active Development　　　　　　　　　　　　33
　　　Enabling Testing and Debugging　　　　　　　　　　　34
　　Setting Up a Development Environment Best Practices　　　34
　　Summary　　　　　　　　　　　　　　　　　　　　35

3. **Monitoring and Logging in Kubernetes**. **37**
　　Metrics Versus Logs　　　　　　　　　　　　　　　　37
　　Monitoring Techniques　　　　　　　　　　　　　　　37
　　Monitoring Patterns　　　　　　　　　　　　　　　　38
　　Kubernetes Metrics Overview　　　　　　　　　　　　39
　　　cAdvisor　　　　　　　　　　　　　　　　　　　39
　　　Metrics Server　　　　　　　　　　　　　　　　　40
　　　kube-state-metrics　　　　　　　　　　　　　　　40
　　What Metrics Do I Monitor?　　　　　　　　　　　　41
　　Monitoring Tools　　　　　　　　　　　　　　　　　42
　　Monitoring Kubernetes Using Prometheus　　　　　　44
　　Logging Overview　　　　　　　　　　　　　　　　48
　　Tools for Logging　　　　　　　　　　　　　　　　49
　　Logging by Using a Loki-Stack　　　　　　　　　　　50
　　Alerting　　　　　　　　　　　　　　　　　　　　53
　　Best Practices for Monitoring, Logging, and Alerting　　54
　　　Monitoring　　　　　　　　　　　　　　　　　　54
　　　Logging　　　　　　　　　　　　　　　　　　　55
　　　Alerting　　　　　　　　　　　　　　　　　　　55
　　Summary　　　　　　　　　　　　　　　　　　　　55

4. **Configuration, Secrets, and RBAC**. **57**
　　Configuration Through ConfigMaps and Secrets　　　　57
　　　ConfigMaps　　　　　　　　　　　　　　　　　　58
　　　Secrets　　　　　　　　　　　　　　　　　　　　58
　　Common Best Practices for the ConfigMap and Secrets APIs　59
　　Best Practices Specific to Secrets　　　　　　　　　　64
　　RBAC　　　　　　　　　　　　　　　　　　　　　65
　　　RBAC Primer　　　　　　　　　　　　　　　　　66
　　　RBAC Best Practices　　　　　　　　　　　　　　68
　　Summary　　　　　　　　　　　　　　　　　　　　69

5. **Continuous Integration, Testing, and Deployment**. **71**
　　Version Control　　　　　　　　　　　　　　　　　72
　　Continuous Integration　　　　　　　　　　　　　　72
　　Testing　　　　　　　　　　　　　　　　　　　　73
　　Container Builds　　　　　　　　　　　　　　　　73

Container Image Tagging   74
Continuous Deployment   75
Deployment Strategies   75
Testing in Production   80
Setting Up a Pipeline and Performing a Chaos Experiment   81
    Setting Up CI   81
    Setting Up CD   84
    Performing a Rolling Upgrade   84
    A Simple Chaos Experiment   85
Best Practices for CI/CD   85
Summary   86

6. Versioning, Releases, and Rollouts. 87
Versioning   88
Releases   88
Rollouts   89
Putting It All Together   90
Best Practices for Versioning, Releases, and Rollouts   93
Summary   94

7. Worldwide Application Distribution and Staging. 95
Distributing Your Image   96
Parameterizing Your Deployment   97
Load-Balancing Traffic Around the World   98
Reliably Rolling Out Software Around the World   98
    Pre-Rollout Validation   99
    Canary Region   102
    Identifying Region Types   103
    Constructing a Global Rollout   103
When Something Goes Wrong   104
Worldwide Rollout Best Practices   105
Summary   106

8. Resource Management. 107
Kubernetes Scheduler   107
    Predicates   107
    Priorities   108
Advanced Scheduling Techniques   109
    Pod Affinity and Anti-Affinity   109
    nodeSelector   110
    Taints and Tolerations   110
Pod Resource Management   112

Resource Request   112
Resource Limits and Pod Quality of Service   113
PodDisruptionBudgets   115
Managing Resources by Using Namespaces   116
ResourceQuota   117
LimitRange   119
Cluster Scaling   120
Application Scaling   121
Scaling with HPA   122
HPA with Custom Metrics   123
Vertical Pod Autoscaler   123
Resource Management Best Practices   124
Summary   124

9. Networking, Network Security, and Service Mesh. 125
Kubernetes Network Principles   125
Network Plug-ins   128
Kubenet   129
Kubenet Best Practices   129
The CNI Plug-in   129
CNI Best Practices   130
Services in Kubernetes   130
Service Type ClusterIP   131
Service Type NodePort   132
Service Type ExternalName   134
Service Type LoadBalancer   134
Ingress and Ingress Controllers   136
Gateway API   137
Services and Ingress Controllers Best Practices   139
Network Security Policy   140
Network Policy Best Practices   142
Service Meshes   143
Service Mesh Best Practices   145
Summary   145

10. Pod and Container Security. 147
Pod Security Admission Controller   147
Enabling Pod Security Admission   148
Pod Security levels   148
Activating Pod Security Using Namespace Labels   149
Workload Isolation and RuntimeClass   150
Using RuntimeClass   151

      Runtime Implementations 151
      Workload Isolation and RuntimeClass Best Practices 152
   Other Pod and Container Security Considerations 153
      Admission Controllers 153
      Intrusion and Anomaly Detection Tooling 153
   Summary 153

11. Policy and Governance for Your Cluster. 155
   Why Policy and Governance Are Important 155
   How Is This Policy Different? 155
   Cloud Native Policy Engine 156
   Introducing Gatekeeper 156
      Example Policies 157
      Gatekeeper Terminology 157
      Defining Constraint Templates 158
      Defining Constraints 159
      Data Replication 160
      UX 161
   Using Enforcement Action and Audit 161
      Mutation 163
      Testing Policies 163
      Becoming Familiar with Gatekeeper 163
   Policy and Governance Best Practices 164
   Summary 165

12. Managing Multiple Clusters. 167
   Why Multiple Clusters? 167
   Multicluster Design Concerns 169
   Managing Multiple Cluster Deployments 171
   Deployment and Management Patterns 171
   The GitOps Approach to Managing Clusters 173
   Multicluster Management Tools 175
   Kubernetes Federation 176
   Managing Multiple Clusters Best Practices 176
   Summary 177

13. Integrating External Services with Kubernetes. 179
   Importing Services into Kubernetes 179
      Selector-Less Services for Stable IP Addresses 180
      CNAME-Based Services for Stable DNS Names 181
      Active Controller-Based Approaches 182
   Exporting Services from Kubernetes 183

     Exporting Services by Using Internal Load Balancers   184
     Exporting Services on NodePorts   184
     Integrating External Machines and Kubernetes   185
  Sharing Services Between Kubernetes   186
  Third-Party Tools   187
  Connecting Cluster and External Services Best Practices   188
  Summary   188

14. Running Machine Learning in Kubernetes. **189**
  Why Is Kubernetes Great for Machine Learning?   189
  Machine Learning Workflow   190
  Machine Learning for Kubernetes Cluster Admins   191
     Model Training on Kubernetes   192
     Distributed Training on Kubernetes   195
     Resource Constraints   195
     Specialized Hardware   196
     Libraries, Drivers, and Kernel Modules   197
     Storage   197
     Networking   198
     Specialized Protocols   198
  Data Scientist Concerns   199
  Machine Learning on Kubernetes Best Practices   199
  Summary   201

15. Building Higher-Level Application Patterns on Top of Kubernetes. **203**
  Approaches to Developing Higher-Level Abstractions   203
  Extending Kubernetes   204
     Extending Kubernetes Clusters   205
     Extending the Kubernetes User Experience   206
     Making Containerized Development Easier   207
     Developing a "Push-to-Deploy" Experience   207
  Design Considerations When Building Platforms   208
     Support Exporting to a Container Image   208
     Support Existing Mechanisms for Service and Service Discovery   209
  Building Application Platforms Best Practices   209
  Summary   210

16. Managing State and Stateful Applications. **211**
  Volumes and Volume Mounts   212
  Volume Best Practices   213
  Kubernetes Storage   213
     PersistentVolume   213

PersistentVolumeClaims   214
StorageClasses   215
Kubernetes Storage Best Practices   216
Stateful Applications   217
StatefulSets   218
Operators   220
StatefulSet and Operator Best Practices   221
Summary   222

17. **Admission Control and Authorization**. **223**
Admission Control   224
What Are They?   224
Why Are They Important?   224
Admission Controller Types   225
Configuring Admission Webhooks   226
Admission Control Best Practices   228
Authorization   231
Authorization Modules   231
Authorization Best Practices   234
Summary   234

18. **GitOps and Deployment**. **235**
What Is GitOps?   236
Why GitOps?   237
GitOps Repo Structure   238
Managing Secrets   240
Setting Up Flux   241
GitOps Tooling   243
GitOps Best Practices   244
Summary   244

19. **Security**. **245**
Cluster Security   246
etcd Access   246
Authentication   246
Authorization   246
TLS   247
Kubelet and Cloud Metadata Access   247
Secrets   247
Logging and Auditing   247
Cluster Security Posture Tooling   248
Cluster Security Best Practices   248

Workload Container Security   248
    Pod Security Admission   249
    Seccomp, AppArmor, and SELinux   249
    Admission Controllers   249
    Operators   249
    Network Policy   250
    Runtime Security   250
    Workload Container Security Best Practices   251
Code Security   251
    Non-Root and Distroless Containers   251
    Container Vulnerability Scanning   252
    Code Repository Security   252
Code Security Best Practices   252
Summary   253

20. Chaos Testing, Load Testing, and Experiments. 255
Chaos Testing   255
    Goals for Chaos Testing   256
    Prerequisites for Chaos Testing   256
    Chaos Testing Your Application's Communication   257
    Chaos Testing Your Application's Operation   258
    Fuzz Testing Your Application for Security and Resiliency   259
    Summary   259
Load Testing   259
    Goals for Load Testing   259
    Prerequisites for Load Testing   260
    Generating Realistic Traffic   261
    Load Testing Your Application   262
    Tuning Your Application Using Load Tests   262
    Summary   263
Experiments   263
    Goals for Experiments   263
    Prerequisites for an Experiment   264
    Setting Up an Experiment   264
    Summary   265
Chaos Testing, Load Testing, and Experiments Summary   266

21. Implementing an Operator. 267
Operator Key Components   268
Custom Resource Definitions   268
Creating Our API   270
Controller Reconciliation   277

Resource Validation   278
Controller Implementation   279
Operator Life Cycle   284
  Version Upgrades   284
  Operator Best Practices   285
Summary   287

22. Conclusion... 289

Index.. 291

Preface

Who Should Read This Book

Kubernetes is the de facto standard for cloud native development. It is a powerful tool that can make your next application easier to develop, faster to deploy, and more reliable to operate. However, unlocking the power of Kubernetes requires using it correctly. This book is intended for anyone who is deploying real-world applications to Kubernetes and is interested in learning patterns and practices they can apply to the applications that they build on top of Kubernetes.

Importantly, this book is not an introduction to Kubernetes. We assume that you have a basic familiarity with the Kubernetes API and tools, and that you know how to create and interact with a Kubernetes cluster. If you are looking to learn Kubernetes, there are numerous great resources out there, such as *Kubernetes: Up and Running* (O'Reilly), that can give you an introduction.

Instead, this book is a resource for anyone who wants to dive deep on how to deploy specific applications and workloads on Kubernetes. It should be useful to you whether you are about to deploy your first application onto Kubernetes or you've been using Kubernetes for years.

Why We Wrote This Book

Between the four of us, we have significant experience helping a wide variety of users deploy their applications onto Kubernetes. Through this experience, we have seen where people struggle, and we have helped them find their way to success. When sitting down to write this book, we attempted to capture these experiences so that many more people could learn by reading the lessons that we learned from these real-world experiences. It's our hope that by committing our experiences to writing, we can scale our knowledge and allow you to be successful deploying and managing your application on Kubernetes on your own.

Navigating This Book

Although you might read this book from cover to cover in a single sitting, that is not really how we intended you to use it. Instead, we designed this book to be a collection of standalone chapters. Each chapter gives a complete overview of a particular task that you might need to accomplish with Kubernetes. We expect people to dive into the book to learn about a specific topic or interest, and then leave the book alone, only to return when a new topic comes up.

Despite this standalone approach, some themes span the book. There are several chapters on developing applications on Kubernetes. Chapter 2 covers developer workflows. Chapter 5 discusses continuous integration and testing. Chapter 15 covers building higher-level platforms on top of Kubernetes, and Chapter 16 discusses managing state and stateful applications. In addition to developing applications, there are several chapters on operating services in Kubernetes. Chapter 1 covers the setup of a basic service, and Chapter 3 covers monitoring and metrics. Chapter 4 covers configuration management, while Chapter 6 covers versioning and releases. Chapter 7 covers deploying your application around the world.

There are also several chapters on cluster management, including Chapter 8 on resource management, Chapter 9 on networking, Chapter 10 on pod security, Chapter 11 on policy and governance, Chapter 12 on managing multiple clusters, and Chapter 17 on admission control and authorization. Finally, some chapters are truly independent; these cover machine learning (Chapter 14) and integrating with external services (Chapter 13).

Though it can be useful to read all the chapters before you actually attempt the topic in the real world, our primary hope is that you will treat this book as a reference. It is intended as a guide as you put these topics to practice in the real world.

New to This Edition

We wanted to complement the 1st edition with four new chapters that cover emerging tools and patterns as Kubernetes continues to mature and provide best practices. These new chapters are Chapter 18 on GitOps, Chapter 19 on security, Chapter 20 on chaos testing, and Chapter 21 on implementing an operator.

Conventions Used in This Book

The following typographical conventions are used in this book:

Italic
    Indicates new terms, URLs, email addresses, filenames, and file extensions.

`Constant width`

> Used for program listings, as well as within paragraphs to refer to program elements such as variable or function names, databases, data types, environment variables, statements, and keywords.

`Constant width bold`

> Shows commands or other text that should be typed literally by the user.

`Constant width italic`

> Shows text that should be replaced with user-supplied values or by values determined by context.

 This element signifies a tip or suggestion.

 This element signifies a general note.

 This element indicates a warning or caution.

Using Code Examples

Supplemental material (code examples, exercises, etc.) is available for download at *https://oreil.ly/KBPsample*.

If you have a technical question or a problem using the code examples, please send email to *bookquestions@oreilly.com*.

This book is here to help you get your job done. In general, if example code is offered with this book, you may use it in your programs and documentation. You do not need to contact us for permission unless you're reproducing a significant portion of the code. For example, writing a program that uses several chunks of code from this book does not require permission. Selling or distributing examples from O'Reilly books does require permission. Answering a question by citing this book and quoting example code does not require permission. Incorporating a significant amount of example code from this book into your product's documentation does require permission.

We appreciate, but generally do not require, attribution. An attribution usually includes the title, author, publisher, and ISBN. For example: "*Kubernetes Best Practices* by Brendan Burns, Eddie Villalba, Dave Strebel, and Lachlan Evenson (O'Reilly). Copyright 2024 Brendan Burns, Eddie Villalba, Dave Strebel, and Lachlan Evenson, 978-1-098-14216-2."

If you feel your use of code examples falls outside fair use or the permission given above, feel free to contact us at *permissions@oreilly.com*.

O'Reilly Online Learning

 For more than 40 years, *O'Reilly Media* has provided technology and business training, knowledge, and insight to help companies succeed.

Our unique network of experts and innovators share their knowledge and expertise through books, articles, conferences, and our online learning platform. O'Reilly's online learning platform gives you on-demand access to live training courses, in-depth learning paths, interactive coding environments, and a vast collection of text and video from O'Reilly and 200+ other publishers. For more information, please visit *http://oreilly.com*.

How to Contact Us

Please address comments and questions concerning this book to the publisher:

O'Reilly Media, Inc.
1005 Gravenstein Highway North
Sebastopol, CA 95472
800-889-8969 (in the United States or Canada)
707-829-7019 (international or local)
707-829-0104 (fax)
support@oreilly.com
https://www.oreilly.com/about/contact.html

We have a web page for this book, where we list errata, examples, and any additional information. You can access this page at *https://oreil.ly/kubernetes-best-practices2*.

For news and information about our books and courses, visit *https://oreilly.com*.

Find us on LinkedIn: *https://linkedin.com/company/oreilly-media*

Follow us on Twitter: *https://twitter.com/oreillymedia*

Watch us on YouTube: *https://youtube.com/oreillymedia*

Acknowledgments

Brendan would like to thank his wonderful family, Robin, Julia, and Ethan, for the love and support of everything he does; the Kubernetes community, without whom none of this would be possible; and his fabulous coauthors, without whom this book would not exist.

Dave would like to thank his beautiful wife, Jen, and their three children, Max, Maddie, and Mason, for all their support. He would also like to thank the Kubernetes community for all the advice and help they have provided over the years. Finally, he would like to thank his coauthors in making this adventure a reality.

Lachlan would like to thank his wife and three children for their love and support. He would also like to thank everyone in the Kubernetes community, including the wonderful individuals who have taken the time to teach him over the years. He also would like to send a special thanks to Joseph Sandoval for his mentorship. And, finally, he would like to thank his fantastic coauthors for making this book possible.

Eddie would like to thank his wife, Sandra, for her undying support, love, and encouragement through the writing process. He would also like to thank his daughter, Giavanna, for giving him the motivation to leave a legacy so she can be proud of her daddy. Finally, he would like to thank the Kubernetes community and his coauthors who have always been guideposts in his journey to be cloud native.

We all would like to thank Virginia Wilson for her work in developing the manuscript and helping us bring all our ideas together, and Jill Leonard for her guidance on the 2nd edition. Finally, we'd like to thank Bridget Kromhout, Bilgin Ibryam, Roland Huß, Justin Domingus, Jess Males, and Jonathan Johnson for their attention to the finishing touches.

## CHAPTER 1

Setting Up a Basic Service

This chapter describes the procedure for setting up a simple multitier application in Kubernetes. The example we'll walk through consists of two tiers: a simple web application and a database. Though this might not be the most complicated application, it is a good place to start when learning to manage an application in Kubernetes.

Application Overview

The application that we will use for our example is fairly straightforward. It's a simple journal service with the following details:

- It has a separate static file server using NGINX.
- It has a RESTful application programming interface (API) https://some-host-name.io/api on the */api* path.
- It has a file server on the main URL, https://some-host-name.io.
- It uses the Let's Encrypt service (*https://oreil.ly/7XN3G*) for managing Secure Sockets Layer (SSL).

Figure 1-1 presents a diagram of this application. Don't be worried if you don't understand all the pieces right away; they will be explained in greater detail throughout the chapter. We'll walk through building this application step by step, first using YAML configuration files and then Helm charts.

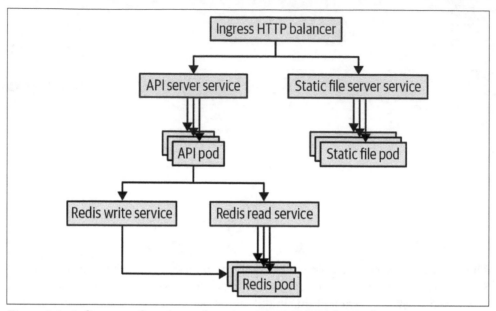

Figure 1-1. A diagram of our journal service as it is deployed in Kubernetes

Managing Configuration Files

Before we get into the details of how to construct this application in Kubernetes, it is worth discussing how we manage the configurations themselves. With Kubernetes, everything is represented *declaratively*. This means that you write down the desired state of the application in the cluster (generally in YAML or JSON files), and these declared desired states define all the pieces of your application. This declarative approach is far preferable to an *imperative* approach in which the state of your cluster is the sum of a series of changes to the cluster. If a cluster is configured imperatively, it is difficult to understand and replicate how the cluster came to be in that state, making it challenging to understand or recover from problems with your application.

When declaring the state of your application, people typically prefer YAML to JSON, though Kubernetes supports them both. This is because YAML is somewhat less verbose and more human editable than JSON. However, it's worth noting that YAML is indentation sensitive; often errors in Kubernetes configurations can be traced to incorrect indentation in YAML. If things aren't behaving as expected, checking your indentation is a good place to start troubleshooting. Most editors have syntax highlighting support for both JSON and YAML. When working with these files it is a good idea to install such tools to make it easier to find both author and file errors in your configurations. There is also an excellent extension for Visual Studio Code that supports richer error checking for Kubernetes files.

Because the declarative state contained in these YAML files serves as the source of truth for your application, correct management of this state is critical to the success of your application. When modifying your application's desired state, you will want to be able to manage changes, validate that they are correct, audit who made changes, and possibly roll things back if they fail. Fortunately, in the context of software engineering, we have already developed the tools necessary to manage both changes to the declarative state as well as audit and rollback. Namely, the best practices around both version control and code review directly apply to the task of managing the declarative state of your application.

These days most people store their Kubernetes configurations in Git. Though the specific details of the version control system are unimportant, many tools in the Kubernetes ecosystem expect files in a Git repository. For code review there is much more heterogeneity; though clearly GitHub is quite popular, others use on-premises code review tools or services. Regardless of how you implement code review for your application configuration, you should treat it with the same diligence and focus that you apply to source control.

When it comes to laying out the filesystem for your application, it's worthwhile to use the directory organization that comes with the filesystem to organize your components. Typically, a single directory is used to encompass an *Application Service*. The definition of what constitutes an Application Service can vary in size from team to team, but generally, it is a service developed by a team of 8–12 people. Within that directory, subdirectories are used for subcomponents of the application.

For our application, we lay out the files as follows:

```
journal/
  frontend/
  redis/
  fileserver/
```

Within each directory are the concrete YAML files needed to define the service. As you'll see later on, as we begin to deploy our application to multiple different regions or clusters, this file layout will become more complicated.

Creating a Replicated Service Using Deployments

To describe our application, we'll begin at the frontend and work downward. The frontend application for the journal is a Node.js application implemented in Type-Script. The complete application (*https://oreil.ly/70kFT*) is too large to include in the book, so we've hosted it on our GitHub. You'll be able to find code for future examples there, too, so it's worth bookmarking. The application exposes an HTTP service on port 8080 that serves requests to the */api/** path and uses the Redis backend to add, delete, or return the current journal entries. If you plan to work through the YAML examples that follow on your local machine, you'll want to build this application into a container image using the Dockerfile and push it to your own image repository. Then, rather than using our example file name, you'll want to include your container image name in your code.

Best Practices for Image Management

Though in general, building and maintaining container images is beyond the scope of this book, it's worthwhile to identify some general best practices for building and naming images. In general, the image build process can be vulnerable to "supply-chain attacks." In such attacks, a malicious user injects code or binaries into some dependency from a trusted source that is then built into your application. Because of the risk of such attacks, it is critical that when you build your images you base them on only well-known and trusted image providers. Alternatively, you can build all your images from scratch. Building from scratch is easy for some languages (e.g., Go) that can build static binaries, but it is significantly more complicated for interpreted languages like Python, JavaScript, or Ruby.

The other best practices for images relate to naming. Though the version of a container image in an image registry is theoretically mutable, you should treat the version tag as immutable. In particular, some combination of the semantic version and the SHA hash of the commit where the image was built is a good practice for naming images (e.g., *v1.0.1-bfeda01f*). If you don't specify an image version, `latest` is used by default. Although this can be convenient in development, it is a bad idea for production usage because `latest` is clearly being mutated every time a new image is built.

Creating a Replicated Application

Our frontend application is *stateless*; it relies entirely on the Redis backend for its state. As a result, we can replicate it arbitrarily without affecting traffic. Though our application is unlikely to sustain large-scale usage, it's still a good idea to run with at least two replicas so that you can handle an unexpected crash or roll out a new version of the application without downtime.

In Kubernetes, the ReplicaSet resource is the one that directly manages replicating a specific version of your containerized application. Since the version of all applications changes over time as you modify the code, it is not a best practice to use a ReplicaSet directly. Instead, you use the Deployment resource. A Deployment combines the replication capabilities of ReplicaSet with versioning and the ability to perform a staged rollout. By using a Deployment you can use Kubernetes' built-in tooling to move from one version of the application to the next.

The Kubernetes Deployment resource for our application looks as follows:

```
apiVersion: apps/v1
kind: Deployment
metadata:
  labels:
    # All pods in the Deployment will have this label
    app: frontend
  name: frontend
  namespace: default
spec:
  # We should always have at least two replicas for reliability
  replicas: 2
  selector:
    matchLabels:
      app: frontend
  template:
    metadata:
      labels:
        app: frontend
    spec:
      containers:
      - image: my-repo/journal-server:v1-abcde
        imagePullPolicy: IfNotPresent
        name: frontend
        # TODO: Figure out what the actual resource needs are
        resources:
          request:
            cpu: "1.0"
            memory: "1G"
          limits:
            cpu: "1.0"
            memory: "1G"
```

There are several things to note in this Deployment. First is that we are using Labels to identify the Deployment as well as the ReplicaSets and the pods that the Deployment creates. We've added the `app: frontend` label to all these resources so that we can examine all resources for a particular layer in a single request. You'll see that as we add other resources, we'll follow the same practice.

Additionally, we've added comments in a number of places in the YAML. Although these comments don't make it into the Kubernetes resource stored on the server, just like comments in code, they serve to guide people who are looking at this configuration for the first time.

You should also note that for the containers in the Deployment we have specified both Request and Limit resource requests, and we've set Request equal to Limit. When running an application, the Request is the reservation that is guaranteed on the host machine where it runs. The Limit is the maximum resource usage that the container will be allowed. When you are starting out, setting Request equal to Limit will lead to the most predictable behavior of your application. This predictability comes at the expense of resource utilization. Because setting Request equal to Limit prevents your applications from overscheduling or consuming excess idle resources, you will not be able to drive maximal utilization unless you tune Request and Limit very, very carefully. As you become more advanced in your understanding of the Kubernetes resource model, you might consider modifying Request and Limit for your application independently, but in general most users find that the stability from predictability is worth the reduced utilization.

Often times, as our comment suggests, it is difficult to know the right values for these resource limits. Starting by overestimating the estimates and then using monitoring to tune to the right values is a pretty good approach. However, if you are launching a new service, remember that the first time you see large-scale traffic, your resource needs will likely increase significantly. Additionally, there are some languages, especially garbage-collected languages, that will happily consume all available memory, which can make it difficult to determine the correct minimum for memory. In this case, some form of binary search may be necessary, but remember to do this in a test environment so that it doesn't affect your production!

Now that we have the Deployment resource defined, we'll check it into version control, and deploy it to Kubernetes:

```
git add frontend/deployment.yaml
git commit -m "Added deployment" frontend/deployment.yaml
kubectl apply -f frontend/deployment.yaml
```

It is also a best practice to ensure that the contents of your cluster exactly match the contents of your source control. The best pattern to ensure this is to adopt a GitOps approach and deploy to production only from a specific branch of your source control, using continuous integration/continuous delivery (CI/CD) automation. In this way you're guaranteed that source control and production match. Though a full CI/CD pipeline might seem excessive for a simple application, the automation by itself, independent of the reliability it provides, is usually worth the time taken to set it up. And CI/CD is extremely difficult to retrofit into an existing, imperatively deployed application.

We'll come back to this application description YAML in later sections to examine additional elements such as the ConfigMap and secret volumes as well as pod Quality of Service.

Setting Up an External Ingress for HTTP Traffic

The containers for our application are now deployed, but it's not currently possible for anyone to access the application. By default, cluster resources are available only within the cluster itself. To expose our application to the world, we need to create a service and load balancer to provide an external IP address and to bring traffic to our containers. For the external exposure we are going to use two Kubernetes resources.

The first is a service that load-balances Transmission Control Protocol (TCP) or User Datagram Protocol (UDP) traffic. In our case, we're using the TCP protocol. And the second is an Ingress resource, which provides HTTP(S) load balancing with intelligent routing of requests based on HTTP paths and hosts. With a simple application like this, you might wonder why we choose to use the more complex Ingress, but as you'll see in later sections, even this simple application will be serving HTTP requests from two different services. Furthermore, having an Ingress at the edge enables flexibility for future expansion of our service.

 The Ingress resource is one of the older resources in Kubernetes, and over the years numerous issues have been raised with the way that it models HTTP access to microservices. This has led to the development of the Gateway API for Kubernetes. The Gateway API has been designed as an extension to Kubernetes and requires additional components to be installed in your cluster. If you find that Ingress doesn't meet your needs, consider moving to the Gateway API.

Before the Ingress resource can be defined, there needs to be a Kubernetes Service for the Ingress to point to. We'll use Labels to direct the Service to the pods that we created in the previous section. The Service is significantly simpler to define than the Deployment and looks as follows:

```
apiVersion: v1
kind: Service
metadata:
  labels:
    app: frontend
  name: frontend
  namespace: default
spec:
  ports:
  - port: 8080
    protocol: TCP
    targetPort: 8080
  selector:
    app: frontend
  type: ClusterIP
```

After you've defined the Service, you can define an Ingress resource. Unlike Service resources, Ingress requires an Ingress controller container to be running in the cluster. There are a number of different implementations you can choose from, either offered by your cloud provider, or implemented using open source servers. If you choose to install an open source Ingress provider, it's a good idea to use the Helm package manager (*https://helm.sh*) to install and maintain it. The nginx or haproxy Ingress providers are popular choices:

```
apiVersion: networking.k8s.io/v1
kind: Ingress
metadata:
  name: frontend-ingress
spec:
  rules:
  - http:
      paths:
      - path: /testpath
        pathType: Prefix
        backend:
          service:
            name: test
            port:
              number: 8080
```

With our Ingress resource created, our application is ready to serve traffic from web browsers around the world. Next, we'll look at how you can set up your application for easy configuration and customization.

Configuring an Application with ConfigMaps

Every application needs a degree of configuration. This could be the number of journal entries to display per page, the color of a particular background, a special holiday display, or many other types of configuration. Typically, separating such configuration information from the application itself is a best practice to follow.

There are several reasons for this separation. The first is that you might want to configure the same application binary with different configurations depending on the setting. In Europe you might want to light up an Easter special, whereas in China you might want to display a special for Chinese New Year. In addition to this environmental specialization, there are agility reasons for the separation. Usually a binary release contains multiple different new features; if you turn on these features via code, the only way to modify the active features is to build and release a new binary, which can be an expensive and slow process.

The use of configuration to activate a set of features means that you can quickly (and even dynamically) activate and deactivate features in response to user needs or application code failures. Features can be rolled out and rolled back on a per-feature basis. This flexibility ensures that you are continually making forward progress with most features even if some need to be rolled back to address performance or correctness problems.

In Kubernetes this sort of configuration is represented by a resource called a ConfigMap. A ConfigMap contains multiple key/value pairs representing configuration information or a file. This configuration information can be presented to a container in a pod via either files or environment variables. Imagine that you want to configure your online journal application to display a configurable number of journal entries per page. To achieve this, you can define a ConfigMap as follows:

```
kubectl create configmap frontend-config --from-literal=journalEntries=10
```

To configure your application, you expose the configuration information as an environment variable in the application itself. To do that, you can add the following to the `container` resource in the Deployment that you defined earlier:

```
...
# The containers array in the PodTemplate inside the Deployment
containers:
  - name: frontend
    ...
    env:
    - name: JOURNAL_ENTRIES
      valueFrom:
        configMapKeyRef:
          name: frontend-config
          key: journalEntries
  ...
```

Although this demonstrates how you can use a ConfigMap to configure your application, in the real world of Deployments, you'll want to roll out regular changes to this configuration at least weekly. It might be tempting to roll this out by simply changing the ConfigMap itself, but this isn't really a best practice, for reasons: the first is that changing the configuration doesn't actually trigger an update to existing pods. The configuration is applied only when the pod is restarted. As a result, the rollout isn't health based and can be ad hoc or random. Another reason is that the only versioning for the ConfigMap is in your version control, and it can be very difficult to perform a rollback.

A better approach is to put a version number in the name of the ConfigMap itself. Instead of calling it `frontend-config`, call it `frontend-config-v1`. When you want to make a change, instead of updating the ConfigMap in place, you create a new v2 ConfigMap, and then update the Deployment resource to use that configuration. When you do this, a Deployment rollout is automatically triggered, using the appropriate health checking and pauses between changes. Furthermore, if you ever need to roll back, the v1 configuration is sitting in the cluster and rollback is as simple as updating the Deployment again.

Managing Authentication with Secrets

So far, we haven't really discussed the Redis service to which our frontend is connecting. But in any real application we need to secure connections between our services. In part, this is to ensure the security of users and their data, and in addition, it is essential to prevent mistakes like connecting a development frontend with a production database.

The Redis database is authenticated using a simple password. It might be convenient to think that you would store this password in the source code of your application, or in a file in your image, but these are both bad ideas for a variety of reasons. The first is that you have leaked your secret (the password) into an environment where you aren't necessarily thinking about access control. If you put a password into your source control, you are aligning access to your source with access to all secrets. This isn't the best course of action because you will probably have a broader set of users who can access your source code than should really have access to your Redis instance. Likewise, someone who has access to your container image shouldn't necessarily have access to your production database.

In addition to concerns about access control, another reason to avoid binding secrets to source control and/or images is parameterization. You want to be able to use the same source code and images in a variety of environments (e.g., development, canary, and production). If the secrets are tightly bound in source code or an image, you need a different image (or different code) for each environment.

Having seen ConfigMaps in the previous section, you might immediately think that the password could be stored as a configuration and then populated into the application as an application-specific configuration. You're absolutely correct to believe that the separation of configuration from application is the same as the separation of secrets from application. But the truth is that a secret is an important concept by itself. You likely want to handle access control, handling, and updates of secrets in a different way than a configuration. More important, you want your developers *thinking* differently when they are accessing secrets than when they are accessing configuration. For these reasons, Kubernetes has a built-in Secret resource for managing secret data.

You can create a secret password for your Redis database as follows:

```
kubectl create secret generic redis-passwd --from-literal=passwd=${RANDOM}
```

Obviously, you might want to use something other than a random number for your password. Additionally, you likely want to use a secret/key management service, either via your cloud provider, like Microsoft Azure Key Vault, or an open source project, like HashiCorp's Vault. When you are using a key management service, they generally have tighter integration with Kubernetes secrets.

After you have stored the Redis password as a secret in Kubernetes, you then need to *bind* that secret to the running application when deployed to Kubernetes. To do this, you can use a Kubernetes Volume. A Volume is effectively a file or directory that can be mounted into a running container at a user-specified location. In the case of secrets, the Volume is created as a tmpfs RAM-backed filesystem and then mounted into the container. This ensures that even if the machine is physically compromised (quite unlikely in the cloud, but possible in the datacenter), the secrets are much more difficult for an attacker to obtain.

 Secrets in Kubernetes are stored unencrypted by default. If you want to store secrets encrypted, you can integrate with a key provider to give you a key that Kubernetes will use to encrypt all the secrets in the cluster. Note that although this secures the keys against direct attacks to the etcd database, you still need to ensure that access via the Kubernetes API server is properly secured.

To add a secret Volume to a Deployment, you need to specify two new entries in the YAML for the Deployment. The first is a volume entry for the pod that adds the Volume to the pod:

```
...
  volumes:
  - name: passwd-volume
    secret:
      secretName: redis-passwd
```

Container Storage Interface (CSI) drivers enable you to use key management systems (KMS) that are located outside of your Kubernetes cluster. This is often a requirement for compliance and security within large or regulated organizations. If you use one of these CSI drivers your Volume would instead look like:

```
...
  volumes:
  - name: passwd-volume
    csi:
      driver: secrets-store.csi.k8s.io
      readOnly: true
      volumeAttributes:
        secretProviderClass: "azure-sync"
  ...
```

Regardless of which method you use, with the Volume defined in the pod, you need to mount it into a specific container. You do this via the volumeMounts field in the container description:

```
...
  volumeMounts:
  - name: passwd-volume
    readOnly: true
    mountPath: "/etc/redis-passwd"
  ...
```

This mounts the secret Volume into the redis-passwd directory for access from the client code. Putting this all together, you have the complete Deployment as follows:

```
apiVersion: apps/v1
kind: Deployment
metadata:
  labels:
    app: frontend
  name: frontend
  namespace: default
spec:
  replicas: 2
  selector:
    matchLabels:
      app: frontend
  template:
    metadata:
      labels:
        app: frontend
    spec:
      containers:
      - image: my-repo/journal-server:v1-abcde
        imagePullPolicy: IfNotPresent
        name: frontend
        volumeMounts:
        - name: passwd-volume
          readOnly: true
          mountPath: "/etc/redis-passwd"
        resources:
          requests:
            cpu: "1.0"
            memory: "1G"
          limits:
            cpu: "1.0"
            memory: "1G"
      volumes:
      - name: passwd-volume
        secret:
          secretName: redis-passwd
```

At this point we have configured the client application to have a secret available to authenticate to the Redis service. Configuring Redis to use this password is similar; we mount it into the Redis pod and load the password from the file.

Deploying a Simple Stateful Database

Although conceptually deploying a stateful application is similar to deploying a client like our frontend, state brings with it more complications. The first is that in Kubernetes a pod can be rescheduled for a number of reasons, such as node health, an upgrade, or rebalancing. When this happens, the pod might move to a different machine. If the data associated with the Redis instance is located on any particular machine or within the container itself, that data will be lost when the container migrates or restarts. To prevent this, when running stateful workloads in Kubernetes it's important to use remote *PersistentVolume*s to manage the state associated with the application.

There are a wide variety of implementations of PersistentVolumes in Kubernetes, but they all share common characteristics. Like secret Volumes described earlier, they are associated with a pod and mounted into a container at a particular location. Unlike secrets, PersistentVolumes are generally remote storage mounted through some sort of network protocol, either file based, such as Network File System (NFS) or Server Message Block (SMB), or block based (iSCSI, cloud-based disks, etc.). Generally, for applications such as databases, block-based disks are preferable because they offer better performance, but if performance is less of a consideration, file-based disks sometimes offer greater flexibility.

 Managing state in general is complicated, and Kubernetes is no exception. If you are running in an environment that supports stateful services (e.g., MySQL as a service, Redis as a service), it is generally a good idea to use those stateful services. Initially, the cost premium of a stateful software as a service (SaaS) might seem expensive, but when you factor in all the operational requirements of state (backup, data locality, redundancy, etc.), and the fact that the presence of state in a Kubernetes cluster makes it difficult to move applications between clusters, it becomes clear that, in most cases, storage SaaS is worth the price premium. In on-premises environments where storage SaaS isn't available, having a dedicated team provide storage as a service to the entire organization is definitely a better practice than allowing each team to build it themselves.

To deploy our Redis service, we use a StatefulSet resource. Added after the initial Kubernetes release as a complement to ReplicaSet resources, a StatefulSet gives slightly stronger guarantees such as consistent names (no random hashes!) and a defined order for scale-up and scale-down. When you are deploying a singleton, this is somewhat less important, but when you want to deploy replicated state, these attributes are very convenient.

To obtain a PersistentVolume for our Redis, we use a PersistentVolumeClaim. You can think of a claim as a "request for resources." Our Redis declares abstractly that it wants 50 GB of storage, and the Kubernetes cluster determines how to provision an appropriate PersistentVolume. There are two reasons for this. The first is so we can write a StatefulSet that is portable between different clouds and on premises, where the details of disks might be different. The other reason is that although many PersistentVolume types can be mounted to only a single pod, we can use Volume claims to write a template that can be replicated and still have each pod assigned its own specific PersistentVolume.

The following example shows a Redis StatefulSet with PersistentVolumes:

```yaml
apiVersion: apps/v1
kind: StatefulSet
metadata:
  name: redis
spec:
  serviceName: "redis"
  replicas: 1
  selector:
    matchLabels:
      app: redis
  template:
    metadata:
      labels:
        app: redis
    spec:
      containers:
      - name: redis
        image: redis:5-alpine
        ports:
        - containerPort: 6379
          name: redis
        volumeMounts:
        - name: data
          mountPath: /data
  volumeClaimTemplates:
  - metadata:
      name: data
    spec:
      accessModes: [ "ReadWriteOnce" ]
      resources:
        requests:
          storage: 10Gi
```

This deploys a single instance of your Redis service, but suppose you want to replicate the Redis cluster for scale-out of reads and resiliency to failures. To do this you obviously need to increase the number of replicas to three, but you also need to ensure that the two new replicas connect to the write master for Redis. We'll see how to make this connection in the following section.

When you create the headless Service for the Redis StatefulSet, it creates a DNS entry redis-0.redis; this is the IP address of the first replica. You can use this to create a simple script that can launch in all the containers:

```sh
#!/bin/sh

PASSWORD=$(cat /etc/redis-passwd/passwd)

if [[ "${HOSTNAME}" == "redis-0" ]]; then
  redis-server --requirepass ${PASSWORD}
else
```

```
    redis-server --slaveof redis-0.redis 6379 --masterauth ${PASSWORD}
      --requirepass ${PASSWORD}
  fi
```

You can create this script as a ConfigMap:

```
kubectl create configmap redis-config --from-file=./launch.sh
```

You then add this ConfigMap to your StatefulSet and use it as the command for the container. Let's also add in the password for authentication that we created earlier in the chapter.

The complete three-replica Redis looks as follows:

```
apiVersion: apps/v1
kind: StatefulSet
metadata:
  name: redis
spec:
  serviceName: "redis"
  replicas: 3
  selector:
    matchLabels:
      app: redis
  template:
    metadata:
      labels:
        app: redis
    spec:
      containers:
      - name: redis
        image: redis:5-alpine
        ports:
        - containerPort: 6379
          name: redis
        volumeMounts:
        - name: data
          mountPath: /data
        - name: script
          mountPath: /script/launch.sh
          subPath: launch.sh
        - name: passwd-volume
          mountPath: /etc/redis-passwd
        command:
        - sh
        - -c
        - /script/launch.sh
      volumes:
      - name: script
        configMap:
          name: redis-config
          defaultMode: 0777
      - name: passwd-volume
```

```
      secret:
        secretName: redis-passwd
volumeClaimTemplates:
- metadata:
    name: data
  spec:
    accessModes: [ "ReadWriteOnce" ]
    resources:
      requests:
        storage: 10Gi
```

Now your Redis is clustered for fault tolerance. If any one of the three Redis replicas fails for any reason, your application can keep running with the two remaining replicas until the third replica is restored.

Creating a TCP Load Balancer by Using Services

Now that we've deployed the stateful Redis service, we need to make it available to our frontend. To do this, we create two different Kubernetes Services. The first is the Service for reading data from Redis. Because Redis is replicating the data to all three members of the StatefulSet, we don't care which read our request goes to. Consequently, we use a basic Service for the reads:

```
apiVersion: v1
kind: Service
metadata:
  labels:
    app: redis
  name: redis
  namespace: default
spec:
  ports:
  - port: 6379
    protocol: TCP
    targetPort: 6379
  selector:
    app: redis
  sessionAffinity: None
  type: ClusterIP
```

To enable writes, you need to target the Redis master (replica #0). To do this, create a *headless* Service. A headless Service doesn't have a cluster IP address; instead, it programs a DNS entry for every pod in the StatefulSet. This means that we can access our master via the redis-0.redis DNS name:

```
apiVersion: v1
kind: Service
metadata:
  labels:
    app: redis-write
```

```
      name: redis-write
spec:
  clusterIP: None
  ports:
  - port: 6379
  selector:
    app: redis
```

Thus, when we want to connect to Redis for writes or transactional read/write pairs, we can build a separate write client connected to the `redis-0.redis-write` server.

Using Ingress to Route Traffic to a Static File Server

The final component in our application is a *static file server*. The static file server is responsible for serving HTML, CSS, JavaScript, and image files. It's both more efficient and more focused for us to separate static file serving from our API serving frontend described earlier. We can easily use a high-performance static off-the-shelf file server like NGINX to serve files while we allow our development teams to focus on the code needed to implement our API.

Fortunately, the Ingress resource makes this sort of mini-microservice architecture very easy. Just like the frontend, we can use a Deployment resource to describe a replicated NGINX server. Let's build the static images into the NGINX container and deploy them to each replica. The Deployment resource looks as follows:

```
apiVersion: apps/v1
kind: Deployment
metadata:
  labels:
    app: fileserver
  name: fileserver
  namespace: default
spec:
  replicas: 2
  selector:
    matchLabels:
      app: fileserver
  template:
    metadata:
      labels:
        app: fileserver
    spec:
      containers:
      # This image is intended as an example, replace it with your own
      # static files image.
      - image: my-repo/static-files:v1-abcde
        imagePullPolicy: Always
        name: fileserver
        terminationMessagePath: /dev/termination-log
        terminationMessagePolicy: File
```

```
        resources:
          requests:
            cpu: "1.0"
            memory: "1G"
          limits:
            cpu: "1.0"
            memory: "1G"
      dnsPolicy: ClusterFirst
      restartPolicy: Always
```

Now that there is a replicated static web server up and running, you will likewise create a Service resource to act as a load balancer:

```
apiVersion: v1
kind: Service
metadata:
  labels:
    app: fileserver
  name: fileserver
  namespace: default
spec:
  ports:
  - port: 80
    protocol: TCP
    targetPort: 80
  selector:
    app: fileserver
  sessionAffinity: None
  type: ClusterIP
```

Now that you have a Service for your static file server, extend the Ingress resource to contain the new path. It's important to note that you must place the / path *after* the /api path, or else it would subsume /api and direct API requests to the static file server. The new Ingress looks like this:

```
apiVersion: networking.k8s.io/v1
kind: Ingress
metadata:
  name: frontend-ingress
spec:
  rules:
  - http:
      paths:
      - path: /api
        pathType: Prefix
        backend:
          service:
            name: fileserver
            port:
              number: 8080
      # NOTE: this should come after /api or else it will hijack requests
      - path: /
```

```
          pathType: Prefix
          backend:
            service:
              name: fileserver
              port:
                number: 80
```

Now that you have set up an Ingress resource for your file server, in addition to the Ingress for the API you set up earlier, the application's user interface is ready to use. Most modern applications combine static files, typically HTML and JavaScript, with a dynamic API server implemented in a server-side programming language like Java, .NET, or Go.

Parameterizing Your Application by Using Helm

Everything that we have discussed so far focuses on deploying a single instance of our service to a single cluster. However, in reality, nearly every service and every service team is going to need to deploy to multiple environments (even if they share a cluster). Even if you are a single developer working on a single application, you likely want to have at least a development version and a production version of your application so that you can iterate and develop without breaking production users. After you factor in integration testing and CI/CD, it's likely that even with a single service and a handful of developers, you'll want to deploy to at least three different environments, and possibly more if you consider handling datacenter-level failures. Let's explore a few options for deployment.

An initial failure mode for many teams is to simply copy the files from one cluster to another. Instead of having a single *frontend/* directory, have a *frontend-production/* and *frontend-development/* pair of directories. While this is a viable option, it's also dangerous because you are now in charge of ensuring that these files remain synchronized with one another. If they were intended to be entirely identical, this might be easy, but some skew between development and production is expected because you will be developing new features. It's critical that the skew is both intentional and easily managed.

Another option to achieve this would be to use branches and version control, with the production and development branches leading off from a central repository and the differences between the branches clearly visible. This can be a viable option for some teams, but the mechanics of moving between branches are challenging when you want to simultaneously deploy software to different environments (e.g., a CI/CD system that deploys to a number of different cloud regions).

Consequently, most people end up with a *templating system*. A templating system combines templates, which form the centralized backbone of the application configuration, with parameters that *specialize* the template to a specific environment configuration. In this way, you can have a generally shared configuration, with intentional (and easily understood) customization as needed. There are a variety of template systems for Kubernetes, but the most popular by far is Helm (*https://helm.sh*).

In Helm, an application is packaged in a collection of files called a *chart* (nautical jokes abound in the world of containers and Kubernetes).

A chart begins with a *chart.yaml* file, which defines the metadata for the chart itself:

```
apiVersion: v1
appVersion: "1.0"
description: A Helm chart for our frontend journal server.
name: frontend
version: 0.1.0
```

This file is placed in the root of the chart directory (e.g., *frontend/*). Within this directory, there is a *templates* directory, which is where the templates are placed. A template is basically a YAML file from the previous examples, with some of the values in the file replaced with parameter references. For example, imagine that you want to parameterize the number of replicas in your frontend. Previously, here's what the Deployment had:

```
...
spec:
  replicas: 2
...
```

In the template file (*frontend-deployment.tmpl*), it instead looks like the following:

```
...
spec:
  replicas: {{ .replicaCount }}
...
```

This means that when you deploy the chart, you'll substitute the value for replicas with the appropriate parameter. The parameters themselves are defined in a *values.yaml* file. There will be one values file per environment where the application should be deployed. The values file for this simple chart would look like this:

```
replicaCount: 2
```

Putting this all together, you can deploy this chart using the helm tool, as follows:

```
helm install path/to/chart --values path/to/environment/values.yaml
```

This parameterizes your application and deploys it to Kubernetes. Over time these parameterizations will grow to encompass the variety of environments for your application.

Deploying Services Best Practices

Kubernetes is a powerful system that can seem complex. But setting up a basic application for success can be straightforward if you use the following best practices:

- Most services should be deployed as Deployment resources. Deployments create identical replicas for redundancy and scale.

- Deployments can be exposed using a Service, which is effectively a load balancer. A Service can be exposed either within a cluster (the default) or externally. If you want to expose an HTTP application, you can use an Ingress controller to add things like request routing and SSL.

- Eventually you will want to parameterize your application to make its configuration more reusable in different environments. Packaging tools like Helm (*https://helm.sh*) are the best choice for this kind of parameterization.

Summary

The application built in this chapter is a simple one, but it contains nearly all the concepts you'll need to build larger, more complicated applications. Understanding how the pieces fit together and how to use foundational Kubernetes components is key to successfully working with Kubernetes.

Laying the correct foundation via version control, code review, and continuous delivery of your service ensures that no matter what you build, it is built solidly. As we go through the more advanced topics in subsequent chapters, keep this foundational information in mind.

## CHAPTER 2

Developer Workflows

Kubernetes was built for reliably operating software. It simplifies deploying and managing applications with an application-oriented API, self-healing properties, and useful tools like Deployments for zero downtime rollout of software. Although all these tools are useful, they don't do much to make it easier to develop applications for Kubernetes. This is where developer workflows come into play. Even though many clusters are designed to run production applications and thus are rarely accessed by developer workflows, it is critical to enable development workflows to target Kubernetes, and this typically means having a cluster or at least part of a cluster that is intended for development. Setting up such a cluster to facilitate easy development of applications for Kubernetes is critical to ensuring success with Kubernetes. If there is no code being built for your cluster, the cluster itself isn't accomplishing much.

Goals

Before we describe the best practices for building out development clusters, it is worth stating our goals for such clusters. Obviously, the ultimate goal is to enable developers to rapidly and easily build applications on Kubernetes, but what does that really mean in practice, and how is that reflected in practical features of the development cluster?

To answer this, let's start by identifying phases of developer interaction with the cluster.

The first phase is *onboarding*. This is when a new developer joins the team. This phase includes giving the user a login to the cluster as well as getting them oriented to their first deployment. The goal for this phase is to get a developer's feet wet in a minimal amount of time. You should set a key performance indicator (KPI) goal for this process. A reasonable goal would be that a user could go from nothing to the current application at HEAD running in less than half an hour. Every time someone is new to the team, test how you are doing against this goal.

The second phase is *developing*. This is the day-to-day activity of the developer. The goal for this phase is to ensure rapid iteration and debugging. Developers need to quickly and repeatedly push code to the cluster. They also need to be able to easily test their code and debug it when it isn't operating properly. The KPI for this phase is more challenging to measure, but you can estimate it by measuring the time to get a pull request (PR) or change up and running in the cluster, or with surveys of the user's perceived productivity, or both. You will also be able to measure this in the overall productivity of your teams.

The third phase is *testing*. This phase is interweaved with developing and is used to validate the code before submission and merging. The goals for this phase are two-fold. First, the developer should be able to run all tests for their environment before a PR is submitted. Second, all tests should automatically run before code is merged into the repository. In addition to these goals you should also set a KPI for the length of time the tests take to run. As your project becomes more complex, it's natural for more and more tests to take a longer time. As this happens, it might become valuable to identify a smaller set of smoke tests that a developer can use for initial validation before submitting a PR. You should also have a very strict KPI around *test flakiness*. A flaky test is one that occasionally (or not so occasionally) fails. In any reasonably active project, a flakiness rate of more than one failure per one thousand runs will lead to developer friction. You need to ensure that your cluster environment does not lead to flaky tests. Whereas sometimes flaky tests occur due to problems in the code, they can also occur because of interference in the development environment (e.g., running out of resources and noisy neighbors). You should ensure that your development environment is free of such issues by measuring test flakiness and acting quickly to fix it.

Building a Development Cluster

When people begin to think about developing on Kubernetes, one of the first choices that occurs is whether to build a single large development cluster or to have one cluster per developer. Note that this choice only makes sense in an environment in which dynamic cluster creation is easy, such as the public cloud. In physical environments, it's possible that one large cluster is the only choice.

If you do have a choice, you should consider the pros and cons of each option. If you choose to have a development cluster per user, the significant downside of this approach is that it will be more expensive and less efficient, and you will have a large number of different development clusters to manage. The extra costs come from the fact that each cluster is likely to be heavily underutilized. Also, with developers creating different clusters, it becomes more difficult to track and garbage-collect resources that are no longer in use. The advantage of the cluster-per-user approach is simplicity: each developer can self-service manage their own cluster, and from isolation, it's much more difficult for different developers to step on one another's toes.

On the other hand, a single development cluster will be significantly more efficient; you can likely sustain the same number of developers on a shared cluster for one-third the price (or less). Plus, it's much easier for you to install shared cluster services, for example, monitoring and logging, which makes it significantly easier to produce a developer-friendly cluster. The downside of a shared development cluster is the process of user management and potential interference between developers. Because the process of adding new users and namespaces to the Kubernetes cluster isn't currently streamlined, you will need to activate a process to onboard new developers. Although Kubernetes resource management and Role-Based Access Control (RBAC) can reduce the probability that two developers conflict, it is always possible that a user will *brick* the development cluster by consuming too many resources so that other applications and developers won't schedule. Additionally, you will still need to ensure that developers don't leak and forget about resources they've created. This is somewhat easier, though, than the approach in which developers each create their own clusters.

Even though both approaches are feasible, generally, our recommendation is to have a single large cluster for all developers. Although there are challenges in interference between developers, they can be managed, and ultimately the cost efficiency and ability to easily add organization-wide capabilities to the cluster outweigh the risks of interference. But you will need to invest in a process for onboarding developers, resource management, and garbage collection. Our recommendation would be to try a single large cluster as a first option. As your organization grows (or if it is already large), you might consider having a cluster per team or group (10 to 20 people) rather than a giant cluster for hundreds of users. This can make both billing and management easier. Moving to multiple clusters can make it more complicated to ensure consistency, but tools like fleet management can make it easier to manage groups of clusters.

Setting Up a Shared Cluster for Multiple Developers

When setting up a large cluster, the primary goal is to ensure that multiple users can simultaneously use the cluster without stepping on one another's toes. The obvious way to separate your different developers is with Kubernetes namespaces. Namespaces can serve as scopes for the deployment of services so that one user's frontend service doesn't interfere with another user's frontend service. Namespaces are also scopes for RBAC, ensuring that one developer cannot accidentally delete another developer's work. Thus, in a shared cluster it makes sense to use a namespace as a developer's workspace. The processes for onboarding users and creating and securing a namespace are described in the following sections.

Onboarding Users

Before you can assign a user to a namespace, you have to onboard that user to the Kubernetes cluster itself. To achieve this, there are two options. You can use certificate-based authentication to create a new certificate for the user and give them a *kubeconfig* file that they can use to log in, or you can configure your cluster to use an external identity system (for example, Microsoft Entra ID or AWS Identity and Access Management [IAM]) for cluster access.

In general, using an external identity system is a best practice because it doesn't require that you maintain two different sources of identity. Additionally, most external systems use short-lived tokens rather than long-lived certificates so the accidental disclosure of a token has a time-bound security impact. If at all possible you should restrict your developers to proving their identity via an external identity provider.

Unfortunately, in some cases this isn't possible and you need to use certificates. Fortunately, you can use the Kubernetes certificate API for creating and managing such certificates. Here's the process for adding a new user to an existing cluster.

First, you need to generate a certificate-signing request to generate a new certificate. Here is a simple Go program to do this:

```go
package main

import (
        "crypto/rand"
        "crypto/rsa"
        "crypto/x509"
        "crypto/x509/pkix"
        "encoding/asn1"
        "encoding/pem"
        "os"
)

func main() {
        name := os.Args[1]
        user := os.Args[2]

        key, err := rsa.GenerateKey(rand.Reader, 1024)
        if err != nil {
                panic(err)
        }
        keyDer := x509.MarshalPKCS1PrivateKey(key)
        keyBlock := pem.Block{
                Type:  "RSA PRIVATE KEY",
                Bytes: keyDer,
        }
```

```go
	keyFile, err := os.Create(name + "-key.pem")
	if err != nil {
		panic(err)
	}
	pem.Encode(keyFile, &keyBlock)
	keyFile.Close()

	commonName := user
	// You may want to update these too
	emailAddress := "someone@myco.com"

	org := "My Co, Inc."
	orgUnit := "Widget Farmers"
	city := "Seattle"
	state := "WA"
	country := "US"

	subject := pkix.Name{
		CommonName:         commonName,
		Country:            []string{country},
		Locality:           []string{city},
		Organization:       []string{org},
		OrganizationalUnit: []string{orgUnit},
		Province:           []string{state},
	}

	asn1, err := asn1.Marshal(subject.ToRDNSequence())
	if err != nil {
		panic(err)
	}
	csr := x509.CertificateRequest{
		RawSubject:         asn1,
		EmailAddresses:     []string{emailAddress},
		SignatureAlgorithm: x509.SHA256WithRSA,
	}

	bytes, err := x509.CreateCertificateRequest(rand.Reader, &csr, key)
	if err != nil {
		panic(err)
	}
	csrFile, err := os.Create(name + ".csr")
	if err != nil {
		panic(err)
	}

	pem.Encode(csrFile, &pem.Block{Type: "CERTIFICATE REQUEST", Bytes: bytes})
	csrFile.Close()
}
```

You can run this as follows:

```
go run csr-gen.go client <user-name>;
```

This creates files called *client-key.pem* and *client.csr*. You can then run the following script to create and download a new certificate:

```bash
#!/bin/bash

csr_name="my-client-csr"
name="${1:-my-user}"

csr="${2}"


cat <<EOF | kubectl create -f -
apiVersion: certificates.k8s.io/v1
kind: CertificateSigningRequest
metadata:
  name: ${csr_name}
spec:
  groups:
  - system:authenticated
  request: $(cat ${csr} | base64 | tr -d '\n')
  usages:
  - key encipherment
  - client auth
EOF

echo
echo "Approving signing request."
kubectl certificate approve ${csr_name}

echo
echo "Downloading certificate."
kubectl get csr ${csr_name} -o jsonpath='{.status.certificate}' \
        | base64 --decode > $(basename ${csr} .csr).crt

echo
echo "Cleaning up"
kubectl delete csr ${csr_name}

echo
echo "Add the following to the 'users' list in your kubeconfig file:"
echo "- name: ${name}"
echo "  user:"
echo "    client-certificate: ${PWD}/$(basename ${csr} .csr).crt"
echo "    client-key: ${PWD}/$(basename ${csr} .csr)-key.pem"
echo
echo "Next you may want to add a role-binding for this user."
```

This script prints out the final information that you can add to a *kubeconfig* file to enable that user. Of course, the user has no access privileges, so you will need to apply Kubernetes RBAC for the user to grant them privileges to a namespace.

Creating and Securing a Namespace

The first step in provisioning a namespace is actually just creating it. You can do this using `kubectl create namespace my-namespace`.

But the truth is that when you create a namespace, you want to attach a bunch of metadata to that namespace, for example, the contact information for the team that builds the component deployed into the namespace. Generally, this is in the form of annotations; you can either generate the YAML file using some templating, such as Jinja (*https://oreil.ly/vvtTF*) or others, or you can create and then annotate the namespace. A simple script to do this looks like:

```
ns='my-namespace'
team='some team'
kubectl create namespace ${ns}
kubectl annotate namespace ${ns} team=${team}
```

When the namespace is created, you want to secure it by ensuring that you can grant access to the namespace to a specific user. To do this, you can bind a role to a user in the context of that namespace. You do this by creating a `RoleBinding` object within the namespace itself. The `RoleBinding` might look like this:

```
apiVersion: rbac.authorization.k8s.io/v1
kind: RoleBinding
metadata:
  name: example
  namespace: my-namespace
roleRef:
  apiGroup: rbac.authorization.k8s.io
  kind: ClusterRole
  name: edit
subjects:
- apiGroup: rbac.authorization.k8s.io
  kind: User
  name: myuser
```

To create it, you simply run `kubectl create -f role-binding.yaml`. Note that you can reuse this binding as much as you want as long as you update the namespace in the binding to point to the correct namespace. If you ensure that the user doesn't have any other role bindings, you can be assured that this namespace is the only part of the cluster to which the user has access. A reasonable practice is to also grant reader access to the entire cluster; in this way developers can see what others are doing in case it is interfering with their work. Be careful in granting such read access, however, because it will include access to secret resources in the cluster. Generally, in a development cluster this is OK because everyone is in the same organization and the secrets are used only for development; however, if this is a concern, then you can create a more fine-grained role that eliminates the ability to read secrets.

If you want to limit the resources consumed by a particular namespace to put a cap on costs or ensure that resources are fairly distributed among developers, you can use the ResourceQuota resource to set a limit to the total number of resources that any particular namespace consumes. For example, the following quota limits the namespace to 10 cores and 100 GB of memory for both Request and Limit for the pods in the namespace:

```
apiVersion: v1
kind: ResourceQuota
metadata:
  name: limit-compute
  namespace: my-namespace
spec:
  hard:
    # These look a little odd because they're not nested
      # but they refer to the requests and limit fields in
      # a Pod
    requests.cpu: "10"
    requests.memory: 100Gi
    limits.cpu: 10
    limits.memory: 100Gi
```

Managing Namespaces

Now that you have seen how to onboard a new user and how to create a namespace to use as a workspace, the question remains how to assign a developer to the namespace. As with many things, there is no single perfect answer; rather, there are two approaches. The first is to give each user their own namespace as part of the onboarding process. This is useful because after a user is onboarded, they always have a dedicated workspace in which they can develop and manage their applications. However, making the developer's namespace too persistent encourages the developer to leave things lying around in the namespace after they are done with them, and garbage-collecting and accounting individual resources is more complicated. An alternate approach is to temporarily create and assign a namespace with a bounded time to live (TTL). This ensures that the developer thinks of the resources in the cluster as transient and that it is easy to build automation around the deletion of entire namespaces when their TTL has expired.

In the bounded TTL model, when the developer wants to begin a new project, they use a tool to allocate a new namespace for the project. When they create the namespace, it has a selection of metadata associated with the namespace for management and accounting. Obviously, this metadata includes the TTL for the namespace, but it also includes the developer to which it is assigned, the resources that should be allocated to the namespace (e.g., CPU and memory), and the team and purpose of the namespace. This metadata ensures that you can both track resource usage and delete the namespace at the right time.

Developing the tooling to allocate namespaces on demand can seem like a challenge, but simple tooling is relatively easy to develop. For example, you can achieve the allocation of a new namespace with a simple script that creates the namespace and prompts for the relevant metadata to attach to the namespace.

If you want to get more integrated with Kubernetes, you can use custom resource definitions (CRDs) to enable users to dynamically create and allocate new namespaces using the kubectl tool. If you have the time and inclination, this is definitely a good practice because it makes namespace management declarative and also enables the use of Kubernetes RBAC.

After you have tooling to enable the allocation of namespaces, you also need to add tooling to reap namespaces when their TTL has expired. Again, you can accomplish this with a simple script that examines the namespaces and deletes those that have an expired TTL.

You can build this script into a container and use a ScheduledJob to run it at an interval like once per hour. These combined tools can ensure that developers can easily allocate independent resources for their project as needed, but those resources will also be reaped at the proper interval to ensure that you don't have wasted resources and that old resources don't get in the way of new development.

Cluster-Level Services

In addition to using tooling to allocate and manage namespaces, there are also useful cluster-level services, and it's a good idea to enable them in your development cluster. The first is log aggregation to a central Logging as a Service (LaaS) system. One of the easiest things for a developer to do to understand the operation of their application is to write something to STDOUT. Although you can access these logs via kubectl logs, that log is limited in length and is not particularly searchable. If you instead automatically ship those logs to a LaaS system such as a cloud service or an Elasticsearch cluster, developers can easily search through logs for relevant information as well as aggregate logging information across multiple containers in their service.

Enabling Developer Workflows

Now that we have successfully set up a shared cluster and we can onboard new application developers to the cluster itself, we need to actually get them developing their application. Remember that one of the KPIs we are measuring is the time from onboarding to an initial application running in the cluster. It's clear that via the just-described onboarding scripts we can quickly authenticate a user to a cluster and allocate a namespace, but what about getting started with the application? Unfortunately, even though a few techniques can help with this process, it generally requires more convention than automation to get the initial application up and running. In the following sections, we describe one approach to achieving this; it is by no means the only approach or the only solution. You can optionally apply the approach as is or be inspired by the ideas to arrive at your own solution.

Initial Setup

One of the main challenges to deploying an application is the installation of all the dependencies. In many cases, especially in modern microservice architectures, to even get started developing on one of the microservices requires the deployment of multiple dependencies, either databases or other microservices. Although the deployment of the application itself is relatively straightforward, the task of identifying and deploying all the dependencies to build the complete application is often a frustrating case of trial and error married with incomplete or out-of-date instructions.

To address this issue, it is often valuable to introduce a convention for describing and installing dependencies. This can be seen as the equivalent of something like `npm install`, which installs all the required JavaScript dependencies. Eventually, there is likely to be a tool similar to `npm` that provides this service for Kubernetes-based applications, but until then, the best practice is to rely on convention within your team.

One such option for a convention is the creation of a *setup.sh* script within the root directory of all project repositories. The responsibility of this script is to create all dependencies within a particular namespace to ensure that all the application's dependencies are correctly created. For example, a setup script might look like the following:

```
kubectl create my-service/database-stateful-set-yaml
kubectl create my-service/middle-tier.yaml
kubectl create my-service/configs.yaml
```

You could then integrate this script with npm by adding the following to your *package.json*:

```
{
    ...
    "scripts": {
        "setup": "./setup.sh",
        ...
    }
}
```

With this setup, a new developer can simply run `npm run setup`, and the cluster dependencies will be installed. Obviously, this particular integration is Node.js/npm specific. In other programming languages, it will make more sense to integrate with the language-specific tooling. For example, in Java you might integrate with a Maven *pom.xml* file instead.

For more generic workflows, both GitHub and Visual Studio Code have recently standardized on "devcontainers," which are containers that are described by a Dockerfile stored in the `.devcontainer/` folder in the repository. When built, they construct a complete environment for starting development on that repository.

Enabling Active Development

Having set up the developer workspace with the required dependencies, the next task is to enable developers to iterate on their application quickly. The first prerequisite for this is the ability to build and push a container image. Let's assume that you have this already set up; if not, you can read how to do this in a number of other online resources and books.

After you have built and pushed a container image, the task is to roll it out to the cluster. Unlike traditional rollouts, in the case of developer iteration, maintaining availability is really not a concern. Thus, the easiest way to deploy new code is to simply delete the Deployment object associated with the previous Deployment and then create a new Deployment pointing to the newly built image. It is also possible to update an existing Deployment in place, but this will trigger the rollout logic in the Deployment resource. Although it is possible to configure a Deployment to roll out code quickly, doing so introduces a difference between the development environment and the production environment that can be dangerous or destabilizing. Imagine, for example, that you accidentally push the development configuration of the Deployment into production; you will suddenly deploy new versions to production without appropriate testing and delays between phases of the rollout. Because of this risk and because there is an alternative, the best practice is to delete and recreate the Deployment.

Just like installing dependencies, it is also a good practice to make a script for performing this Deployment. An example *deploy.sh* script might look like the following:

```
kubectl delete -f ./my-service/deployment.yaml
perl -pi -e 's/${old_version}/${new_version}/' ./my-service/deployment.yaml
kubectl create -f ./my-service/deployment.yaml
```

As before, you can integrate this with existing programming language tooling so that (for example) a developer can simply run `npm run deploy` to deploy their new code into the cluster.

As you build this automation it is often useful to integrate it into a continuous integration and delivery (CI/CD) tool such as GitHub Actions, Azure DevOps, or Jenkins. Integration with a CI/CD tool makes it much easier to enable further automation like automatic deployment on merging a developer's PR.

Enabling Testing and Debugging

After a user has successfully deployed the development version of their application, they need to test it and, if there are problems, debug any issues with the application. This can also be a hurdle when developing in Kubernetes because it is not always clear how to interact with your cluster. The kubectl command line is a veritable Swiss Army knife of tools to achieve this, from kubectl logs to kubectl exec and kubectl port-forward, but learning how to use all the different options and achieving familiarity with the tool can take a considerable amount of experience. Furthermore, because the tool runs in the terminal, it often requires the composition of multiple windows to simultaneously examine both the source code for the application and the running application itself.

To streamline the testing and debugging experience, Kubernetes tooling is increasingly being integrated into development environments, for example, the open source extension for Visual Studio (VS) Code for Kubernetes. The extension is easily installed for free from the VS Code marketplace. When installed, it automatically discovers any clusters that you already have in your *kubeconfig* file and provides a tree-view navigation pane for you to see the contents of your cluster at a glance.

In addition to being able to see your cluster state at a glance, the integration allows a developer to use the tools available via kubectl in an intuitive, discoverable way. From the tree view, if you right-click a Kubernetes pod, you can immediately use port forwarding to bring a network connection from the pod directly to the local machine. Likewise, you can access the logs for the pod or even get a terminal within the running container.

The integration of these commands with prototypical user interface expectations (e.g., right-click shows a context menu), as well as the integration of these experiences alongside the code for the application itself, enables developers with minimal Kubernetes experience to rapidly become productive in the development cluster.

Of course this VS Code extension isn't the only integration between Kubernetes and a development environment; there are several others that you can install depending on your choice of programming environment and style (vi, emacs, etc.).

Setting Up a Development Environment Best Practices

Setting up development workflows on Kubernetes is key to productivity and is pivotal for productive and happy development teams. Following these best practices will help to ensure that developers are up and running quickly:

- Think about developer experience in three phases: onboarding, developing, and testing. Make sure that the development environment you build supports all three of these phases.

- When building a development cluster, you can choose between one large cluster and a cluster per developer. There are pros and cons to each, but generally a single large cluster is a better approach.

- When you add users to a cluster, add them with their own identity and access to their own namespace. Use resource limits to restrict how much of the cluster they can use.

- When managing namespaces, think about how you can reap old, unused resources. Developers will have bad hygiene about deleting unused things. Use automation to clean it up for them.

- Think about cluster-level services like logs and monitoring that you can set up for all users. Sometimes, cluster-level dependencies like databases are also useful to set up on behalf of all users using templates like Helm charts.

Summary

We've reached a place where creating a Kubernetes cluster, especially in the cloud, is a relatively straightforward exercise, but enabling developers to productively use such a cluster is significantly less obvious and easy. When thinking about enabling developers to successfully build applications on Kubernetes, it's important to think about the key goals around onboarding, iterating, testing, and debugging applications. Likewise, it pays to invest in some basic tooling specific to user onboarding, namespace provisioning, and cluster services like basic log aggregation. Viewing a development cluster and your code repositories as an opportunity to standardize and apply best practices will ensure that you have happy and productive developers successfully building code to deploy to your production Kubernetes clusters.

## CHAPTER 3

Monitoring and Logging in Kubernetes

In this chapter, we discuss best practices for monitoring and logging in Kubernetes. We'll dive into the details of different monitoring patterns, important metrics to collect, and building dashboards from these raw metrics. We then wrap up with examples of implementing monitoring for your Kubernetes cluster.

Metrics Versus Logs

You first need to understand the difference between log collection and metrics collection. They are complementary but serve different purposes:

Metrics
> A series of numbers measured over a period of time.

Logs
> Logs keep track of what happens while a program is running, including any errors, warnings, or notable events that occur.

A example of where you would need to use both metrics and logging is when an application is performing poorly. Our first indication of the issue might be an alert of high latency on the pods hosting the application, but the metrics might not give a good indication of the issue. We then can look into our logs to investigate errors that are being emitted from the application.

Monitoring Techniques

Closed-box monitoring focuses on monitoring from the outside of an application and is what's been used traditionally when monitoring systems for components like CPU, memory, storage, and so on. Closed-box monitoring can still be useful for monitoring at the infrastructure level, but it lacks insights and context into how the application is operating. For example, to test whether a cluster is healthy, we might schedule a pod, and if it's successful, we know that the scheduler and service discovery are healthy within our cluster, so we can assume the cluster components are healthy.

Open-box monitoring focuses on the details in the context of the application state, such as total HTTP requests, number of 500 errors, latency of requests, and so on. With open-box monitoring, we can begin to understand the *why* of our system state. It allows us to ask, "Why did the disk fill up?" and not just state, "The disk filled up."

Monitoring Patterns

You might look at monitoring and say, "How difficult can this be? We've always monitored our systems." The concept of monitoring isn't new, and we have many tools at our disposal to help us understand how our systems are performing. But platforms like Kubernetes are much more dynamic and transient, so you'll need to change your thinking about how to monitor these environments. For example, when monitoring a virtual machine (VM) you expect that VM to be up 24/7 and all its state preserved. In Kubernetes, pods can be very dynamic and short-lived, so you need to have monitoring in place that can handle this dynamic and transient nature.

There are two monitoring patterns to focus on when monitoring distributed systems. The *USE* method, popularized by Brendan Gregg, focuses on the following:

- U—Utilization
- S—Saturation
- E—Errors

This method is focused on infrastructure monitoring because there are limitations on using it for application-level monitoring. The USE method is described as "For every resource, check utilization, saturation, and error rates." This method lets you quickly identify resource constraints and error rates of your systems. For example, to check the health of the network for your nodes in the cluster, you will want to monitor the utilization, saturation, and error rate to be able to easily identify any network bottlenecks or errors in the network stack. The USE method is a tool in a larger toolbox and is not the only method you will utilize to monitor your systems.

Another monitoring approach, called the *RED* method, was popularized by Tom Wilkie. The RED method approach is focused on the following:

- R—Rate
- E—Errors
- D—Duration

The philosophy was taken from Google's *Four Golden Signals*:

Latency
> How long it takes to serve a request

Traffic
> How much demand is placed on your system

Errors
> The rate of requests that are failing

Saturation
> How utilized your service is

As an example, you could use this method to monitor a frontend service running in Kubernetes to calculate the following:

- How many requests is my frontend service processing?
- How many 500 errors are users of the service receiving?
- Is the service overutilized by requests?

As you can see from the previous example, this method is more focused on the users' experience with the service.

The USE and RED methods are complementary given that the USE method focuses on the infrastructure components and the RED method focuses on monitoring the end-user experience for the application.

Kubernetes Metrics Overview

Now that we know the different monitoring techniques and patterns, let's look at what components you should be monitoring in your Kubernetes cluster. A Kubernetes cluster consists of control-plane components and node components. The control-plane components consist of the API server, etcd, scheduler, and controller manager. The nodes consist of the kubelet, container runtime, kube-proxy, kube-dns, and pods. You need to monitor all these components to ensure a healthy cluster and application.

Kubernetes exposes these metrics in a variety of ways, so let's look at different components that you can use to collect metrics within your cluster.

cAdvisor

Container Advisor, or cAdvisor, is an open source project that collects resources and metrics for containers running on a node. cAdvisor is built into the Kubernetes kubelet, which runs on every node in the cluster. It collects memory and CPU metrics through the Linux control group (cgroup) tree. If you are not familiar with cgroups, it's a Linux kernel feature that allows isolation of resources for CPU, disk I/O, or network I/O. cAdvisor will also collect disk metrics through statfs, which is built into the Linux kernel. These are implementation details you don't really need to worry about, but you should understand how these metrics are exposed and the type of information you can collect. You should consider cAdvisor as the source of truth for all container metrics.

Metrics Server

The Kubernetes metrics server and Metrics Server API replace the deprecated Heapster. Heapster had some architectural disadvantages with how it implemented the data sink, which caused a lot of vendored solutions in the core Heapster code base. This issue was solved by implementing a resource and Custom Metrics API as an aggregated API in Kubernetes. This allows implementations to be switched out without changing the API.

There are two aspects to understand in the Metrics Server API and metrics server.

First, the canonical implementation of the Resource Metrics API is the metrics server. The metrics server gathers resource metrics such as CPU and memory. It gathers these metrics from the kubelet's API and then stores them in memory. Kubernetes uses these resource metrics in the scheduler, Horizontal Pod Autoscaler (HPA), and Vertical Pod Autoscaler (VPA).

Second, the Custom Metrics API allows monitoring systems to collect arbitrary metrics. This allows monitoring solutions to build custom adapters that will allow for extending outside the core resource metrics. For example, Prometheus built one of the first custom metrics adapters, which allows you to use the HPA based on a custom metric. This opens up better scaling based on your use case because now you can bring in metrics like queue size and scale based on a metric that might be external to Kubernetes.

Now that there is a standardized Metrics API, this opens up many possibilities to scale outside the plain old CPU and memory metrics.

kube-state-metrics

kube-state-metrics is a Kubernetes add-on that monitors the object stored in Kubernetes. Where cAdvisor and Metrics Server are used to provide detailed metrics on resource usage, kube-state-metrics is focused on identifying conditions on Kubernetes objects deployed to your cluster.

Following are some questions that kube-state-metrics can answer for you:

- Pods
  - — How many pods are deployed to the cluster?
  - — How many pods are in a pending state?
  - — Are there enough resources to serve a pods request?
- Deployments
  - — How many pods are in a running state versus a desired state?
  - — How many replicas are available?
  - — What deployments have been updated?
- Nodes
  - — What's the status of my nodes?
  - — What are the allottable CPU cores in my cluster?
  - — Are there any nodes that are unschedulable?
- Jobs
  - — When did a job start?
  - — When did a job complete?
  - — How many jobs failed?

As of this writing, kube-state-metrics tracks many object types. These are always expanding, and you can find the documentation in the GitHub repository (*https:// oreil.ly/bdTp2*).

What Metrics Do I Monitor?

The easy answer is "everything," but if you try to monitor too much, you can create noise that filters out the real signals into which you need to have insight. When we think about monitoring in Kubernetes, we want a layered approach that takes into account the following:

- Physical or virtual nodes
- Cluster components
- Cluster add-ons
- End-user applications

Using this layered approach to monitoring allows you to more easily identify the correct signals in your monitoring system. It allows you to approach issues in a more targeted way. For example, if you have pods going into a pending state, you can start with resource utilization of the nodes, and if all is OK, you can target cluster-level components.

Following are metrics you would want to target in your system:

- Nodes
  - CPU utilization
  - Memory utilization
  - Network utilization
  - Disk utilization
- Cluster components
  - etcd latency
- Cluster add-ons
  - Cluster Autoscaler
  - Ingress controller
- Application
  - Container memory utilization and saturation
  - Container CPU utilization
  - Container network utilization and error rate
  - Application framework–specific metrics

Monitoring Tools

Many monitoring tools can integrate with Kubernetes, and more arrive every day, building on their feature set to better integrate with Kubernetes. Following are a few popular tools that integrate with Kubernetes:

Prometheus

Prometheus is an open source systems monitoring and alerting toolkit originally built at SoundCloud. Since its inception in 2012, many companies and organizations have adopted Prometheus, and the project has a very active developer and user community. It is now a standalone open source project and maintained independent of any company. To emphasize this, and to clarify the project's governance structure, Prometheus joined the Cloud Native Computing Foundation (CNCF) in 2016 as the second hosted project, after Kubernetes.

InfluxDB

InfluxDB is a time-series database designed to handle high write and query loads. It is an integral component of the TICK (Telegraf, InfluxDB, Chronograf, and Kapacitor) stack. InfluxDB is meant to be used as a backing store for any use case involving large amounts of timestamped data, including DevOps monitoring, application metrics, IoT sensor data, and real-time analytics.

Datadog

Datadog provides a monitoring service for cloud-scale applications, providing monitoring of servers, databases, tools, and services through a SaaS-based data analytics platform.

Sysdig

Sysdig Monitor is a commercial tool that provides Docker monitoring and Kubernetes monitoring for container-native apps. Sysdig also allows you to collect, correlate, and query Prometheus metrics with direct Kubernetes integration.

Cloud provider tools

All major cloud providers provide monitoring tools for their different solutions. These tools are typically integrated into the cloud provider's ecosystem and provide a good starting point for monitoring your Kubernetes cluster. Following are some examples of cloud provider tools:

GCP Stackdriver

Stackdriver Kubernetes Engine Monitoring is designed to monitor Google Kubernetes Engine (GKE) clusters. It manages monitoring and logging services together and its interface provides a dashboard customized for GKE clusters. Stackdriver Monitoring provides visibility into the performance, uptime, and overall health of cloud-powered applications. It collects metrics, events, and metadata from Google Cloud Platform (GCP), Amazon Web Services (AWS), hosted uptime probes, and application instrumentation.

Microsoft Azure Monitor for containers

Azure Monitor for containers is a feature designed to monitor the performance of container workloads deployed to either Azure Container Instances or managed Kubernetes clusters hosted on Azure Kubernetes Service. Monitoring your containers is critical, especially when you're running a production cluster, at scale, with multiple applications. Azure Monitor for containers gives you performance visibility by collecting memory and processor metrics from controllers, nodes, and containers that are available in Kubernetes through the Metrics API. Container logs are also collected. After you enable monitoring from Kubernetes clusters, metrics and logs are automatically collected for you through a containerized version of the Log Analytics agent for Linux.

AWS Container Insights

If you use Amazon Elastic Container Service (ECS), Amazon Elastic Kubernetes Service, or other Kubernetes platforms on Amazon EC2, you can use CloudWatch Container Insights to collect, aggregate, and summarize metrics and logs from your containerized applications and microservices. The metrics include utilization for resources such as CPU, memory, disk, and network. Container Insights also provides diagnostic information, such as container restart failures, to help you isolate issues and resolve them quickly.

One important aspect when looking at implementing a tool to monitor metrics is to look at how the metrics are stored. Tools that provide a time-series database with key/value pairs will give you a higher degree of attributes for the metric.

 Always evaluate monitoring tools you already have, because taking on a new monitoring tool has a learning curve and a cost due to the operational implementation of the tool. Many of the monitoring tools now have integration into Kubernetes, so evaluate which ones you have today and whether they will meet your requirements.

Monitoring Kubernetes Using Prometheus

In this section we focus on monitoring metrics with Prometheus, which provides good integrations with Kubernetes labeling, service discovery, and metadata. The high-level concepts we implement throughout the chapter will also apply to other monitoring systems.

Prometheus is an open source project hosted by the CNCF. It was originally developed at SoundCloud, and a lot of its concepts are based on Google's internal monitoring system, Borgmon. It implements a multidimensional data model with keypairs that work much like how the Kubernetes labeling system works. Prometheus exposes metrics in a human-readable format, as in the following example:

```
# HELP node_cpu_seconds_total Seconds the CPU is spent in each mode.
# TYPE node_cpu_seconds_total counter
node_cpu_seconds_total{cpu="0",mode="idle"} 5144.64
node_cpu_seconds_total{cpu="0",mode="iowait"} 117.98
```

To collect metrics, Prometheus uses a pull model in which it scrapes a metrics endpoint to collect and ingest the metrics into the Prometheus server. Systems like Kubernetes already expose their metrics in a Prometheus format, making it simple to collect metrics. Many other Kubernetes ecosystem projects (NGINX, Traefik, Istio, Linkerd, etc.) also expose their metrics in a Prometheus format. Prometheus also can use exporters, which allow you to take emitted metrics from your service and translate them to Prometheus-formatted metrics.

Prometheus has a very simplified architecture, as depicted in Figure 3-1.

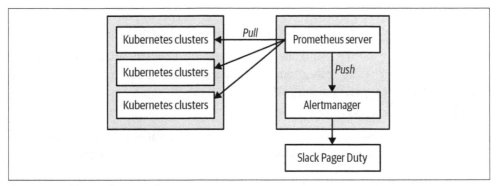

Figure 3-1. Prometheus architecture

 You can install Prometheus within the cluster or outside the cluster. It's a good practice to monitor your cluster from a "utility cluster" to avoid a production issue also affecting your monitoring system. Tools like Thanos (*https://oreil.ly/7e6Wf*) provide high availability for Prometheus and allow you to export metrics into an external storage system.

A deep dive into the Prometheus architecture is beyond the scope of this book, and you should refer to one of the dedicated books on this topic. *Prometheus: Up & Running* (O'Reilly) is a good in-depth book to get you started.

So, let's dive in and get Prometheus set up on our Kubernetes cluster. There are many different ways to deploy Prometheus, and the deployment will depend on your specific implementation. We will install the Prometheus Operator with Helm:

Prometheus server
    Pulls and stores metrics being collected from systems.

Prometheus Operator
    Makes the Prometheus configuration Kubernetes native, and manages and oper-ates Prometheus and Alertmanager clusters. Allows you to create, destroy, and configure Prometheus resources through native Kubernetes resource definitions.

Node Exporter
    Exports host metrics from Kubernetes nodes in the cluster.

kube-state-metrics
    Collects Kubernetes-specific metrics.

Alertmanager
    Allows you to configure and forward alerts to external systems.

Grafana

Provides visualization on dashboard capabilities for Prometheus.

First, we'll start by getting minikube setup to deploy Prometheus to. We are using Macs so we'll use `brew` to install minikube. You can also install minikube from the minikube website (*https://oreil.ly/BgFFL*).

```
brew install minikube
```

Now we'll install kube-prometheus-stack (formerly Prometheus Operator) and prepare our cluster to start monitoring the Kubernetes API server for changes.

Create a namespace for monitoring:

```
kubectl create ns monitoring
```

Add the prometheus-community Helm chart repository:

```
helm repo add prometheus-community
    https://prometheus-community.github.io/helm-charts
```

Add the Helm Stable chart repository:

```
helm repo add stable https://charts.helm.sh/stable
```

Update the chart repository:

```
helm repo update
```

Install the kube-prometheus-stack chart:

```
helm install --namespace monitoring prometheus
    prometheus-community/kube-prometheus-stack
```

Let's check to ensure that all the pods are running:

```
kubectl get pods -n monitoring
```

If installed correctly you should see the following pods:

```
kubectl get pods -n monitoring
```

NAME	READY	STATUS	RESTARTS	AGE
alertmanager-prometheus-kube-prometheus-alertm...	2/2	Running	1	79s
prometheus-grafana-6f7cf9b968-xtnzj	3/3	Running	0	97s
prometheus-kube-prometheus-operator-7bdb94567b...	1/1	Running	0	97s
prometheus-kube-state-metrics-6bdd65d76-s5r5j	1/1	Running	0	97s
prometheus-prometheus-kube-prometheus-promethe...	2/2	Running	0	78s
prometheus-prometheus-node-exporter-dgrlf	1/1	Running	0	98s

Now we'll create a tunnel to the Grafana instance that is included with kube-prometheus-stack. This will allow us to connect to Grafana from our local machine.

This creates a tunnel to our localhost on port 3000. Now we can open a web browser and connect to Grafana on *http://127.0.0.1:3000*.

We talked earlier in the chapter about employing the USE method, so let's gather some node metrics on CPU utilization and saturation. Kube-prometheus-stack provides visualizations for these common USE method metrics we want to track. The great thing about the kube-prometheus-stack you installed is that it comes with prebuilt Grafana dashboards you can use.

Now we'll create a tunnel to the Grafana instance that is included with kube-prometheus-stack. This will allow us to connect to Grafana from our local machine:

```
kubectl port-forward -n monitoring svc/prometheus-grafana 3000:80
```

Point your web browser at *http://localhost:3000* and log in using the following credentials:

- Username: admin
- Password: prom-operator

Under the Grafana dashboards you'll find a dashboard called Kubernetes / USE Method / Cluster. This dashboard gives you a good overview of the utilization and saturation of the Kubernetes cluster, which is at the heart of the USE method. Figure 3-2 presents an example of the dashboard.

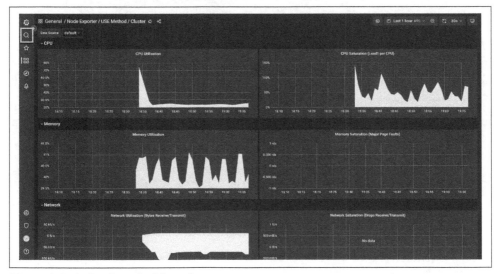

Figure 3-2. A Grafana dashboard

Go ahead and take some time to explore the different dashboards and metrics that you can visualize in Grafana.

Avoid creating too many dashboards (aka "The Wall of Graphs") because this can be difficult for engineers to reason with in trouble-shooting situations. You might think having more information in a dashboard means better monitoring, but the majority of the time it causes more confusion for a user looking at the dashboard. Focus your dashboard design on outcomes and time to resolution.

Logging Overview

Up to this point, we have discussed a lot about metrics and Kubernetes, but to get the full picture of your environment, you also need to collect and centralize logs from the Kubernetes cluster and the applications deployed to your cluster. With logging, it might be easy to say, "Let's just log everything," but this can cause two issues:

- There is too much noise to find issues quickly.
- Logs can consume a lot of resources and come with a high cost.

There is no clear-cut answer to what exactly you should log because debug logs become a necessary evil. Over time you'll start to understand your environment better and learn what noise you can tune out from the logging system. Also, to address the ever-increasing number of logs stored, you will need to implement a retention and archival policy. From an end-user experience, having somewhere between 30 and 45 days' worth of historical logs is a good fit. This allows for investigation of problems that manifest over a longer period of time but also reduces the amount of resources needed to store logs. If you require longer-term storage for compliance reasons, you'll want to archive the logs to more cost-effective resources.

In a Kubernetes cluster, there are multiple components to log. Following is a list of components from which you should be collecting metrics:

- Node logs
- Kubernetes control-plane logs
  - API server
  - Controller manager
  - Scheduler
- Kubernetes audit logs
- Application container logs

With node logs, you want to collect events that happen to essential node services. For example, you will want to collect logs from the Docker daemon running on the nodes. A healthy Docker daemon is essential for running containers on the node. Collecting these logs will help you diagnose any issues that you might run into with the Docker daemon, and it will give you information into any underlying issues with the daemon. There are also other essential services that you will want to log from the underlying node.

The Kubernetes control plane consists of several components from which you'll need to collect logs to give you more insight into underlying issues within it. The Kubernetes control plane is core to a healthy cluster, and you'll want to aggregate the logs that it stores on the host in */var/log/kube-APIserver.log*, */var/log/kube-scheduler.log*, and */var/log/kube-controller-manager.log*. The controller manager is responsible for creating objects defined by the end user. As an example, as a user you create a Kubernetes service with type LoadBalancer and it just sits in a pending state; the Kubernetes events might not give all the details to diagnose the issue. If you collect the logs in a centralized system, it will give you more detail into the underlying issue and a quicker way to investigate it.

You can think of Kubernetes audit logs as security monitoring because they give you insight into who did what within the system. These logs can be very noisy, so you'll want to tune them for your environment. In many instances these logs can cause a huge spike in your logging system when first initialized, so make sure that you follow the Kubernetes documentation guidance on audit log monitoring.

Application container logs give you insight into the actual logs your application is emitting. You can forward these logs to a central repository in multiple ways. The first and recommended way is to send all application logs to STDOUT because this gives you a uniform way of application logging, and a monitoring daemon set can gather the logs directly from the Docker daemon. The other way is to use a *sidecar* pattern and run a log-forwarding container next to the application container in a Kubernetes pod. You might need to use this pattern if your application logs to the filesystem.

There are many options and configurations for managing Kubernetes audit logs. These audit logs can be very noisy and it can be expensive to log all actions. You should consider looking at the audit logging documentation (*https://oreil.ly/L84dM*) so that you can fine-tune these logs for your environment.

Tools for Logging

As with collecting metrics, there are many tools to collect logs from Kubernetes and applications running in the cluster. You might already have tooling for this, but be aware of how the tool implements logging. The tool should have the capability to run as a Kubernetes DaemonSet, and have a solution to run as a sidecar for applications that don't send logs to STDOUT. An advantage of using an existing tool is that you will already have operational knowledge of the tool.

Some of the more popular tools with Kubernetes integration are:

- Loki
- Elastic Stack
- Datadog
- Sumo Logic
- Sysdig
- Cloud provider services (GCP Stackdriver, Azure Monitor for containers, and Amazon CloudWatch)

When looking for a tool to centralize logs, hosted solutions can provide a lot of value because they offload a lot of the operational cost. Hosting your own logging solution seems great on day N, but as the environment grows, it can be very time consuming to maintain the solution.

Logging by Using a Loki-Stack

For the purposes of this book, we use a Loki-Stack with prom-tail for logging for our cluster. Implementing a Loki-Stack can be a good way to get started, but at some point you'll probably ask yourself, "Is it really worth managing my own logging platform?" Typically, it's not worth the effort because self-hosted logging solutions are great at first, but become overly complex with time. Self-hosted logging solutions become more operationally complex as your environment scales. There is no one correct answer, so evaluate whether your business requirements need you to host your own solution. There is also a hosted Loki solution (provided by Grafana), so you can always move pretty easily if you choose not to host it yourself.

We will use the following for the logging stack:

- Loki
- prom-tail
- Grafana

Deploy Loki-Stack with Helm to your Kubernetes cluster with the following steps.

Add Loki-Stack Helm repo:

```
helm repo add grafana https://grafana.github.io/helm-charts
```

Update Helm repo:

```
helm repo update

helm upgrade --install loki --namespace=monitoring grafana/loki-stack
```

This deploys Loki with prom-tail, which will allow us to forward logs to Loki and visualize the logs using Grafana.

You should see the following pods deployed to your cluster:

```
kubectl get pods -n monitoring

NAME                 READY  STATUS   RESTARTS  AGE
loki-0               1/1    Running  0         93s
loki-promtail-x7nw8  1/1    Running  0         93s
```

After all pods are "Running," go ahead and connect to Grafana through port forwarding to our localhost:

```
kubectl port-forward -n monitoring svc/prometheus-grafana 3000:80
```

Now, point your web browser at *http://localhost:3000* and log in using the following credentials:

- Username: admin
- Password: prom-operator

Under the Grafana configuration you'll find data sources, as shown in Figure 3-3. We'll then add Loki as a `Data Source`.

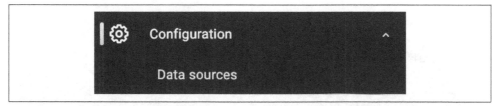

Figure 3-3. The Grafana data source

We will then add a new data source and add Loki as the data source (see Figure 3-4).

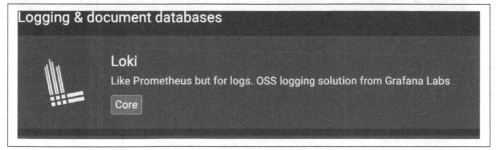

Figure 3-4. Loki datasource

In the Loki settings page (Figure 3-5), fill in the URL with http://loki:3100, then click the Save & Test button.

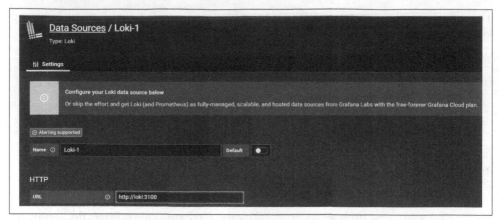

Figure 3-5. Loki configuration

In Grafana, you can perform ad hoc queries on the logs, and you can build out dashboards to give you an overview of the environment.

To explore the logs that the Loki-Stack has collected we can use the *Explore* function in Grafana, as shown in Figure 3-6. This will allow us to run a query against the logs that have been collected.

Figure 3-6. Explore Loki logs

For the label filter you will need the following filter:

```
namespace = kube-system
```

Go ahead and take some time to explore the different logs that you can visualize from Loki and Grafana.

Alerting

Alerting is a double-edged sword, and you need to strike a balance between what you alert on versus what should just be monitored. Alerting on too much causes alert fatigue, and important events will be lost in all the noise. An example would be generating an alert any time a pod fails. You might be asking, "Why wouldn't I want to monitor for a pod failure?" Well, the beauty of Kubernetes is that it provides features to automatically check the health of a container and restart the container automatically. You really want to focus alerting on events that affect your Service-Level Objectives (SLOs). SLOs are specific measurable characteristics such as availability, throughput, frequency, and response time that you agree upon with the end user of your service. Setting SLOs sets expectations with your end users and provides clarity on how the system should behave. Without an SLO, users can form their opinion, which might be an unrealistic expectation of the service. Alerting in a system like Kubernetes needs an entirely new approach from what we are typically accustomed to and needs to focus on how the end user is experiencing the service. For example, if your SLO for a frontend service is a 20-ms response time and you are seeing higher latency than average, you want to be alerted on the problem.

You need to decide what alerts are good and require intervention. In typical monitoring, you might be accustomed to alerting on high CPU usage, memory usage, or processes not responding. These might seem like good alerts, but they probably don't indicate an issue that someone needs to take immediate action on and that requires notifying an on-call engineer. An alert to an on-call engineer should be an issue that needs immediate human attention and is affecting the UX of the application. If you have ever experienced a "that issue resolved itself" scenario, then that is a good indication that the alert did not need to contact an on-call engineer.

One way to handle alerts that don't need immediate action is to focus on automating the remediation of the cause. For example, when a disk fills up, you could automate the deletion of logs to free up space on the disk. Also, utilizing Kubernetes *liveness probes* in your app deployment can help auto-remediate issues with a process that is not responding in the application.

When building alerts, you also need to consider *alert thresholds*; if you set thresholds too short, then you can get a lot of false positives with your alerts. It's generally recommended to set a threshold of at least five minutes to help eliminate false positives. Coming up with standard thresholds can help define a standard and avoid micromanaging many different thresholds. For example, you might want to follow a specific pattern of 5 minutes, 10 minutes, 30 minutes, 1 hour, and so on.

When building notifications for alerts, you want to ensure that you provide relevant information in the notification. For example, you might provide a link to a "playbook" that gives troubleshooting or other helpful information on resolving the issue. You should also include information on the datacenter, region, app owner, and affected system in notifications. Providing all this information will allow engineers to quickly formulate a theory around the issue.

You also need to build notification channels to route alerts that are fired. When thinking about "Who do I notify when an alert is triggered?" you should ensure that notifications are not just sent to a distribution list or team emails. What tends to happen if alerts are sent to larger groups is that they end up getting filtered out because users see these as noise. You should route notifications to the user who is going to take responsibility for the issue.

With alerting, you'll never get it perfect on day one, and we could argue it might never be perfect. You just want to make sure that you incrementally improve on alerting to preclude alert fatigue, which can cause many issues with staff burnout and your systems.

 For further insight on how to approach alerting on and managing systems, read "My Philosophy on Alerting" (*https://oreil.ly/YPxju*) by Rob Ewaschuk, which is based on Rob's observations as a site reliability engineer (SRE) at Google.

Best Practices for Monitoring, Logging, and Alerting

Following are the best practices that you should adopt regarding monitoring, logging, and alerting.

Monitoring

- Monitor nodes and all Kubernetes components for utilization, saturation, and error rates, and monitor applications for rate, errors, and duration.
- Use closed-box monitoring to monitor for symptoms and not predictive health of a system.
- Use open-box monitoring to inspect the system and its internals with instrumentation.
- Implement time-series-based metrics to gain high-precision metrics that also allow you to have insight into the behavior of your application.
- Utilize monitoring systems like Prometheus that provide key labeling for high dimensionality; this will give a better signal to symptoms of an impacting issue.
- Use average metrics to visualize subtotals and metrics based on factual data. Utilize sum metrics to visualize the distribution across a specific metric.

Logging

- You should use logging in combination with metrics monitoring to get the full picture of how your environment is operating.
- Be cautious of storing logs for more than 30 to 45 days; if needed, use cheaper resources for long-term archiving.
- Limit usage of log forwarders in a sidecar pattern, as they will utilize a lot more resources. Opt for using a DaemonSet for the log forwarder and sending logs to STDOUT.

Alerting

- Be cautious of alert fatigue because it can lead to bad behaviors in people and processes.
- Always look at incrementally improving on alerting and accept that it will not always be perfect.
- Alert for symptoms that affect your SLOs and customers and not for transient issues that don't need immediate human attention.

Summary

In this chapter we discussed the patterns, techniques, and tools that can be used for monitoring our systems with metrics and log collection. The most important piece to take away from this chapter is that you need to rethink how you perform monitoring and do it from the outset. Too many times we see this implemented after the fact, and it can get you into a very bad place in understanding your system. Monitoring is all about having better insight into a system and being able to provide better resiliency, which in turn provides a better end-user experience for your application. Monitoring distributed applications and distributed systems like Kubernetes requires a lot of work, so you must be ready for it at the beginning of your journey.

## CHAPTER 4

Configuration, Secrets, and RBAC

The composable nature of containers allows us as operators to introduce configuration data into a container at runtime. This makes it possible for us to decouple an application's function from the environment it runs in. By means of the conventions allowed in the container runtime to pass through either environment variables or mount external volumes into a container at runtime, you can effectively change the configuration of the application upon its instantiation. As a developer, it is important to consider the dynamic nature of this behavior and allow for the use of environment variables or the reading of configuration data from a specific path available to the application runtime user.

When moving sensitive data such as secrets into a native Kubernetes API object, it is important to understand how Kubernetes secures access to the API. The most commonly implemented security method in use in Kubernetes is Role-Based Access Control (RBAC) to implement a fine-grained permission structure around actions that can be taken against the API by specific users or groups. This chapter covers some of the best practices regarding RBAC and also provides a small primer.

Configuration Through ConfigMaps and Secrets

Kubernetes allows you to natively provide configuration information to our applications through ConfigMaps or secret resources. The main differentiator between the two is the way a pod stores the receiving information and how the data is stored in the etcd data store.

ConfigMaps

It is very common to have applications consume configuration information through some type of mechanism such as command-line arguments, environment variables, or files that are available to the system. Containers allow the developer to decouple this configuration information from the application, which allows for true application portability. The ConfigMap API allows for the injection of supplied configuration information. ConfigMaps are very adaptable to the application's requirements and can provide key/value pairs or complex bulk data such as JSON, XML, or proprietary configuration data.

The ConfigMaps not only provide configuration information for pods, but they can also provide information to be consumed for more complex system services such as controllers, CRDs, operators, and so on. As mentioned earlier, the ConfigMap API is meant more for string data that is not really sensitive data. If your application requires more sensitive data, the Secrets API is more appropriate.

For your application to use the ConfigMap data, it can be injected as either a volume mounted into the pod or as environment variables.

Secrets

Many of the attributes and reasons for which you would want to use a ConfigMap apply to secrets. The main differences lie in the fundamental nature of a secret. Secret data should be stored and handled in a way that can be easily hidden and possibly encrypted at rest if the environment is configured as such. The secret data is represented as base64-encoded information, and it is critical to understand that this is not encrypted. As soon as the secret is injected into the pod, the pod itself can see the secret data in plain text.

Secret data is meant to be small amounts of data, limited by default in Kubernetes to 1 MB in size for the base64-encoded data, so ensure that the actual data is approximately 750 KB because of the overhead of the encoding. There are three types of secrets in Kubernetes:

generic
> This is typically just regular key/value pairs that are created from a file, a directory, or from string literals using the `--from-literal=` parameter, as follows:

```
kubectl create secret generic mysecret --from-literal=key1=$3cr3t1
    --from-literal=key2=@3cr3t2
```

docker-registry
> This is used by the kubelet when passed in a pod template if there is an `image Pullsecret` to provide the credentials needed to authenticate to a private Docker registry:

```
kubectl create secret docker-registry registryKey --docker-server
    myreg.azurecr.io --docker-username myreg --docker-password
    $up3r$3cr3tP@ssw0rd --docker-email ignore@dummy.com
```

tls

This creates a Transport Layer Security (TLS) secret from a valid public/private key pair. As long as the cert is in a valid PEM format, the key pair will be encoded as a secret and can be passed to the pod to use for SSL/TLS needs:

```
kubectl create secret tls www-tls --key=./path_to_key/wwwtls.key
    --cert=./path_to_crt/wwwtls.crt
```

Secrets are also mounted into tmpfs only on the nodes that have a pod that requires the secret and are deleted when the pod that needs the secret is gone. This prevents any secrets from being left behind on the disk of the node. Although this might seem secure, it is important to know that, by default, secrets are stored in the etcd data store of Kubernetes in plain text, and it is important that the system administrators or cloud service provider take efforts to ensure the security of the etcd environment, including mTLS between the etcd nodes and enabling encryption at rest for the etcd data. More recent versions of Kubernetes use etcd3 and have the ability to enable etcd native encryption; however, this is a manual process that must be configured in the API server configuration by specifying a provider and the appropriate key media to properly encrypt secret data held in etcd. As of Kubernetes v1.10 (it has been promoted to beta in v1.12), we have the KMS provider, which promises to provide a more secure key process by using third-party KMS systems to hold the proper keys.

Common Best Practices for the ConfigMap and Secrets APIs

The majority of issues that arise from the use of a ConfigMap or secret are incorrect assumptions about how changes are handled when the data held by the object is updated. By understanding the rules of the road and adding a few tricks to make it easier to abide by those rules, you can steer away from trouble:

- To support dynamic changes to your application without having to redeploy new versions of the pods, mount your ConfigMaps/Secrets as a volume and configure your application with a file watcher to detect the changed file data and reconfigure itself as needed. The following code shows a Deployment that mounts a ConfigMap and a Secret file as a volume:

```
apiVersion: v1
kind: ConfigMap
metadata:
    name: nginx-http-config
    namespace: myapp-prod
data:
```

```yaml
  config: |
    http {
      server {
        location / {
        root /data/html;
        }

        location /images/ {
          root /data;
        }
      }
    }

apiVersion: v1
kind: Secret
metadata:
  name: myapp-api-key
type: Opaque
data:
  myapikey: YWRtd5thSaW4=

apiVersion: apps/v1
kind: Deployment
metadata:
  name: mywebapp
  namespace: myapp-prod
spec:
  containers:
  - name: nginx
    image: nginx
    ports:
    - containerPort: 8080
    volumeMounts:
    - mountPath: /etc/nginx
      name: nginx-config
    - mountPath: /usr/var/nginx/html/keys
      name: api-key
  volumes:
    - name: nginx-config
      configMap:
        name: nginx-http-config
        items:
        - key: config
          path: nginx.conf
    - name: api-key
      secret:
        name: myapp-api-key
        secretname: myapikey
```

There are a couple of things to consider when using `volumeMounts`. First, as soon as the ConfigMap/Secret is created, add it as a volume in your pod's specification. Then mount that volume into the container's filesystem. Each property name in the ConfigMap/Secret will become a new file in the mounted directory, and the contents of each file will be the value specified in the ConfigMap/Secret. Second, avoid mounting ConfigMaps/Secrets using the `volumeMounts.subPath` property. This will prevent the data from being dynamically updated in the volume if you update a ConfigMap/Secret with new data.

- ConfigMaps/Secrets must exist in the namespace for the pods that will consume them prior to the pod being deployed. The optional flag can be used to prevent the pods from not starting if the ConfigMap/Secret is not present.
- Use an admission controller to ensure specific configuration data or to prevent deployments that do not have specific configuration values set. An example would be if you require all production Java workloads to have certain JVM properties set in production environments.
- If you're using Helm to release applications into your environment, you can use a life cycle hook to ensure the ConfigMap/Secret template is deployed before the Deployment is applied.
- Some applications require their configuration to be applied as a single file such as a JSON or YAML file. ConfigMap/Secret allows an entire block of raw data by using the | symbol, as demonstrated here:

```
apiVersion: v1
kind: ConfigMap
metadata:
  name: config-file
data:
  config: |
    {
      "iotDevice": {
        "name": "remoteValve",
        "username": "CC:22:3D:E3:CE:30",
        "port": 51826,
        "pin": "031-45-154"
      }
    }
```

- If the application uses system environment variables to determine its configuration, you can use the injection of the ConfigMap data to create an environment variable mapping into the pod. There are two main ways to do this: mounting every key/value pair in the ConfigMap as a series of environment variables into the pod using `envFrom` and then using `configMapRef` or `secretRef`, or assigning individual keys with their respective values using the `configMapKeyRef` or `secretKeyRef`.

- If you're using the `configMapKeyRef` or `secretKeyRef` method, be aware that if the actual key does not exist, this will prevent the pod from starting.

- If you're loading all the key/value pairs from the ConfigMap/Secret into the pod using `envFrom`, any keys that are considered invalid environment values will be skipped; however, the pod will be allowed to start. The event for the pod will have an event with reason `InvalidVariableNames` and the appropriate message about which key was skipped. The following code is an example of a Deployment with a ConfigMap and Secret reference as an environment variable:

```
apiVersion: v1
kind: ConfigMap
metadata:
  name: mysql-config
data:
  mysqldb: myappdb1
  user: mysqluser1

apiVersion: v1
kind: Secret
metadata:
  name: mysql-secret
type: Opaque
data:
  rootpassword: YWRtJasdhaW4=
  userpassword: MWYyZDigKJGUyfgKJBmU2N2Rm

apiVersion: apps/v1
kind: Deployment
metadata:
  name: myapp-db-deploy
spec:
  selector:
    matchLabels:
      app: myapp-db
  template:
    metadata:
      labels:
        app: myapp-db
    spec:
      containers:
      - name: myapp-db-instance
        image: mysql
        resources:
          limits:
            memory: "128Mi"
            cpu: "500m"
        ports:
        - containerPort: 3306
```

```
    env:
      - name: MYSQL_ROOT_PASSWORD
        valueFrom:
          secretKeyRef:
            name: mysql-secret
            key: rootpassword
      - name: MYSQL_PASSWORD
        valueFrom:
          secretKeyRef:
            name: mysql-secret
            key: userpassword
      - name: MYSQL_USER
        valueFrom:
          configMapKeyRef:
            name: mysql-config
            key: user
      - name: MYSQL_DB
        valueFrom:
          configMapKeyRef:
            name: mysql-config
            key: mysqldb
```

- If there is a need to pass command-line arguments to your containers, environment variable data can be sourced using $(ENV_KEY) interpolation syntax:

```
[...]
spec:
  containers:
  - name: load-gen
    image: busybox
    command: ["/bin/sh"]
args: ["-c", "while true; do curl $(WEB_UI_URL); sleep 10;done"]
    ports:
    - containerPort: 8080
    env:
    - name: WEB_UI_URL
      valueFrom:
        configMapKeyRef:
          name: load-gen-config
          key: url
```

- When consuming ConfigMap/Secret data as environment variables, it is very important to understand that updates to the data in the ConfigMap/Secret will *not* update in the pod and will require a pod restart. This can be done either by deleting the pods and letting the ReplicaSet controller create a new pod, or by triggering a Deployment update, which will follow the proper application update strategy as declared in the Deployment specification.

- It is easier to assume that all changes to a ConfigMap/Secret require an update to the entire Deployment; this ensures that even if you're using environment variables or volumes, the code will take the new configuration data. To make this easier, you can use a CI/CD pipeline to update the `name` property of the ConfigMap/Secret and also update the reference in the Deployment, which will then trigger a Deployment update through normal Kubernetes update strategies. We will explore this in the following example code. If you're using Helm to release your application code into Kubernetes, you can take advantage of an annotation in the Deployment template to check the `sha256` checksum of the ConfigMap/Secret. This triggers Helm to update the Deployment using the `helm upgrade` command when the data within a ConfigMap/Secret is changed:

```
apiVersion: apps/v1
kind: Deployment
[...]
spec:
  template:
    metadata:
      annotations:
        checksum/config: {{ include (print $.Template.BasePath "/configmap.yaml")
            . | sha256sum }}
[...]
```

Best Practices Specific to Secrets

Because of the nature of sensitive data of the Secrets API, there are naturally more specific best practices, which are mainly around the security of the data itself:

- If your workload does not need to access the Kubernetes API directly it is good practice to block the automounting of the API Credential for the Service Account (Default or operator created). This will reduce the API calls to the API server as a watch is used to update the API credential data upon the credential expiring. In very large clusters or clusters with a lot of pods, this will reduce the calls to the Control Plane thus reducing a possible cause of performance degradation. This can be defined on the ServiceAccount or the Pod Spec itself:

```
apiVersion: v1
kind: ServiceAccount
metadata:
  name: app1-svcacct
automountServiceAccountToken: false
[...]

apiVersion: v1
kind: Pod
metadata:
  name: app1-pod
```

```
spec:
  serviceAccountName: app1-svcacct
  automountServiceAccountToken: false
[...]
```

- The original specification for the Secrets API outlined a pluggable architecture to allow the actual storage of the secret to be configurable based on requirements. Solutions such as HashiCorp Vault, Aqua Security, Twistlock, AWS Secrets Manager, Google Cloud KMS, or Azure Key Vault allow the use of external storage systems for secret data using a higher level of encryption and auditability than what is offered natively in Kubernetes. The Linux Foundation project ExternalSecrets Operator provides a native way to provide this functionality.

- Assign an `imagePullSecrets` to a `serviceaccount` that the pod will use to automatically mount the secret without having to declare it in the `pod.spec`. You can patch the default service account for the namespace of your application and add the `imagePullSecrets` to it directly. This automatically adds it to all pods in the namespace:

```
Create the docker-registry secret first
kubectl create secret docker-registry registryKey --docker-server
myreg.azurecr.io --docker-username myreg --docker-password $up3r$3cr3tP@ssw0rd
--docker-email ignore@dummy.com

patch the default serviceaccount for the namespace you wish to configure
kubectl patch serviceaccount default -p '{"imagePullSecrets": [{"name":
"registryKey"}]}'
```

- Use CI/CD capabilities to get secrets from a secure vault or encrypted store with a Hardware Security Module (HSM) during the release pipeline. This allows for separation of duties. Security management teams can create and encrypt the secrets, and developers just need to reference the names of the secret expected. This is also the preferred DevOps process to ensure a more dynamic application delivery process.

RBAC

When working in large, distributed environments, it is very common that some type of security mechanism is needed to prevent unauthorized access to critical systems. There are numerous strategies around how to limit access to resources in computer systems, but the majority all go through the same phases. Using an analogy of a common experience such as flying to a foreign country can help explain the processes that happen in systems like Kubernetes. We can use the common traveler's experience with a passport, travel visa, and customs or border guards to show the process:

Passport (subject authentication)

Usually you need to have a passport issued by some government agency that will offer some sort of verification as to who you are. This would be equivalent to a user account in Kubernetes. Kubernetes relies on an external authority to authenticate users; however, service accounts are a type of account that is managed directly by Kubernetes.

Visa or travel policy (authorization)

Countries will have formal agreements to accept travelers holding passports from other countries through formal short-term agreements such as visas. The visas will also outline what the visitor may do and for how long they may stay in the visiting country, depending on the specific type of visa. This would be equivalent to authorization in Kubernetes. Kubernetes has different authorization methods, but RBAC is the one used most. This allows very granular access to different API capabilities.

Border patrol or customs (admission control)

When entering a foreign country, usually there is a body of authority that will check the requisite documents, including the passport and visa, and, in many cases, inspect what is being brought into the country to ensure it abides by that country's laws. In Kubernetes this is equivalent to admission controllers. Admission controllers can allow, deny, or change the requests into the API based upon rules and policies that are defined. Kubernetes has many built-in admission controllers such as PodSecurity, ResourceQuota, and ServiceAccount controllers. Kubernetes also allows for dynamic controllers through the use of validating or mutating admission controllers.

The focus of this section is the least understood and the most avoided of these three areas: RBAC. Before we outline some of the best practices, we first must present a primer on Kubernetes RBAC.

RBAC Primer

The RBAC process in Kubernetes has three main components that need to be defined: the subject, the rule, and the role binding.

Subjects

The first component is the subject, the item that is actually being checked for access. The subject is usually a user, a service account, or a group. As mentioned earlier, users as well as groups are handled outside of Kubernetes by the authorization module used. We can categorize these as basic authentication, x.509 client certificates, or bearer tokens. The most common implementations use either x.509 client certificates or some type of bearer token using something like an OpenID Connect system such as Azure Active Directory (Azure AD), Salesforce, or Google.

Service accounts in Kubernetes are different from user accounts in that they are namespace bound and internally stored in Kubernetes; they are meant to represent processes, not people, and are managed by native Kubernetes controllers.

Rules

Simply stated, this is the actual list of actions that can be performed on a specific object (resource) or a group of objects in the API. Verbs align to typical create, read, update, and delete (CRUD) type operations but with some added capabilities in Kubernetes such as `watch`, `list`, and `exec`. The objects align to the different API components and are grouped together in categories. Pod objects, as an example, are part of the core API and can be referenced with `apiGroup: ""`, whereas deployments are under the app API group. This is the real power of the RBAC process and probably what intimidates and confuses people when creating proper RBAC controls.

Roles

Roles allow the definition of scope of the rules defined. Kubernetes has two types of roles, `role` and `clusterRole`, the difference being that `role` is specific to a namespace, and `clusterRole` is a cluster-wide role across all namespaces. An example role definition with namespace scope would be as follows:

```
kind: Role
apiVersion: rbac.authorization.k8s.io/v1
metadata:
  namespace: default
  name: pod-viewer
rules:
- apiGroups: [""] # "" indicates the core API group
  resources: ["pods"]
  verbs: ["get", "watch", "list"]
```

RoleBindings

The RoleBinding allows a mapping of a subject like a user or group to a specific role. Bindings also have two modes: `roleBinding`, which is specific to a namespace, and `clusterRoleBinding`, which is across the entire cluster. Here's an example RoleBinding with namespace scope:

```
kind: RoleBinding
apiVersion: rbac.authorization.k8s.io/v1
metadata:
  name: noc-helpdesk-view
  namespace: default
subjects:
- kind: User
  name: helpdeskuser@example.com
```

```
  apiGroup: rbac.authorization.k8s.io
roleRef:
  kind: Role #this must be Role or ClusterRole
  name: pod-viewer # this must match the name of the Role or ClusterRole
                   # to bind to
  apiGroup: rbac.authorization.k8s.io
```

RBAC Best Practices

RBAC is a critical component of running a secure, dependable, and stable Kubernetes environment. The concepts underlying RBAC can be complex; however, adhering to a few best practices can ease some of the major stumbling blocks:

- Applications that are developed to run in Kubernetes rarely ever need an RBAC role and RoleBinding associated to them. Only if the application code interacts directly with the Kubernetes API does the application require RBAC configuration.

- If the application does need to directly access the Kubernetes API to perhaps change configuration depending on endpoints being added to a service, or if it needs to list all the pods in a specific namespace, the best practice is to create a new service account that is then specified in the pod specification. Then, create a role that has the least amount of privileges needed to accomplish its goal.

- Use an OpenID Connect service that enables identity management and, if needed, two-factor authentication. This will allow for a higher level of identity authentication. Map user groups to roles that have the least amount of privileges needed to accomplish the job.

- Along with the aforementioned practice, you should use Just in Time (JIT) access systems to allow site reliability engineers (SREs), operators, and those who might need to have escalated privileges for a short period of time to accomplish a very specific task. Alternatively, these users should have different identities that are more heavily audited for sign-on, and those accounts should have more elevated privileges assigned by the user account or group bound to a role.

- Specific service accounts should be used for CI/CD tools that deploy into your Kubernetes clusters. This ensures auditability within the cluster and an understanding of who might have deployed or deleted any objects in a cluster.

- If you're still using Helm v2 to deploy applications, the default service account is Tiller, deployed to kube-system. It is better to deploy Tiller into each namespace with a service account specifically for Tiller that is scoped for that namespace. In the CI/CD tool that calls the Helm install/upgrade command, as a prestep, initialize the Helm client with the service account and the specific namespace for the Deployment. The service account name can be the same for each namespace, but the namespace should be specific. It is advised to move to Helm v3 because one of its core principles is that Tiller is no longer needed to run in a cluster. The new architecture is completely client based and uses the RBAC access of the user calling the Helm commands. This is in alignment with the preferred approach of client-based tooling to the Kubernetes API.

- Limit any applications that require `watch` and `list` on the Secrets API. This basically allows the application or the person who deployed the pod to view the secrets in that namespace. If an application needs to access the Secrets API for specific secrets, limit using `get` on any specific secrets that the application needs to read outside of those that it is directly assigned.

Summary

Principles for developing applications for cloud native delivery is a topic for another day, but it is universally accepted that strict separation of configuration from code is a key principle for success. With native objects for nonsensitive data, the ConfigMap API, and for sensitive data, the Secrets API, Kubernetes can now manage this process in a declarative approach. As more and more critical data is represented and stored natively in the Kubernetes API, it is critical to secure access to those APIs through proper gated security processes such as RBAC and integrated authentication systems.

As you'll see throughout the rest of this book, these principles permeate every aspect of the proper deployment of services into a Kubernetes platform to build a stable, reliable, secure, and robust system.

## CHAPTER 5

Continuous Integration, Testing, and Deployment

In this chapter, we look at the key concepts of how to integrate a continuous integration/continuous deployment (CI/CD) pipeline to deliver your applications to Kubernetes. Building a well-integrated pipeline will enable you to deliver applications to production with confidence, so here we look at the methods, tools, and processes to enable CI/CD in your environment. The goal of CI/CD is to have a fully automated process, from a developer checking in code to rolling out the new code to production. You want to avoid manually rolling out updates to your apps deployed to Kubernetes because it can be very error prone. Manually managing application updates in Kubernetes leads to configuration drift and fragile deployment updates, and overall agility delivering an application is lost.

We cover the following topics in this chapter:

- Version control
- Continuous integration
- Testing
- Container builds
- Container image tagging
- Continuous deployment
- Deployment strategies
- Testing in production
- Chaos testing

We also go through an example CI/CD pipeline, which consists of the following tasks:

- Pushing code changes to the Git repository
- Running a build of the application code
- Running test against the code
- Building a container image on a successful test
- Pushing the container image to a container registry
- Deploying the application to Kubernetes
- Running a test against a deployed application
- Performing rolling upgrades on Deployments

Version Control

Every CI/CD pipeline starts with version control, which maintains a running history of application and configuration code changes. Git has become the industry standard as a source-control management platform, and every Git repository will contain a *main branch*. A main branch contains your production code. You will have other branches for feature and development work that eventually will be merged to your main branch. There are many ways to set up a branching strategy, and the setup will be very dependent on the organization structure and separation of duties. We find that including both application code and configuration code, such as a Kubernetes manifest or Helm charts, helps promote good DevOps principles of communication and collaboration. Having both application developers and operation engineers collaborate in a single repository builds confidence in a team to deliver an application to production.

Continuous Integration

CI is the process of integrating code changes continuously into a version-control repository. Instead of committing large changes less often, you commit smaller changes more often. Each time a code change is committed to the repository, a build is kicked off. This allows you to have a quicker feedback loop into what might have broken the application if problems indeed arise. Many solutions provide CI, with Jenkins being one of the more popular tools. At this point you might be asking, "Why do I need to know about how the application is built; isn't that the application developer's role?" Traditionally, this might have been the case, but as companies move toward embracing a DevOps culture, the operations team comes closer to the application code and software development workflows.

Testing

The goal of running tests in the pipeline is to quickly provide a feedback loop for code changes that break the build. The language that you're using will determine the testing framework you use. For example, Go applications can use `go test` for running a suite of unit tests against your code base. Having an extensive test suite helps to avoid delivering bad code into your production environment. You'll want to ensure that if tests fail in the pipeline, the build fails after the test suite runs. You don't want to build the container image and push it to a registry if you have failing tests against your code base.

Again, you might be asking, "Isn't creating tests a developer's job?" As you begin automating the delivery of infrastructure and applications to production, you need to think about running automated tests against all of the pieces of the code base. For example, in Chapter 2, we talked about using Helm to package applications for Kubernetes. Helm includes a tool called `helm lint`, which runs a series of tests against a chart to examine any potential issues with the chart provided. Many different tests need to be run in an end-to-end pipeline. Some are the developer's responsibility, like unit testing for the application, but others, like smoke testing, will be a joint effort. Testing the code base and its delivery to production is a team effort and needs to be implemented end to end.

Container Builds

When building your images, you should optimize the size of the image. Having a smaller image decreases the time it takes to pull and deploy the image, and also increases the security of the image. There are multiple ways of optimizing the image size, but some do have trade-offs. The following strategies will help you build the smallest image possible for your application:

Multistage builds
: These allow you to remove the dependencies not needed for your applications to run. For example, with Golang, we don't need all the build tools used to build the static binary, so multistage builds allow you to run a build step in a single Dockerfile with the final image containing only the static binary that's needed to run the application.

Distroless base images
: These remove all the unneeded binaries and shells from the image. This reduces the size of the image and increases the security. The trade-off with distroless images is you don't have a shell, so you can't attach a debugger to the image. You might think this is great, but it can be a pain to debug an application. Distroless images contain no package manager, shell, or other typical OS packages, so you

might not have access to the debugging tools you are accustomed to with a typical OS.

Optimized base images

These are images that focus on removing the cruft out of the OS layer and provide a slimmed-down image. For example, Alpine provides a base image that starts at just 10 MB, and it allows you to attach a local debugger for local development. Other distros also typically offer an optimized base image, such as Debian's Slim image. This might be a good option for you because its optimized images give you the capabilities you expect for development while also optimizing for image size and lower security exposure.

Optimizing your images is extremely important and often overlooked by users. You might have obstacles due to company standards for OSes that are approved for use in the enterprise, but push back on these so that you can maximize the value of containers.

We have found that companies starting out with Kubernetes tend to be successful with initially using their current OS but then choose a more optimized image, like Debian Slim. After you mature in operationalizing and developing against a container environment, you'll be comfortable with distroless images.

Container Image Tagging

Another step in the CI pipeline is to build a container image so that you have an image artifact to deploy to an environment. It's important to have an image-tagging strategy so that you can easily identify the versioned images you have deployed to your environments. We can't preach enough about one of the most important things: do not use "latest" as an image tag. Using that as an image tag is not a *version* and will lead to not having the ability to identify what code change belongs to the rolled-out image. Every image that is built in the CI pipeline should have a unique tag.

There are multiple strategies we've found to be effective when tagging images in the CI pipeline. The following strategies allow you to easily identify the code changes and the build with which they are associated:

BuildID

When a CI build kicks off, it has a buildID associated with it. Using this part of the tag allows you to reference which build assembled the image.

Build System-buildID

This tag is the same as BuildID but adds the Build System for users who have multiple build systems.

Git hash

> On new code commits, a Git hash is generated, and using the hash for the tag allows you to easily reference which commit generated the image.

githash-buildID

> This allows you to reference both the code commit and the buildID that generated the image. The only caution here is that the tag can be kind of long.

Continuous Deployment

CD is the process by which changes that have passed successfully through the CI pipeline are deployed to production without human intervention. Containers provide a great advantage for deploying changes into production. Container images become an immutable object that can be promoted through dev and staging and into production. For example, a major issue we've always had has been maintaining consistent environments. Almost everyone has experienced a Deployment that works fine in staging, but when it gets promoted to production, it breaks. This is due to having *configuration drift*, with libraries and versioning of components differing in each environment. Kubernetes gives us a declarative way to describe our Deployment objects that can be versioned and deployed consistently.

One thing to keep in mind is that you need a solid CI pipeline set up before focusing on CD. If you don't have a robust set of tests to catch issues early in the pipeline, you'll end up rolling bad code to all your environments.

Deployment Strategies

Now that we learned the principles of CD, let's look at the different rollout strategies you can use. Kubernetes provides multiple strategies to roll out new versions of your application. And even though it has a built-in mechanism to provide rolling updates, you can also utilize more advanced strategies. Here, we examine the following strategies to deliver updates to your application:

- Rolling updates
- Blue/green deployments
- Canary deployments

Rolling updates are built into Kubernetes and allow you to trigger an update to the currently running application without downtime. For example, if you took your frontend app that is currently running frontend:v1 and updated the Deployment to frontend:v2, Kubernetes would update the replicas in a rolling fashion to frontend:v2. Figure 5-1 depicts a rolling update.

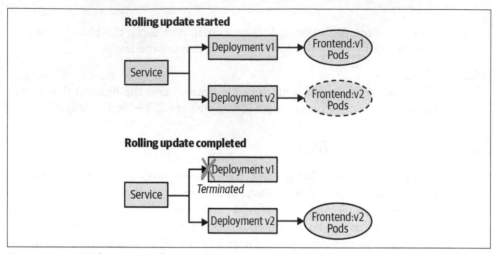

Figure 5-1. A Kubernetes rolling update

A Deployment object also lets you configure the maximum amount of replicas to be updated and the maximum unavailable pods during the rollout. The following manifest is an example of how you specify the rolling update strategy:

```
kind: Deployment
apiVersion: apps/v1
metadata:
  name: frontend
  labels:
    app: frontend
spec:
  replicas: 3
  selector:
    matchLabels:
      app: frontend
  template:
    metadata:
      labels:
        app: frontend
    spec:
      containers:
      - name: frontend
        image: brendanburns/frontend:v1
  strategy:
    type: RollingUpdate
    rollingUpdate:
      maxSurge: 1 # Maximum amount of replicas to update at one time
      maxUnavailable: 1 # Maximum amount of replicas unavailable during rollout
```

You need to be cautious with rolling updates because using this strategy can cause dropped connections. To deal with this issue, you can utilize *readiness probes* and *preStop* life-cycle hooks. The readiness probe ensures that the new version deployed is ready to accept traffic, whereas the preStop hook can ensure that connections are drained on the current deployed application. The life-cycle hook is called before the container exits and is synchronous, so it must complete before the final termination signal is given. The following example implements a readiness probe and life-cycle hook:

```
kind: Deployment
apiVersion: apps/v1
metadata:
  name: frontend
  labels:
    app: frontend
spec:
  replicas: 3
  selector:
    matchLabels:
      app: frontend
  template:
    metadata:
      labels:
        app: frontend
    spec:
      containers:
      - name: frontend
        image: brendanburns/frontend:v1
        livenessProbe:
          # ...
        readinessProbe:
          httpGet:
            path: /readiness # probe endpoint
            port: 8888
        lifecycle:
          preStop:
            exec:
              command: ["/usr/sbin/nginx","-s","quit"]
  strategy:
    # ...
```

The preStop life-cycle hook in this example will gracefully exit NGINX, whereas a SIGTERM conducts a nongraceful, quick exit.

Another concern with rolling updates is that you now have two versions of the application running at the same time during the rollover. Your database schema needs to support both versions of the application. You can also use a feature flag strategy in which your schema indicates the new columns created by the new app version. After the rolling update has completed, the old columns can be removed.

We have also defined a readiness and liveness probe in our Deployment manifest. A readiness probe will ensure that your application is ready to serve traffic before putting it behind the service as an endpoint. The liveness probe ensures that your application is healthy and running, and it restarts the pod if it fails its liveness probe. Kubernetes can automatically restart a failed pod only if the pod exits on error. For example, the liveness probe can check its endpoint and restart it if we had a deadlock from which the pod did not exit.

Blue/green deployments allow you to release your application predictably. With blue/green deployments, you control when the traffic is shifted over to the new environment, so it gives you a lot of control over the rollout of a new version of your application. With blue/green deployments, you are required to have the capacity to deploy both the existing and new environment at the same time. These types of deployments have a lot of advantages, such as easily switching back to your previous version of the application. There are some things that you need to consider with this deployment strategy, however:

- Database migrations can become difficult with this deployment option because you need to consider in-flight transactions and schema update compatibility.
- There is the risk of accidental deletion of both environments.
- You need extra capacity for both environments.
- There are coordination issues for hybrid deployments in which legacy apps can't handle the deployment.

Figure 5-2 depicts a blue/green deployment.

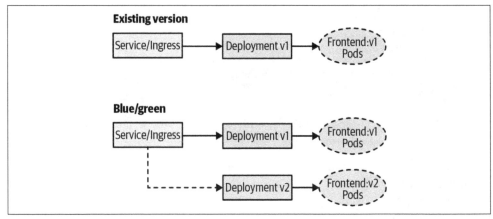

Figure 5-2. A blue/green deployment

Canary deployments are very similar to blue/green deployments, but they give you much more control over shifting traffic to the new release. Most modern Ingress implementations will give you the ability to release a percentage of traffic to a new release, but you can also implement a service mesh technology, like Istio, Linkerd, or HashiCorp Consul, which gives you a number of features that help implement this deployment strategy.

Canary deployments allow you to test new features for only a subset of users. For example, you might roll out a new version of an application and want to test the deployment for only 10% of your user base. This allows you to reduce the risk of a bad deployment or broken features to a much smaller subset of users. If there are no errors with the deployment or new features, you can begin shifting a greater percentage of traffic to the new version of the application. There are also more advanced techniques that you can use with canary deployments in which you release to only a specific region of users or only target users with a specific profile. These types of releases are often referred to as A/B or dark releases because users are unaware they are testing new feature deployments.

With canary deployments, you have some of the same considerations that you have with blue/green deployments, but there are some additional considerations as well. You must have:

- The ability to shift traffic to a percentage of users
- A firm knowledge of steady state to compare against a new release
- Metrics to understand whether the new release is in a "good" or "bad" state

Figure 5-3 provides an example of a canary deployment.

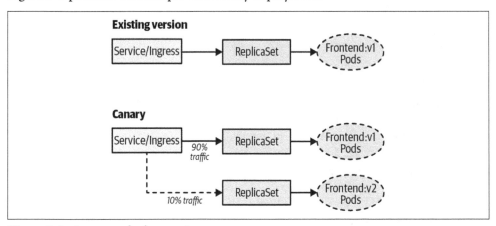

Figure 5-3. A canary deployment

Canary releases also suffer from having multiple versions of the application running at the same time. Your database schema needs to support both versions of the application. When using these strategies, you'll need to focus on how to handle dependent services and having multiple versions running. This includes having strong API contracts and ensuring that your data services support the multiple versions you have deployed at the same time.

Testing in Production

Testing in production helps you to build confidence in the resiliency, scalability, and UX of your application. This comes with the caveat that *testing in production* doesn't come without challenges and risk, but it's worth the effort to ensure reliability in your systems. There are important aspects you need to address up front when embarking on the implementation. You need to ensure that you have an in-depth observability strategy in place, in which you have the ability to identify the effects of testing in production. Without being able to observe metrics that affect the end users' experience of your applications, you won't have a clear indication of what to focus on when trying to improve the resiliency of your system. You also need a high degree of automation in place to be able to automatically recover from failures that you inject into your systems.

You'll need to implement many tools to reduce risk and effectively test your systems when they're in production. We have discussed some tools in this chapter, but there are some new ones, like distributed tracing, instrumentation, chaos engineering, and traffic shadowing. To recap, here are the tools we have already mentioned:

- Canary deployments
- Blue/green deployments
- Traffic shifting
- Feature flags

Chaos engineering was developed by Netflix. It is the practice of deploying experiments into live production systems to discover weaknesses within those systems. Chaos engineering allows you to learn about the behavior of your system by observing it during a controlled experiment. Following are the steps that you want to implement before doing a "game-day" experiment:

1. Build a hypothesis and learn about your steady state.
2. Have a varying degree of real-world events that can affect the system.

3. Build a control group and experiment to compare to steady state.

4. Perform experiments to test the hypothesis.

It's extremely important that when you're running experiments, you minimize the "blast radius" to ensure that the issues that might arise are minimal. You'll also want to ensure that when you're building experiments, you focus on automating them, given that running experiments can be labor intensive.

By this point, you might be asking, "Why wouldn't I just test in staging?" We find there are some inherent problems when testing in staging, such as the following:

- Nonidentical deployment of resources.
- Configuration drift from production.
- Traffic and user behavior tend to be generated synthetically.
- The number of requests generated don't mimic a real workload.
- Lack of monitoring implemented in staging.
- The data services deployed contain differing data and load than in production.

We can't stress this enough: ensure that you have solid confidence in the monitoring you have in place for production, because this practice tends to fail users who don't have adequate observability of their production systems. Also, starting with smaller experiments to first learn about your experiments and their effects will help build confidence.

Setting Up a Pipeline and Performing a Chaos Experiment

The first step in the process is to fork a GitHub repository so that you can have your own repository to use throughout the chapter. You will need to use the GitHub interface to fork the sample application repository (*https://oreil.ly/TtJfd*).

Setting Up CI

Now that you have learned about CI, you will set up a build of the code that we cloned previously.

For this example, we use the hosted *drone.io*. You'll need to sign up for a free account (*https://cloud.drone.io*). Log in with your GitHub credentials (this registers your repositories in Drone and allows you to synchronize the repositories). After you're logged in to Drone, select Activate on your forked repository. The first thing that you need to do is add some secrets to your settings so that you can push the app to your Docker Hub registry and also deploy the app to your Kubernetes cluster.

Under your repository in Drone, click Settings and add the following secrets (see Figure 5-4):

- docker_username
- docker_password
- kubernetes_server
- kubernetes_cert
- kubernetes_token

Figure 5-4. Drone secrets configuration

The Docker username and password will be whatever you used to register on Docker Hub. The following steps show how to create a Kubernetes service account and certificate and retrieve the token.

For the Kubernetes server, you will need a publicly available Kubernetes API endpoint.

 You will need cluster-admin privileges on your Kubernetes cluster to perform the steps in this section.

You can retrieve your API endpoint by using the following command:

```
kubectl cluster-info
```

You should see something like the following: Kubernetes master is running at https://kbp.centralus.azmk8s.io:443. You'll store this in the `kubernetes_server` secret.

Now let's create a service account that Drone will use to connect to the cluster. Use the following command to create the `serviceaccount`:

```
kubectl create serviceaccount drone
```

Next, use the following command to create a `clusterrolebinding` for the `service account`:

```
kubectl create clusterrolebinding drone-admin \
  --clusterrole=cluster-admin \
  --serviceaccount=default:drone
```

Now retrieve your `serviceaccount` token:

```
TOKENNAME=`kubectl -n default get serviceaccount/drone
    -o jsonpath='{.secrets[0].name}'`
TOKEN=`kubectl -n default get secret $TOKENNAME -o jsonpath='{.data.token}' |
    base64 -d`
echo $TOKEN
```

You'll want to store the output of the token in the `kubernetes_token` secret.

You will also need the user certificate to authenticate to the cluster, so use the following command and paste the `ca.crt` for the `kubernetes_cert` secret:

```
kubectl get secret $TOKENNAME -o yaml | grep 'ca.crt:'
```

Now, build your app in a Drone pipeline and then push it to Docker Hub.

The first step is the *build step*, which will build your Node.js frontend. Drone utilizes container images to run its steps, which gives you a lot of flexibility in what you can do with it. For the build step, use a Node.js image from Docker Hub:

```
pipeline:
  build:
    image: node
    commands:
      - cd frontend
      - npm i redis --save
```

When the build completes, you'll want to test it, so we include a *test step*, which will run `npm` against the newly built app:

```
test:
    image: node
    commands:
      - cd frontend
```

```
- npm i redis --save
- npm test
```

Now that you have successfully built and tested your app, you will move on to a *publish step* to create a container image of the app and push it to Docker Hub.

In the *.drone.yml* file, make the following code change:

```
repo: <your-registry>/frontend

publish:
    image: plugins/docker
    dockerfile: ./frontend/Dockerfile
    context: ./frontend
    repo: dstrebel/frontend
    tags: [latest, v2]
    secrets: [ docker_username, docker_password ]
```

After the Docker build step finishes, it will push the image to your Docker registry.

Setting Up CD

For the deployment step in your pipeline, you will push your application to your Kubernetes cluster. You will use the deployment manifest that is under the frontend app folder in your repository:

```
kubectl:
    image: dstrebel/drone-kubectl-helm
    secrets: [ kubernetes_server, kubernetes_cert, kubernetes_token ]
    kubectl: "apply -f ./frontend/deployment.yaml"
```

After the pipeline finishes its deployment, you will see the pods running in your cluster. Run the following command to confirm that the pods are running:

```
kubectl get pods
```

You can also add a test step that will retrieve the status of the deployment by adding the following step in your Drone pipeline:

```
test-deployment:
    image: dstrebel/drone-kubectl-helm
    secrets: [ kubernetes_server, kubernetes_cert, kubernetes_token ]
    kubectl: "get deployment frontend"
```

Performing a Rolling Upgrade

Let's demonstrate a rolling upgrade by changing a line in the frontend code. In the *server.js* file, change the following line and then commit the change:

```
console.log('api server is running.');
```

You will see the deployment rolling out and rolling updates happening to the existing pods. After the rolling update finishes, you'll have the new version of the application deployed.

A Simple Chaos Experiment

A variety of tools in the Kubernetes ecosystem can help with performing chaos experiments in your environment. They range from sophisticated hosted Chaos as a Service solutions to basic chaos experiment tools that kill pods in your environment. Following are some of the successful tools:

Gremlin
Hosted chaos service that provides advanced features for running chaos experiments

PowerfulSeal
Open source project that provides advanced chaos scenarios

Chaos Toolkit
Open source project with a mission to provide a free, open, and community-driven toolkit and API to all the various forms of chaos engineering tools

KubeMonkey
Open source tool that provides basic resiliency testing for pods in your cluster

Let's set up a quick chaos experiment to test the resiliency of your application by automatically terminating pods. For this experiment, we'll use Chaos Toolkit:

```
pip install -U chaostoolkit

pip install chaostoolkit-kubernetes

export FRONTEND_URL="http://$(kubectl get svc frontend
    -o jsonpath="{.status.loadBalancer.ingress[*].ip}"):8080/api/"

chaos run experiment.json
```

Best Practices for CI/CD

Your CI/CD pipeline won't be perfect on day one, but consider some of the following best practices to iteratively improve on the pipeline:

- With CI, focus on automation and providing quick builds. Optimizing the build speed will provide developers quick feedback if their changes have broken the build.
- Focus on providing reliable tests in your pipeline. This will give developers rapid feedback on issues with their code. The faster the feedback loop to developers, the more productive they'll become in their workflow.

- When deciding on CI/CD tools, ensure that the tools allow you to define the pipeline as code. This will allow you to version-control the pipeline with your application code.

- Ensure that you optimize your images so that you can reduce the size of the image and also reduce the attack surface when running the image in production. Multistage Docker builds allow you to remove packages not needed for the application to run. For example, you might need Maven to build the application, but you don't need it for the actual running image.

- Avoid using "latest" as an image tag, and utilize a *tag* that can be referenced back to the buildID or Git commit.

- If you are new to CD, utilize Kubernetes rolling updates to start. They are easy to use and will get you comfortable with deployment. As you become more comfortable and confident with CD, look at utilizing blue/green and canary deployment strategies.

- With CD, ensure that you test how client connections and database schema upgrades are handled in your application.

- Testing in production will help you build reliability into your application and ensure that you have good monitoring in place. With testing in production, also start at a small scale and limit the blast radius of the experiment.

Summary

In this chapter, we discussed the stages of building a CI/CD pipeline for your applications, which let you reliably deliver software with confidence. CI/CD pipelines help reduce risk and increase throughput of delivering applications to Kubernetes. We also discussed the different deployment strategies that can be utilized for delivering applications.

## CHAPTER 6

Versioning, Releases, and Rollouts

One of the main complaints of traditional monolithic applications is that over time they begin to grow too large and unwieldy to properly upgrade, version, or modify at the speed the business requires. Many can argue that this is one of the critical factors that led to more Agile development practices and the advent of microservice architectures. Being able to quickly iterate on new code, solve new problems, or fix hidden problems before they become major issues, as well as the promise of zero-downtime upgrades, are all goals that development teams strive for. Practically, these issues can be solved with proper processes and procedures in place, no matter the type of system, but this usually comes at a much higher cost of both technology and human capital to maintain.

When designing systems, isolation and composability are important variables. The adoption of containers as the runtime for application code allows for this but still requires a high level of human automation or system management to maintain at a dependable level for large systems. Over time, the system grew, more brittleness was introduced, and systems engineers began to build complex automation processes to deliver on complex release, upgrade, and failure detection mechanisms. Service orchestrators such as Apache Mesos, HashiCorp Nomad, and even specialized container-based orchestrators such as Kubernetes and Docker Swarm have evolved these processes into more primitive components directly into their runtimes. Now, systems engineers can solve more complex system problems as the table stakes have been elevated to include the versioning, release, and deployment of applications into the system.

Versioning

This section is not meant to be a primer on software versioning and the history behind it; there are countless articles and computer science course books on the subject. The main thing is to pick a pattern and stick with it. The majority of software companies and developers have agreed that some form of *semantic versioning* is the most useful, especially in a microservice architecture in which a team that writes a certain microservice will depend on the API compatibility of other microservices that make up the system.

For those new to semantic versioning, the basics are that it follows a three-part version number in a pattern of *major version*, *minor version*, and *patch*, usually expressed in a *dot notation* such as 1(major).2(minor).3(patch). The patch signifies an incremental release that includes a bug fix or very minor change that has no API changes. The minor version signifies updates that might have new API changes but it is backward compatible with the previous version. This is a key attribute for developers working with other microservices they might not be involved in developing. Knowing that I have my service written to communicate with version 1.4.7 of another microservice that has been recently upgraded to 1.5.7 should signify that I might not need to change my code unless I want to take advantage of any new API features. The major version is a breaking change increment to the code. In most cases, the API is no longer compatible between major versions of the same code. There are many slight modifications to this process, including a "4" version to indicate the stage of the software in its development life cycle, such as 1.4.7.0 for alpha code and 1.4.7.3 for release. The most important thing is that there is consistency across the system.

Releases

In truth, Kubernetes does not really have a release controller, so there is no native concept of a release. This is usually added to a Deployment `metadata.labels` specification and/or in the `pod.spec.template.metadata.label` specification. When to include either is very important, and based on how CD is used to update changes to deployments, it can have varied effects. When Helm for Kubernetes was introduced, one of its main concepts was the notion of a release to differentiate the running instance of the same Helm chart in a cluster. This concept is easily reproducible without Helm; however, Helm natively keeps track of releases and their history, so many CD tools integrate Helm into their pipelines to be the actual release service. Again, the key here is consistency in how versioning is used and where it is surfaced in the system state of the cluster.

Release names can be quite useful if there is institutional agreement as to the definition of certain names. Often, labels such as `stable` or `canary` are used, which helps to give some operational control when tools such as service meshes are added to make

---

fine-grained routing decisions. Large organizations that drive numerous changes for different audiences will also adopt a ring architecture that can be denoted as ring-0, ring-1, and so on.

This topic requires a little side trip into the specifics of labels in the Kubernetes declarative model. Labels themselves are very much free form and can be any key/value pair that follows the syntactical rules of the API. The key is not really the content but how each controller handles labels, changes to labels, and selector matching of labels. Jobs, Deployments, ReplicaSets, and DaemonSets support selector-based matching of pods via labels through direct mapping or set-based expressions. It is important to understand that label selectors are immutable after they are created, which means if you add a new selector and the pod's labels have a corresponding match, a new ReplicaSet is made, not an upgrade to an existing ReplicaSet. This becomes very important to understand when dealing with rollouts, discussed next.

Rollouts

Prior to the Deployment controller being introduced in Kubernetes, the only mechanism that existed to control how applications were rolled out by the Kubernetes controller process was using the command-line interface (CLI) command kubectl rolling-update on the specific replicaController that was to be updated. This was very difficult for declarative CD models because this was not part of the state of the original manifest. One had to carefully ensure that manifests were updated correctly, versioned properly so as to not accidentally roll the system back, and archived when no longer needed. The Deployment controller added the ability to automate this update process using a specific strategy and then allowing the system to read the declarative new state based on changes to the spec.template of the Deployment. This last fact is often misunderstood by new users of Kubernetes and causes frustration when they change a label in the Deployment metadata fields, reapply a manifest, and no update has been triggered. The Deployment controller is able to determine changes to the specification and will take action to update the Deployment based on a strategy that is defined by the specification. Kubernetes Deployments support two strategies, rollingUpdate and recreate, the former being the default.

If a rolling update is specified, the Deployment will create a new ReplicaSet to scale to the number of required replicas, and the old ReplicaSet will scale down to zero based on specific values for maxUnavailble and maxSurge. In essence, those two values will prevent Kubernetes from removing older pods until a sufficient number of newer pods have come online, and Kubernetes will not create new pods until a certain number of old pods have been removed. The nice thing is that the Deployment controller will keep a history of the updates, and through the CLI, you can roll back Deployments to previous versions.

The `recreate` strategy is a valid strategy for certain workloads that can handle a complete outage of the pods in a ReplicaSet with little to no degradation of service. In this strategy the Deployment controller will create a new ReplicaSet with the new configuration and will delete the prior ReplicaSet before bringing the new pods online. Services that sit behind queue-based systems are an example of a service that could handle this type of disruption, because messages will queue while waiting for the new pods to come online, and message processing will resume as soon as the new pods come online.

Putting It All Together

Within a single service Deployment, a few key areas are affected by versioning, release, and rollout management. Let's examine an example Deployment and then break down the specific areas of interest as they relate to best practices:

```
# Web Deployment
apiVersion: apps/v1
kind: Deployment
metadata:
  name: gb-web-deploy
  labels:
    app: guest-book
    appver: 1.6.9
    environment: production
    release: guest-book-stable
    release number: 34e57f01
spec:
  strategy:
    type: rollingUpdate
    rollingUpdate:
      maxUnavailbale: 3
      maxSurge: 2
  selector:
    matchLabels:
      app: gb-web
      ver: 1.5.8
    matchExpressions:
      - {key: environment, operator: In, values: [production]}
  template:
    metadata:
      labels:
        app: gb-web
        ver: 1.5.8
        environment: production
    spec:
      containers:
      - name: gb-web-cont
        image: evillgenius/gb-web:v1.5.5
        env:
```

```yaml
        - name: GB_DB_HOST
          value: gb-mysql
        - name: GB_DB_PASSWORD
          valueFrom:
            secretKeyRef:
              name: mysql-pass
              key: password
        resources:
          limits:
            memory: "128Mi"
            cpu: "500m"
        ports:
        - containerPort: 80
---
# DB Deployment
apiVersion: apps/v1
kind: Deployment
metadata:
  name: gb-mysql
  labels:
    app: guest-book
    appver: 1.6.9
    environment: production
    release: guest-book-stable
    release number: 34e57f01
spec:
  selector:
    matchLabels:
      app: gb-db
      tier: backend
  strategy:
    type: Recreate
  template:
    metadata:
      labels:
        app: gb-db
        tier: backend
        ver: 1.5.9
        environment: production
    spec:
      containers:
      - image: mysql:5.6
        name: mysql
        env:
        - name: MYSQL_PASSWORD
          valueFrom:
            secretKeyRef:
              name: mysql-pass
              key: password
        ports:
        - containerPort: 3306
          name: mysql
```

```
      volumeMounts:
      - name: mysql-persistent-storage
        mountPath: /var/lib/mysql
    volumes:
    - name: mysql-persistent-storage
      persistentVolumeClaim:
        claimName: mysql-pv-claim
---
# DB Backup Job
apiVersion: batch/v1
kind: Job
metadata:
  name: db-backup
  labels:
    app: guest-book
    appver: 1.6.9
    environment: production
    release: guest-book-stable
    release number: 34e57f01
  annotations:
    "helm.sh/hook": pre-upgrade
    "helm.sh/hook": pre-delete
    "helm.sh/hook": pre-rollback
    "helm.sh/hook-delete-policy": hook-succeeded
spec:
  template:
    metadata:
      labels:
        app: gb-db-backup
        tier: backend
        ver: 1.6.1
        environment: production
    spec:
      containers:
      - name: mysqldump
        image: evillgenius/mysqldump:v1
        env:
        - name: DB_NAME
          value: gbdb1
        - name: GB_DB_HOST
          value: gb-mysql
        - name: GB_DB_PASSWORD
          valueFrom:
            secretKeyRef:
              name: mysql-pass
              key: password
        volumeMounts:
        - mountPath: /mysqldump
          name: mysqldump
      volumes:
      - name: mysqldump
        hostPath:
```

```
           path: /home/bck/mysqldump
       restartPolicy: Never
    backoffLimit: 3
```

Upon first inspection, things might look a little off. How can a Deployment have a version tag and the container image the Deployment uses have a different version tag? What will happen if one changes and the other does not? What does release mean in this example, and what will be the effect on the system if it changes? If a certain label is changed, when will it trigger an update to my Deployment? We can find the answers to these questions by looking at some of the best practices for versioning, releases, and rollouts.

Best Practices for Versioning, Releases, and Rollouts

Effective CI/CD and the ability to offer reduced- or zero-downtime deployments depend on using consistent practices for versioning and release management. The following best practices can help to define consistent parameters that can assist DevOps teams in delivering smooth software deployments:

- Use semantic versioning for the application that differs from the version of the containers and the version of the pods Deployment that make up the entire application. This allows for independent life cycles of the containers that make up the application and the application as a whole. This can be quite confusing at first, but if a principled hierarchical approach is taken for when one changes the other, you can easily track it. In the previous example, the container itself is currently on v1.5.5; however, the pod specification is 1.5.8, which could mean that changes were made to the pod specification, such as new ConfigMaps, additional secrets, or updated replica values, but the specific container used has not changed its version. The application itself, the entire guestbook application, and all its services, is at 1.6.9, which could mean that operations made changes along the way that were beyond just this specific service, such as other services that make up the entire application.

- Use a release and release version/number label in your deployment metadata to track releases from CI/CD pipelines. The release name and release number should coordinate with the actual release in the CI/CD tool records. This allows for both traceability through the CI/CD process into the cluster and easier roll-back identification. In the previous example, the release number comes directly from the release ID of the CD pipeline that created the manifest.

- If Helm is being used to package services for deployment into Kubernetes, take special care to bundle together those services that need to be rolled back or upgraded together into the same Helm chart. Helm allows for easy rollback of all components of the application to bring the state back to what it was before the upgrade. Because Helm actually processes the templates and all the Helm directives before passing a flattened YAML configuration, the use of life-cycle hooks allows for proper ordering of the application of specific templates. Operators can use proper Helm life-cycle hooks to ensure that upgrades and rollback will happen correctly. The previous example for the `Job` specification uses Helm life-cycle hooks to ensure that the template runs a backup of the database before a rollback, upgrade, or delete of the Helm release. It also ensures that the `Job` is deleted after the job is run successfully, which, until the TTL Controller comes out of alpha in Kubernetes, would require manual cleanup.

- Agree on a release nomenclature that makes sense for the operational tempo of the organization. Simple `stable`, `canary`, and `alpha` states are quite adequate for most situations.

Summary

Kubernetes has allowed for more complex Agile development processes to be adopted within companies large and small. The ability to automate many of the complex processes that would usually require large amounts of human and technical capital has now been democratized so that even startups can take advantage of this cloud pattern with relative ease. The true declarative nature of Kubernetes really shines when planning the proper use of labels and using native Kubernetes controller capabilities. By properly identifying operational and development states within the declarative properties of the applications deployed into Kubernetes, organizations can tie in tooling and automation to more easily manage the complex processes of upgrades, rollouts, and rollbacks of capabilities.

## CHAPTER 7

Worldwide Application Distribution and Staging

To this point in the book, we have seen a number of different practices for building, developing, and deploying applications, but a whole different set of concerns arises when deploying and managing an application with a global footprint.

There are many different reasons why an application might need to scale to a global deployment. The first and most obvious one is simply scale. It might be that your application is so successful or mission critical that it simply needs to be deployed around the world to provide the capacity necessary for its users. Examples of such applications include a worldwide API gateway for a public cloud provider, a large-scale IoT product with a worldwide footprint, a highly successful social network, and more.

Although relatively few of us will build out systems that require worldwide scale, many more applications require a worldwide footprint for latency. Even with containers and Kubernetes there is no getting around the speed of light. To minimize latency between clients and our applications, it is sometimes necessary to distribute our applications around the world to minimize the physical distance between the application and its users.

Finally, an even more common reason for global distribution is locality. Either for reasons of bandwidth (e.g., a remote sensing platform) or data privacy (e.g., geographic restrictions), it is sometimes necessary to deploy an application in specific locations for the application to be possible or successful. As more and more countries and regions implement data privacy and sovereignty laws and regulations, it is becoming a common business necessity to deploy your application in specific locations to serve users who reside in that location.

In all these cases, your application is no longer simply present in a small handful of production clusters. Instead it is distributed across tens to hundreds of different geographic locations. The management of these locations, as well as the demands of rolling out a globally reliable service, is a significant challenge. This chapter covers approaches and practices for doing this successfully.

Distributing Your Image

Before you can even consider running your application around the world, you need to have that image available to clusters located around the globe. The first thing to consider is whether your image registry has automatic geo-replication. Many image registries supplied by cloud providers will automatically distribute your image around the world and resolve a request for that image to the storage location nearest to the cluster from which you are pulling the image. Many clouds enable you to decide where you want to replicate the image; for example, you might know of locations where you are not going to be present. An example of such a registry is the Microsoft Azure container registry (*https://oreil.ly/4jWNh*), but others provide similar services. If you use a cloud-provided registry that supports geo-replication, distributing your image around the world is simple. You push the image into the registry, select the regions for geo-distribution, and the registry takes care of the rest.

If you are not using a cloud registry, or your provider does not support automatic geo-distribution of images, you will need to solve that problem yourself. One option is to use a registry situated in a specific location. There are several concerns about such an approach. Image pull latency often dictates the speed with which you can launch a container in a cluster. This in turn can determine how quickly you can respond to a machine failure, given that generally in the case of a machine failure, you will need to pull the container image down to a new machine.

Another concern about a single registry is that it can be a single point of failure. If the registry is located in a single region or a single datacenter, it's possible that the registry could go offline due to a large-scale incident in that datacenter. If your registry goes offline, your CI/CD pipeline will stop working, and you'll be unable to deploy new code. This obviously has a significant impact on both developer productivity and application operations. Additionally, a single registry can be much more expensive because you will be using significant bandwidth each time you launch a new container, and even though container images are generally fairly small, the bandwidth can add up. Despite these negatives, a single registry solution can be the appropriate answer for small-scale applications running in only a few global regions. It certainly is simpler to set up than full-scale image replication.

If you cannot use cloud-provided geo-replication and you need to replicate your image, you are on your own to craft a solution for image replication. To implement such a service, you have two options. The first is to use geographic names for each image registry (e.g., `us.my-registry.io`, `eu.my-registry.io`, etc.). The advantage of this approach is that it is simple to set up and manage. Each registry is entirely independent, and you can simply push to all registries at the end of your CI/CD pipeline. The downside is that each cluster will require a slightly different configuration to pull the image from the nearest geographic location. However, given that you likely will have geographic differences in your application configurations anyway, this downside is relatively easy to manage and likely already present in your environment.

The second option is to use a networking configuration to connect your image pulls to a specific repository. In this approach you still push your image to multiple registries, but instead of giving them each a unique name, you give them all a single DNS endpoint (e.g., `my-registry.io`). You can use geography-aware DNS (GeoDNS), which will respond to DNS requests from different geographic regions with different IP addresses, or if you have the right networking infrastructure, you can use multicast IP addresses. In multicast, all your registries share the same IP address, but it is advertised to the internet in multiple physical locations, and shortest-path network routing is relied on to take traffic to the server that provides the nearest image registry. Both of these network configurations are tricky to implement correctly. The best answer is definitely to use a cloud-based registry, even if you are pulling to on-premises servers. If you really want to run your own registry (and take on the operational burden that implies), we strongly suggest you use the regional server approach discussed in the previous paragraph unless you have prior network experience with replicated services. The next section describes how you can parameterize your deployment to, for example, use different registries in different regions.

Parameterizing Your Deployment

When you have replicated your image everywhere, you need to parameterize your deployments for different global locations. Whenever you are deploying to a variety of different regions, there are bound to be differences in the configuration of your application in those regions. For example, if you don't have a geo-replicated registry, you might need to tweak the image name for different regions. However, even if you have a geo-replicated image, it's likely that different geographic locations will present different load on your application, and thus the size (e.g., the number of replicas) as well as other configuration can be different between regions. Managing this complexity in a manner that doesn't incur undue toil is key to successfully managing a worldwide application.

The first thing to consider is how to organize your different configurations on disk. A common way to achieve this is by using a different directory for each global region. Given these directories, it might be tempting to simply copy the same configurations into each directory, but doing this is guaranteed to lead to drift and changes between configurations in which some regions are modified and other regions are forgotten.

Instead, use a template-based approach so that most of the configuration is retained in a single template that is shared by all regions, and then parameters are applied to that template to produce the region-specific templates. Helm (*https://helm.sh*) is a commonly used tool for this sort of templating (for details, see Chapter 1).

Load-Balancing Traffic Around the World

Now that your application is running around the world, the next step is to determine how to direct traffic to the application. In general, you want to take advantage of geographic proximity to ensure low-latency access to your service. But you also want to failover across geographic regions in case of an outage or any other source of service failure. Correctly setting up the balancing of traffic to your various regional deployments is key to establishing both a performant and reliable system.

Let's begin with the assumption that you have a single hostname that you want to use for your service, for example, *myapp.myco.com*. One initial decision that you need to make is whether you want to use the Domain Name System (DNS) protocol to implement load balancing across your regional endpoints. If you use DNS for load balancing, the IP address that is returned when a user makes a DNS query to *myapp.myco.com* is based on both the location of the user accessing your service as well as the current availability of your service. The other alternative is multicast IP addresses, where the same IP address is advertised from multiple locations on the internet. When a user looks up *myapp.myco.com*, the DNS always returns this fixed IP address, but the actual routing of packets varies depending on where the connection is in the network.

Reliably Rolling Out Software Around the World

After you have templatized your application so that you have proper configurations for each region, the next important problem is how to deploy these configurations around the world. It might be tempting to simultaneously deploy your application worldwide so that you can efficiently and quickly iterate your application, but this, although Agile, is an approach that can easily leave you with a global outage. Any errors that you accidentally roll out to the world are immediately present for all users in all regions. Instead, for most production applications, a more carefully staged approach to rolling out your software around the world is more appropriate. When combined with things like global load balancing, these approaches can maintain high availability even in the face of major application failures.

 Overall, when approaching the problem of a global rollout, the goal is to roll out software as quickly as possible, while simultaneously detecting issues quickly—ideally before they affect many users.

Let's assume that by the time you are performing a global rollout, your application has already passed basic functional and load testing. Before a particular image (or images) is certified for a global rollout, it should have gone through enough testing that you believe the application is operating correctly. It is important to note that this *does not* mean that your application *is* operating correctly. Though testing catches many problems, in the real world, application problems are often first noticed when they are rolled out to production traffic. This is because the true nature of production traffic is often difficult to simulate with perfect fidelity. For example, you might test with only English-language inputs, whereas in the real world, you see input from a variety of languages. Or your set of test inputs may not be comprehensive for the real-world data your application ingests. Of course, any time that you do see a failure in production that wasn't caught by testing, it is a strong indicator that you need to extend and expand your testing. Nonetheless, it is still true that many problems are caught during a production rollout.

With this in mind, each region that you roll out to is an opportunity to discover a new problem. And because the region is a production region, it is also a potential outage to which you will need to react. These factors combine to set the stage for how you should approach regional rollouts.

 Throughout this discussion we talk about rolling out software to a geographic region, but this sort of progressive rollout is only one form of progressive exposure control. An alternative way to roll out a feature is to use feature flags to do progressive exposure. With feature flags, a new feature is first rolled out via a release that follows a geographic rollout as described next; however, the feature is flagged "off" by default. Once the release is in all regions, the flag is gradually turned on by (for example) activating the feature for 10% of all users, followed by 20%, and so on until the feature is fully rolled out. There are numerous configuration systems for doing flag-based experiments and progressive rollouts. And combining flags with geographic releases is a very stable way to release new features while being able to quickly respond to failures.

Pre-Rollout Validation

Before you even consider rolling out a particular version of your software around the world, it's critically important to validate that software in some sort of synthetic testing environment. If you have your CD pipeline set up correctly, all code prior to a particular release build will have undergone some form of unit testing, and possibly limited integration testing. However, even with this testing in place, it's important to consider two other sorts of tests for a release before it begins its journey through the release pipeline. The first is complete integration testing. This means that you assemble the entirety of your stack into a full-scale deployment of your application but without any real-world traffic. This complete stack generally will include either a copy of your production data or simulated data on the same size and scale as your true production data. If in the real world, the data in your application is 500 GB, it's critical that in preproduction testing your dataset is roughly the same size (and possibly even literally the same dataset).

Generally speaking, setting up a complete integration testing environment is a significant challenge. Often, production data is present only in production, and generating a synthetic dataset of the same size and scale is quite difficult. Because of this complexity, setting up a realistic integration testing dataset is a great example of a task that it pays to do early on in the development of an application. If you set up a synthetic copy of your dataset early, when the dataset itself is quite small, your integration test data grows gradually at the same pace as your production data. This is generally significantly more manageable than if you attempt to duplicate your production data when you are already at scale.

Sadly, many people don't realize that they need a copy of their data until they are already at a large scale and the task is difficult. In such cases it might be possible to deploy a read/write-deflecting layer in front of your production data store. Obviously, you don't want your integration tests writing to production data, but it is often possible to set up a proxy in front of your production data store that reads from production but stores writes in a side table that is also consulted on subsequent reads.

Of course, it is also extremely important that if you use your production data for testing and development you are very careful with the security of that data. Numerous data leaks have been associated with developers accidentally placing their production user data in insecure locations.

Regardless of how you manage to set up your integration testing environment, the goal is the same: to validate that your application behaves as expected when given a series of test inputs and interactions. There are a variety of ways to define and execute these tests—from the most manual, a worksheet of tests and human effort (not recommended because it is fairly error prone), through tests that simulate browsers and user interactions, like clicks and so forth. In the middle are tests that probe RESTful APIs but don't necessarily test the web UI built on top of those APIs. Regardless of how you define your integration tests, the goal should be the same: an automated test suite that validates the correct behavior of your application in response to a complete set of real-world inputs. For simple applications it may be possible to perform this validation in premerge testing, but for most large-scale real-world applications, a complete integration environment is required.

Integration testing will validate the correct operation of your application, but you should also load-test the application. It is one thing to demonstrate that the application behaves correctly; it is quite another to demonstrate that it stands up to real-world load. In any reasonably high-scale system, a significant regression in performance—for example, a 20% increase in request latency—has a significant impact on the UX of the application and, in addition to frustrating users, can cause an application to completely fail. Thus, it is critical to ensure that such performance regressions do not happen in production.

Like integration testing, identifying the correct way to load-test an application can be a complex proposition; after all, it requires that you generate a load similar to production traffic but in a synthetic and reproducible way. One of the easiest ways to do this is to simply replay the logs of traffic from a real-world production system. Doing this can be a great way to perform a load test whose characteristics match what your application will experience when deployed. However, using replay isn't always foolproof. For example, if your logs are old, and your application or dataset has changed, it's possible that the performance on old, replayed logs will be different than the performance on fresh traffic. Additionally, if you have real-world dependencies that you haven't mocked, it's possible that the old traffic will be invalid when sent over to the dependencies (e.g., the data might no longer exist).

As with production data it is critical to safeguard the security of any recorded real-world requests. Just like the production databases, production requests often contain private information or secure credentials (or both!), and it is critical that the security of any recordings be treated the same as the actual user requests.

Because of the challenges associated with saving, securing, and managing this test data, many systems, even critical systems, are developed for a long time without a load test. Like modeling your production data, this is a clear example of something that is easier to maintain if you start earlier. If you build a load test when your application has only a handful of dependencies, and improve and iterate the load test as you adapt your application, you will have a far easier time than if you attempt to retrofit load testing onto an existing large-scale application.

Assuming that you have crafted a load test, the next question is the metrics to watch when load-testing your application. The obvious ones are requests per second and request latency because those are clearly the user-facing metrics.

When measuring latency, it's important to realize that this is actually a distribution, and you need to measure both the mean latency as well as the outlier percentiles (like the 90th and 99th percentiles) since they represent the "worst" UX of your application. Problems with very long latencies can be hidden if you just look at the averages, but if 10% of your users are having a bad time, it can have a significant impact on the success of your product.

In addition, it's worth looking at the resource usage (CPU, memory, network, disk) of the application under load test. Though these metrics do not directly contribute to the UX, large changes in resource usage for your application should be identified and understood in preproduction testing. If your application is suddenly consuming twice as much memory, it's something you will want to investigate, even if you pass your load test, because eventually such significant resource growth will affect the quality and availability of your application. Depending on the circumstances, you might continue bringing a release to production, but at the same time, you need to understand why the resource footprint of your application is changing.

Canary Region

When your application appears to be operating correctly, the first step should be a *canary region*. A canary region is a deployment that receives real-world traffic from people and teams who want to validate your release. These can be internal teams that depend on your service, or they might be external customers who are using your service. Canaries exist to give a team some early warning about changes that you are about to roll out that might break them. No matter how good your integration and load testing, it's always possible that a bug will slip through that isn't covered by your tests but is critical to some user or customer. In such cases, it is much better to catch these issues in a space where everyone using or deploying against the service understands that there is a higher probability of failure. This is the canary region.

 Canary is also a great place for your team or company to *dogfood* or self-test the early release before it goes further in production. A great best practice is to set up an HTTP redirector so that requests from within your company are redirected to an instance of your product that is running in canary. That way every person on your team becomes an end-to-end tester before the release proceeds to external users.

Canaries must be treated as a production region in terms of monitoring, scale, features, and so on. However, because it is the first stop on the release process, it is also the location most likely to see a broken release. This is OK; in fact it is precisely the point. Your customers will knowingly use a canary for lower-risk use cases (e.g., development or internal users) so that they can get an early indication of any breaking changes that you might be rolling out as part of a release.

Because the goal of a canary is to get early feedback on a release, it is a good idea to leave the release in the canary region for a few days. This enables a broad collection of customers to access it before you move on to additional regions. This length of time is needed because sometimes a bug is probabilistic (e.g., affects 1% of requests), or it manifests only in an edge case that takes some time to present itself. It might not even be severe enough to trigger automated alerts, but there might be a problem in business logic that is visible only via customer interactions.

Identifying Region Types

When you begin thinking about rolling out your software across the world, it's important to think about the different characteristics of your different regions. After you begin rolling out software to production regions, you need to run it through integration testing as well as initial canary testing. This means that any subsequent issues you find will be issues that did not manifest in either of these settings. Think about your different regions. Do some get more traffic than others? Are some accessed in a different way? An example of a difference might be that in the developing world, traffic is more likely to come from mobile web browsers. Thus, a region that is geographically close to more developing countries might have significantly more mobile traffic than your test or canary regions.

Another example might be input language. Regions in non-English-speaking areas of the world might send more Unicode characters that could manifest bugs in string or character handling. If you are building an API-driven service, some APIs might be more popular in some regions versus others. All these things are examples of differences that might be present in your application and might be different than your canary traffic. Each of these differences is a possible source of a production incident. Build a table of different characteristics that you think are important. Identifying these characteristics will help you plan your global rollout.

Constructing a Global Rollout

Having identified the characteristics of your regions, you want to identify a plan for rolling out to all regions. Obviously, you want to minimize the impact of a production outage, so a great first region to start with is a region that looks mostly like your canary and has light user traffic. Such a region is very unlikely to have problems, but if they do occur, the impact is also smaller because the region receives less traffic.

With a successful rollout to the first production region, you need to decide how long to wait before moving on to the next region. The reason for waiting is not to artificially delay your release; rather, it's to wait long enough for a fire to send up smoke. This time-to-smoke period is a measure of how long it generally takes between a rollout completing and your monitoring seeing some sign of a problem. Clearly if a rollout contains a problem, the minute the rollout completes, the problem is present in your infrastructure. But even though it is present, it can take some time to manifest. For example, a memory leak might take an hour or more before the impact of the leaked memory is clearly discernible in monitoring or is affecting users. The time-to-smoke is the probability distribution that indicates how long you should wait to have a strong probability that your release is operating correctly. Generally speaking, a decent rule of thumb is doubling the average time it took for a problem to manifest in the past.

If, over the past six months, each outage took an average of an hour to show up, waiting two hours between regional rollouts gives you a decent probability that your release is successful. If you want to derive richer (and more meaningful) statistics based on the history of your application, you can estimate this time-to-smoke even more closely.

Having successfully rolled out to a canary-like, low-traffic region, it's time to roll out to a canary-like, high-traffic region. This is a region where the input data looks like that in your canary, but it receives a large volume of traffic. Because you successfully rolled out to a similar-looking region with lower traffic, at this point the only thing you are testing is your application's ability to scale. If you safely perform this rollout, you can have strong confidence in the quality of your release.

After you have rolled out to a high-traffic region receiving canary-like data, you should follow the same pattern for other potential differences in traffic. For example, you might roll out to a low-traffic region in Asia or Europe next. At this point, it might be tempting to accelerate your rollout, but it is critically important to roll out only to a single region that represents any significant change in either input or load to your release. After you are confident that you have tested all the potential variability in the production input to your application, then you can start parallelizing the release to speed it up with strong confidence that it is operating correctly and your rollout can complete successfully.

When Something Goes Wrong

So far, we have seen the pieces that go into setting up a worldwide rollout for your software system, and we have seen the ways that you can structure this rollout to minimize the chances that something goes wrong. But what do you do when something actually does go wrong? All emergency responders know that in the heat and panic of a crisis, your brain is significantly stressed and it is much more difficult to remember even the simplest processes. Add to this pressure the knowledge that when an outage happens, everyone in the company from the CEO down is going to be feverishly waiting for the "all clear" signal, and you can see how easy it is to make a mistake. Additionally, in such circumstances, a simple mistake, like forgetting a particular step in a recovery process, or rolling out a "fixed" build that actually has more problems, can make a bad situation an order of magnitude worse.

For all these reasons, it is critical that you are capable of responding quickly, calmly, and correctly when a problem happens with a rollout. To ensure that everything necessary is done, and done in the correct order, it pays to have a clear checklist of tasks organized in the order in which they are to be executed as well as the expected output for each step. Write down every step, no matter how obvious it might seem. In the heat of the moment, even the most obvious and easy steps can be the ones that are forgotten and accidentally skipped.

The way that first responders ensure a correct response in a high-stress situation is to practice that response without the stress of the emergency. The same practice applies to all the activities that you might take in response to a problem with your rollout. You begin by identifying all the steps needed to respond to an issue and perform a rollback. Ideally, the first response is to "stop the bleeding," to move user traffic away from the impacted region(s) and into a region where the rollout hasn't happened and your system is operating correctly. This is the first thing you should practice. Can you successfully direct traffic away from a region? How long does it take?

The first time you attempt to move traffic using a DNS-based traffic load balancer, you will realize just how long and in how many ways our computers cache DNS entries. It can take nearly a day to fully drain traffic away from a region using a DNS-based traffic shaper. Regardless of how your first attempt to drain traffic goes, take notes. What worked well? What went poorly? Given this data, set a goal for how long a traffic drain should take in terms of time to drain a percentage of traffic, for example, being able to drain 99% of traffic in less than 10 minutes. Keep practicing until you can achieve that goal. You might need to make architectural changes to make this possible. You might need to add automation so that humans aren't cutting and pasting commands. Regardless of necessary changes, practice will ensure that you are more capable when responding to an incident and that you will learn where your system design needs to be improved.

The same sort of practice applies to every action that you might take on your system. Practice a full-scale data recovery. Practice a global rollback of your system to a previous version. Set goals for the length of time it should take. Note any places where you made mistakes, and add validation and automation to eliminate the possibility of mistakes. Achieving your incident reaction goals in practice gives you confidence that you will be able to respond correctly in a real incident. But just like every emergency responder continues to train and learn, you too need to set up a regular cadence of practice to ensure that everyone on a team stays well versed in the proper responses and (perhaps more important) that your responses stay up to date as your system changes.

Worldwide Rollout Best Practices

Rolling out your software around the world, especially if you have never done it before, can be a significant challenge. Here are some best practices based on our years of production experience for how to manage the global deployment of mission critical software:

- Distribute each image around the world. A successful rollout depends on the release bits (binaries, images, etc.) being nearby to where they will be used. This also ensures reliability of the rollout in the presence of networking slowdowns or irregularities. Geographic distribution should be a part of your automated release pipeline for guaranteed consistency.

- Shift as much of your testing as possible to the left by having as much extensive integration and replay testing of your application as possible. You want to start a rollout only with a release that you strongly believe to be correct.

- Begin a release in a canary region, which is a preproduction environment in which other teams or large customers can validate *their* use of your service before you begin a larger-scale rollout.

- Identify different characteristics of the regions where you are rolling out. Each difference can be one that causes a failure and a full or partial outage. Try to roll out to low-risk regions first.

- Document and practice your response to any problem or process (e.g., a rollback) that you might encounter. Trying to remember what to do in the heat of the moment is a recipe for forgetting something and making a bad problem worse.

Summary

It might seem unlikely today, but most of us will end up running a worldwide scale system sometime during our careers. This chapter described how you can gradually build and iterate your system to be a truly global design. It also discussed how you can set up your rollout to ensure minimal downtime of the system while it is being updated. Finally, we covered setting up and practicing the processes and procedures necessary to react when (note that we didn't say "if") something goes wrong.

## CHAPTER 8

Resource Management

In this chapter, we focus on the best practices for managing and optimizing Kubernetes resources. We discuss workload scheduling, cluster management, pod resource management, namespace management, and scaling applications. We also dive into some of the advanced scheduling techniques that Kubernetes provides through affinity, anti-affinity, taints, tolerations, and nodeSelectors.

We show you how to implement resource limits, resource requests, pod Quality of Service, `PodDisruptionBudgets`, `LimitRangers`, and anti-affinity policies.

Kubernetes Scheduler

The Kubernetes scheduler is one of the main components that is hosted in the control plane. The scheduler allows Kubernetes to make placement decisions for pods deployed to the cluster. It deals with optimization of resources based on constraints of the cluster as well as user-specified constraints. It uses a scoring algorithm that is based on predicates and priorities.

Predicates

The first function Kubernetes uses to make a scheduling decision is the predicate function, which determines what nodes the pods can be scheduled on. It implies a hard constraint, so it returns a value of true or false. An example would be when a pod requests 4 GB of memory and a node cannot satisfy this requirement. The node would return a false value and would be removed from viable nodes for the pod to be scheduled to. Another example would be if the node is set to unschedulable; it would then be removed from the scheduling decision.

The scheduler checks the predicates based on order of restrictiveness and complexity. As of this writing, the following are the predicates that the scheduler checks for:

```
CheckNodeConditionPred,
CheckNodeUnschedulablePred,
GeneralPred,
HostNamePred,
PodFitsHostPortsPred,
MatchNodeSelectorPred,
PodFitsResourcesPred,
NoDiskConflictPred,
PodToleratesNodeTaintsPred,
PodToleratesNodeNoExecuteTaintsPred,
CheckNodeLabelPresencePred,
CheckServiceAffinityPred,
MaxEBSVolumeCountPred,
MaxGCEPDVolumeCountPred,
MaxCSIVolumeCountPred,
MaxAzureDiskVolumeCountPred,
MaxCinderVolumeCountPred,
CheckVolumeBindingPred,
NoVolumeZoneConflictPred,
CheckNodeMemoryPressurePred,
CheckNodePIDPressurePred,
CheckNodeDiskPressurePred,
MatchInterPodAffinityPred
```

Priorities

Whereas predicates indicate a true or false value and dismiss a node for scheduling, the priority value ranks all the valid nodes based on a relative value. The following priorities are scored for nodes:

```
EqualPriority
MostRequestedPriority
RequestedToCapacityRatioPriority
SelectorSpreadPriority
ServiceSpreadingPriority
InterPodAffinityPriority
LeastRequestedPriority
BalancedResourceAllocation
NodePreferAvoidPodsPriority
NodeAffinityPriority
TaintTolerationPriority
ImageLocalityPriority
ResourceLimitsPriority
```

The scores will be added, and then a node is given its final score to indicate its priority. For example, if a pod requires 600 millicores and there are two nodes, one with 900 millicores available and one with 1,800 millicores, the node with 1,800 millicores available will have a higher priority.

If nodes are returned with the same priority, the scheduler will use a selectHost() function, which selects a node in a round-robin fashion.

Advanced Scheduling Techniques

For most cases, Kubernetes does a good job of optimally scheduling pods for you. It takes into account pods that are placed only on nodes that have sufficient resources. It also tries to spread pods from the same ReplicaSet across nodes to increase availability and will balance resource utilization. When this is not good enough, Kubernetes gives you the flexibility to influence how resources are scheduled. For example, you might want to schedule pods across availability zones to mitigate a zonal failure causing downtime to your application. You might also want to colocate pods to a specific host for performance benefits.

Pod Affinity and Anti-Affinity

Pod affinity and anti-affinity let you set rules to place pods relative to other pods. These rules allow you to modify the scheduling behavior and override the scheduler's placement decisions.

For example, an anti-affinity rule would allow you to spread pods from a ReplicaSet across multiple datacenter zones. It does this by utilizing keylabels set on the pods. Setting the key/value pairs instructs the scheduler to schedule the pods on the same node (affinity) or prevent the pods from scheduling on the same nodes (anti-affinity).

Following is an example of setting a pod anti-affinity rule:

```
apiVersion: apps/v1
kind: Deployment
metadata:
  name: nginx
spec:
  selector:
    matchLabels:
      app: frontend
  replicas: 4
  template:
    metadata:
      labels:
        app: frontend
    spec:
      affinity:
        podAntiAffinity:
          requiredDuringSchedulingIgnoredDuringExecution:
          - labelSelector:
              matchExpressions:
              - key: app
                operator: In
                values:
                - frontend
            topologyKey: "kubernetes.io/hostname"
      containers:
```

```
      - name: nginx
        image: nginx:alpine
```

This manifest of an NGINX deployment has four replicas and the selector label app=frontend. The deployment has a PodAntiAffinity stanza configured that will ensure that the scheduler does not colocate replicas on a single node. This ensures that if a node fails, there are still enough replicas of NGINX to serve data from its cache.

nodeSelector

A nodeSelector is the easiest way to schedule pods to a particular node. It uses label selectors with key/value pairs to make the scheduling decision. For example, you might want to schedule pods to a specific node that has specialized hardware, such as a GPU. You might ask, "Can't I do this with a node taint?" The answer is, yes, you can. The difference is that you use a nodeSelector when you want to *request* a GPU-enabled node, whereas a taint *reserves* a node for only GPU workloads. You can use both node taints and nodeSelectors together to reserve the nodes for only GPU workloads, and use the nodeSelector to automatically select a node with a GPU.

Following is an example of labeling a node and using a nodeSelector in the pod specification:

```
kubectl label node <node_name> disktype=ssd
```

Now, let's create a pod specification with a nodeSelector key/value of disktype: ssd:

```
apiVersion: v1
kind: Pod
metadata:
  name: redis
  labels:
    env: prod
spec:
  containers:
  - name: frontend
    image: nginx:alpine
    imagePullPolicy: IfNotPresent
  nodeSelector:
    disktype: ssd
```

Using the nodeSelector schedules the pod to only nodes that have the label disktype=ssd:

Taints and Tolerations

Taints are used on nodes to repel pods from being scheduled on them. But isn't that what anti-affinity is for? Yes, but taints take a different approach than pod anti-affinity and serve a different use case. For example, you might have pods that

---

require a specific performance profile, and you do not want to schedule any other pods to the specific node. Taints work in conjunction with *tolerations*, which allow you to override tainted nodes. The combination of the two gives you fine-grained control over anti-affinity rules.

In general, you will use taints and tolerations for the following use cases:

- Specialized node hardware
- Dedicated node resources
- Avoiding degraded nodes

Multiple taint types affect scheduling and running containers:

NoSchedule
    A hard taint that prevents scheduling on the node

PreferNoSchedule
    Schedules only if pods cannot be scheduled on other nodes

NoExecute
    Evicts pods already running on the node

NodeCondition
    Taints a node if it meets a specific condition

Figure 8-1 shows an example of a node that is tainted with `gpu=true:NoSchedule`. Pod Spec 1 has a toleration key with `gpu`, so it will be scheduled to the tainted node. Pod Spec 2 has a toleration key of `no-gpu`, so it will not be scheduled to the node.

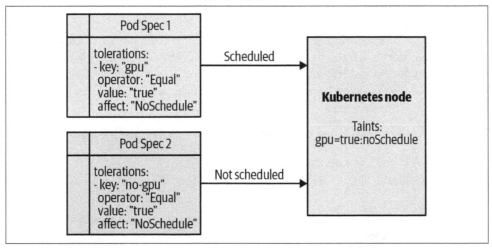

Figure 8-1. Kubernetes taints and tolerations

When a pod cannot be scheduled due to tainted nodes, you'll see an error message like the following:

```
Warning:  FailedScheduling  10s (x10 over 2m)  default-scheduler
0/2 nodes are available: 2 node(s) had taints that the pod did not tolerate.
```

Now that we've seen how we can manually add taints to affect scheduling, there is also the powerful concept of *taint-based eviction*, which allows the eviction of running pods. For example, if a node becomes unhealthy due to a bad disk drive, the taint-based eviction can reschedule the pods on the host to another healthy node in the cluster.

Pod Resource Management

One of the most important aspects of managing applications in Kubernetes is appropriately managing pod resources. Managing pod resources consists of managing CPU and memory to optimize the overall utilization of your Kubernetes cluster. You can manage these resources at the container level and at the namespace level. There are other resources, such as network and storage, but Kubernetes doesn't yet have a way to set requests and limits for those resources.

For the scheduler to optimize resources and make intelligent placement decisions, it needs to understand the requirements of an application. As an example, if a container (application) needs a minimum of 2 GB to perform, we need to define this in our pod specification so the scheduler knows that the container requires 2 GB of memory on the host to which it schedules the container.

Resource Request

A Kubernetes resource *request* defines that a container requires X amount of CPU or memory to be scheduled. If you were to specify in the pod specification that a container requires 8 GB for its resource request and all your nodes have 7.5 GB of memory, the pod would not be scheduled. If the pod is not able to be scheduled, it will go into a *pending* state until the required resources are available. So let's look at how this works in our cluster.

To determine the available free resources in your cluster, use kubectl top:

```
kubectl top nodes
```

The output should look like this (the memory size might be different for your cluster):

```
NAME                      CPU(cores)  CPU%  MEMORY(bytes)  MEMORY%
aks-nodepool1-14849087-0  524m        27%   7500Mi         33%
aks-nodepool1-14849087-1  468m        24%   3505Mi         27%
aks-nodepool1-14849087-2  406m        21%   3051Mi         24%
aks-nodepool1-14849087-3  441m        22%   2812Mi         22%
```

As this example shows, the largest amount of memory available to a host is 7,500 Mi, so let's schedule a pod that requests 8,000 Mi of memory:

```
apiVersion: v1
kind: Pod
metadata:
  name: memory-request
spec:
  containers:
  - name: memory-request
    image: polinux/stress
    resources:
      requests:
        memory: "8000Mi"
```

Notice that the pod will stay pending, and if you look at the events on the pods, you'll see that no nodes are available to schedule the pods:

```
kubectl describe pods memory-request
```

The output of the event should look like this:

```
Events:
  Type     Reason      Age              From            Message
  Warning  FailedSch...  27s (x2 over 27s)  default-sched...  0/3 nodes are
                                                            available: 3
                                                            Insufficient memory
```

Resource Limits and Pod Quality of Service

Kubernetes resource *limits* define the maximum CPU or memory that a pod is given. When you specify limits for CPU and memory, each takes a different action when it reaches the specified limit. With CPU limits, the container is throttled from using more than its specified limit. With memory limits, the pod is restarted if it reaches its limit. The pod might be restarted on the same host or a different host within the cluster.

Specifying limits for containers is a best practice to ensure that applications are allotted their fair share of resources within the cluster:

```
apiVersion: v1
kind: Pod
metadata:
  name: cpu-demo
  namespace: cpu-example
spec:
  containers:
  - name: frontend
    image: nginx:alpine
    resources:
      limits:
        cpu: "1"
```

```
      requests:
        cpu: "0.5"

apiVersion: v1
kind: Pod
metadata:
  name: qos-demo
  namespace: qos-example
spec:
  containers:
  - name: qos-demo-ctr
    image: nginx:alpine
    resources:
      limits:
        memory: "200Mi"
        cpu: "700m"
      requests:
        memory: "200Mi"
        cpu: "700m"
```

When a pod is created, it's assigned one of the following Quality of Service (QoS) classes:

- Guaranteed
- Burstable
- Best effort

The pod is assigned a QoS of *guaranteed* when CPU and memory both have request and limits that match. A *burstable* QoS is when the limits are set higher than the request, meaning that the container is guaranteed its request, but it can also burst to the limit set for the container. A pod is assigned *best effort* when no request or limits are set for the containers in the pod.

Figure 8-2 depicts how QoS is assigned to pods.

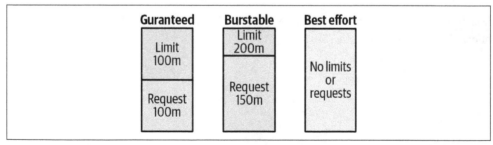

Figure 8-2. Kubernetes QoS

With guaranteed QoS, if you have multiple containers in your pod, you'll need to have memory request and limits set for each container, and you'll also need CPU request and limits set for each container. If the request and limits are not set for all containers, they will not be assigned guaranteed QoS.

PodDisruptionBudgets

At some point in time, Kubernetes might need to *evict* pods from a host. There are two types of evictions: *voluntary* and *involuntary* disruptions. Involuntary disruptions can be caused by hardware failure, network partitions, kernel panics, or a node being out of resources. Voluntary evictions can be caused by performing maintenance on the cluster, the Cluster Autoscaler deallocating nodes, or updating pod templates. To minimize the impact to your application, you can set a `PodDisruptionBudget` to ensure uptime of the application when pods need to be evicted. A `PodDisruption Budget` allows you to set a policy on the minimum available and maximum unavailable pods during voluntary eviction events. An example of a voluntary eviction would be when draining a node to perform maintenance on the node.

For example, you might specify that no more than 20% of pods belonging to your application can be down at a given time. You could also specify this policy in terms of X number of replicas that must always be available.

Minimum available

In the following example, we set a `PodDisruptionBudget` to handle a minimum available to 5 for app: frontend:

```
apiVersion: policy/v1
kind: PodDisruptionBudget
metadata:
  name: frontend-pdb
spec:
  minAvailable: 5
  selector:
    matchLabels:
      app: frontend
```

In this example, the `PodDisruptionBudget` specifies that for the frontend app there must always be five replica pods available at any given time. In this scenario, an eviction can evict as many pods as it wants, as long as five are available.

Maximum unavailable

In the next example, we set a `PodDisruptionBudget` to handle a maximum unavailable to 20% for the frontend app:

```
apiVersion: policy/v1
kind: PodDisruptionBudget
metadata:
  name: frontend-pdb
spec:
  maxUnavailable: 20%
  selector:
    matchLabels:
      app: frontend
```

In this example, the `PodDisruptionBudget` specifies that no more than 20% of replica pods can be unavailable at any given time. In this scenario, an eviction can evict a maximum of 20% of pods during a voluntary disruption.

It's essential that when designing your Kubernetes cluster you think about the sizing of the cluster resources so that you can handle a number of failed nodes. For example, if you have a four-node cluster and one node fails, you will be losing a quarter of your cluster capacity.

When specifying a `PodDisruptionBudget` as a percentage, it might not correlate to a specific number of pods. For example, if your application has seven pods and you specify `maxAvailable` to 50%, it's not clear whether that is three or four pods. In this case, Kubernetes rounds up to the closest integer, so the `maxAvailable` would be four pods.

Managing Resources by Using Namespaces

Namespaces in Kubernetes give you a nice logical separation of resources deployed to a cluster. This allows you to set resource quotas per namespace, Role-Based Access Control (RBAC) per namespace, and also network policies per namespace. It gives you soft multitenancy features so you can separate out workloads in a cluster without dedicating specific infrastructure to a team or application. This allows you to get the most out of your cluster resource while also maintaining a logical form of separation.

For example, you could create a namespace per team and give each team a quota on the number of resources that it can utilize, such as CPU and memory.

When designing how you want to configure a namespace, you should think about how you want to control access to a specific set of applications. If you have multiple teams that will be using a single cluster, it is typically best to allocate a namespace to each team. If the cluster is dedicated to only one team, it might make sense to allocate a namespace for each service deployed to the cluster. There's no single solution to this; your team organization and responsibilities will drive the design.

After deploying a Kubernetes cluster, you'll see the following namespaces in your cluster:

kube-system
> Kubernetes internal components are deployed here, such as coredns, kube-proxy, and metrics-server.

default
> This is the default namespace that is used when you don't specify a namespace in the resource object.

kube-public
> Used for anonymous and unauthenticated content, and reserved for system usage.

You'll want to avoid using the default namespace because users are not mandated to deploy applications within specific resource constraints, and it can lead to resource contention. You should also avoid using the kube-system namespace for your applications because it is used for Kubernetes internal components.

When working with namespaces, you need to use the –namespace flag, or -n for short, when working with kubectl:

```
kubectl create ns team-1

kubectl get pods --namespace team-1
```

You can also set your kubectl context to a specific namespace, which is useful so that you don't need to add the –namespace flag with every command. You can set your namespace context by using the following command:

```
kubectl config set-context my-context --namespace=team-1
```

> When dealing with multiple namespaces and clusters, it can be a pain to set different namespaces and cluster context. We've found that using kubens (*https://oreil.ly/ryavL*) and kubectx (*https://oreil.ly/kVBiL*) can help make it easy to switch between these different namespaces and contexts.

ResourceQuota

When multiple teams or applications share a single cluster, it's important to set up ResourceQuotas on your namespaces. ResourceQuotas allow you to divvy up the cluster in logical units so that no single namespace can consume more than its share of resources in the cluster. The following resources can have a quota set for them:

- Compute resources:
  - `requests.cpu`: Sum of CPU requests cannot exceed this amount
  - `limits.cpu`: Sum of CPU limits cannot exceed this amount
  - `requests.memory`: Sum of memory requests cannot exceed this amount
  - `limit.memory`: Sum of memory limits cannot exceed this amount
- Storage resources:
  - `requests.storage`: Sum of storage requests cannot exceed this value
  - `persistentvolumeclaims`: The total number of PersistentVolume claims that can exist in the namespace
  - `storageclass.request`: Volume claims associated with the specified storage-class cannot exceed this value
  - `storageclass.pvc`: The total number of PersistentVolume claims that can exist in the namespace
- Object count quotas (only an example set):
  - count/pvc
  - count/services
  - count/deployments
  - count/replicasets

As you can see from this list, Kubernetes gives you fine-grained control over how you carve up resource quotas per namespace. This allows you to more efficiently operate resource usage in a multitenant cluster.

Let's see how these quotas actually work by setting up a quota on a namespace. Apply the following YAML file to the `team-1` namespace:

```
apiVersion: v1
kind: ResourceQuota
metadata:
  name: mem-cpu-demo
  namespace: team-1
spec:
  hard:
    requests.cpu: "1"
    requests.memory: 1Gi
    limits.cpu: "2"
    limits.memory: 2Gi
    persistentvolumeclaims: "5"
    requests.storage: "10Gi"

kubectl apply quota.yaml -n team-1
```

This example sets quotas for CPU, memory, and storage on the `team-1` namespace.

Now let's try to deploy an application to see how the resource quotas affect the deployment:

```
kubectl run nginx-quotatest --image=nginx --restart=Never --replicas=1 --port=80
    --requests='cpu=500m,memory=4Gi' --limits='cpu=500m,memory=4Gi' -n team-1
```

This deployment will fail with the following error due to the memory quota exceeding 2 Gi of memory:

```
Error from server (Forbidden): pods "nginx-quotatest" is forbidden:
    exceeded quota: mem-cpu-demo
```

As this example demonstrates, setting resource quotas can let you deny deployment of resources based on policies you set for the namespace.

LimitRange

We've discussed setting `request` and `limits` at the container level, but what happens if the user forgets to set these in the pod specification? Kubernetes provides an admission controller that allows you to automatically set these when none are indicated in the specification.

First, create a namespace to work with quotas and `LimitRanges`:

```
kubectl create ns team-1
```

Apply a `LimitRange` to the namespace to apply `defaultRequest` in `limits`:

```
apiVersion: v1
kind: LimitRange
metadata:
  name: team-1-limit-range
spec:
  limits:
  - default:
      memory: 512Mi
    defaultRequest:
      memory: 256Mi
    type: Container
```

Save this to *limitranger.yaml* and then run `kubectl apply`:

```
kubectl apply -f limitranger.yaml -n team-1
```

Verify that the `LimitRange` applies default limits and requests:

```
kubectl run team-1-pod --image=nginx -n team-1
```

Next, let's describe the pod to see what requests and limits were set on it:

```
kubectl describe pod team-1-pod -n team-1
```

You should see the following requests and limits set on the pod specification:

```
Limits:
        memory:  512Mi
     Requests:
        memory:  256Mi
```

It's important to use `LimitRange` when using `ResourceQuotas`, because if no request or limits are set in the specification, the deployment will be rejected.

Cluster Scaling

One of the first decisions you need to make when deploying a cluster is the instance size you'll want to use within your cluster. This becomes more of an art than science, especially when you're mixing workloads in a single cluster. You'll first want to identify a good starting point for the cluster; aiming for a good balance of CPU and memory is one option. After you've decided on a sensible size for the cluster, you can use a couple of Kubernetes core primitives to manage the scaling of your cluster.

Manual scaling

Kubernetes makes it easy to scale your cluster, especially if you're using tools like Kops or a managed Kubernetes offering. Scaling your cluster manually is typically just choosing a new number of nodes, and the service will add the new nodes to your cluster.

These tools also allow you to create node pools, which allows you to add new instance types to an already running cluster. This becomes very useful when running mixed workloads within a single cluster. For example, one workload might be more CPU driven, whereas the other workloads might be memory-driven applications. Node pools allow you to mix multiple instance types within a single cluster.

But perhaps you don't want to manually do this and want it to autoscale. There are things that you need to take into consideration with cluster autoscaling, and we have found that most users are better off starting with just manually scaling their nodes proactively when resources are needed. If your workloads are highly variable, cluster autoscaling can be very useful.

Cluster autoscaling

Kubernetes provides a Cluster Autoscaler add-on that allows you to set the minimum nodes available to a cluster and also the maximum number of nodes to which your cluster can scale. The Cluster Autoscaler bases its scale decision on when a pod goes pending. For example, if the Kubernetes scheduler tries to schedule a pod with a memory request of 4,000 Mib and the cluster has only 2,000 Mib available, the pod will go into a pending state. After the pod is pending, the Cluster Autoscaler will add a node to the cluster. As soon as the new node is added to the cluster, the pending pod is scheduled to the node. The downside of the Cluster Autoscaler is that a new node is added only before a pod goes pending, so your workload may end up waiting for a new node to come online when it is scheduled. As of Kubernetes v1.15, the Cluster Autoscaler doesn't support scaling based on custom metrics.

The Cluster Autoscaler can also reduce the size of the cluster after resources are no longer needed. When the resources are no longer needed, it will drain the node and reschedule the pods to new nodes in the cluster. You'll want to use a PodDisruption Budget to ensure that you don't negatively affect your application when it performs its drain operation to remove the node from the cluster.

Application Scaling

Kubernetes provides multiple ways to scale applications in your cluster. You can scale an application by manually changing the number of replicas within a deployment. You can also change the ReplicaSet or replication controller, but we don't recommend managing your applications through those implementations. Manual scaling is perfectly fine for workloads that are static or when you know the times that the workload spikes, but for workloads that experience sudden spikes or workloads that are not static, manual scaling is not ideal for the application. Happily, Kubernetes also provides a Horizontal Pod Autoscaler (HPA) to automatically scale workloads for you.

Let's first look at how you can manually scale a deployment by applying the following Deployment manifest:

```
apiVersion: apps/v1
kind: Deployment
metadata:
  name: frontend
spec:
  replicas: 3
  selector:
    matchlables:
      app: frontend
  template:
    metadata:
      name: frontend
      labels:
        app: frontend
    spec:
      containers:
      - image: nginx:alpine
        name: frontend
        resources:
          requests:
            cpu: 100m
```

This example deploys three replicas of our frontend service. We then can scale this deployment by using the `kubectl scale` command:

```
kubectl scale deployment frontend --replicas 5
```

This results in five replicas of our frontend service. This is great, but let's look at how we can add some intelligence and automatically scale the application based on metrics.

Scaling with HPA

The Kubernetes HPA allows you to scale your deployments based on CPU, memory, or custom metrics. It performs a watch on the deployment and pulls metrics from the Kubernetes `metrics-server`. It also allows you to set the minimum and maximum number of pods available. For example, you can define an HPA policy that sets the minimum number of pods to 3 and the maximum number of pods to 10, and it scales when the deployment reaches 80% CPU usage. Setting the minimum and maximum is critical because you don't want the HPA to scale the replicas to an infinite amount due to an application bug or issue.

The HPA has the following default setting for sync metrics, upscaling, and downscaling replicas:

`horizontal-pod-autoscaler-sync-period`
    Default of 30 seconds for syncing metrics

`horizontal-pod-autoscaler-upscale-delay`
    Default of three minutes between two upscale operations

`horizontal-pod-autoscaler-downscale-delay`
    Default of five minutes between two downscale operations

You can change the defaults by using their relative flags, but you need to be careful when doing so. If your workload is extremely variable, it's worth playing around with the settings to optimize them for your specific use case.

Let's go ahead and set up an HPA policy for the frontend application you deployed in the previous exercise.

First, expose the deployment on port 80:

```
kubectl expose deployment frontend --port 80
```

Next, set the autoscale policy:

```
kubectl autoscale deployment frontend --cpu-percent=50 --min=1 --max=10
```

This sets the policy to scale your app from a minimum of 1 replica to a maximum of 10 replicas and will invoke the scale operation when the CPU load reaches 50%.

Let's generate some load so that we can see the deployment autoscale:

```
kubectl run -i --tty load-generator --image=busybox /bin/sh

Hit enter for command prompt
while true; do wget -q -O- http://frontend.default.svc.cluster.local; done

kubectl get hpa
```

You might need to wait a few minutes to see the replicas scale up automatically.

HPA with Custom Metrics

In Chapter 4, we introduced the role that the metrics server plays in monitoring our systems in Kubernetes. With the Metrics Server API, we can also support scaling our applications with custom metrics. The Custom Metrics API and Metrics Aggregator allow third-party providers to plug in and extend the metrics, and HPA can then scale based on these external metrics. For example, instead of just basic CPU and memory metrics, you could scale based on a metric you're collecting on an external storage queue. By utilizing custom metrics for autoscaling, you have the ability to scale application-specific metrics or external service metrics.

Vertical Pod Autoscaler

The Vertical Pod Autoscaler (VPA) differs from the HPA in that it doesn't scale replicas; instead, it automatically scales requests. Earlier in the chapter, we talked about setting requests on our pods and how that guarantees X amount of resources for a given container. The VPA frees you from manually adjusting these requests and automatically scales up and scales down pod requests for you. For workloads that can't scale out due to their architecture, this works well for automatically scaling the resources. For example, a MySQL database doesn't scale the same way as a stateless web frontend. With MySQL, you might want to set the Master nodes to automatically scale up based on workload.

The VPA is more complex than the HPA, and it consists of three components:

Recommender
> Monitors the current and past resource consumption, and provides recommended values for the container's CPU and memory requests

Updater
> Checks which of the pods have the correct resources set, and if they don't, kills them so that they can be re-created by their controllers with the updated requests

Admission Plugin
> Sets the correct resource requests on new pods

Vertical scaling has two objectives:

- Reducing the maintenance cost, by automating configuration of resource requirements.
- Improving utilization of cluster resources, while minimizing the risk of containers running out of memory or getting CPU starved.

Resource Management Best Practices

- Utilize pod anti-affinity to spread workloads across multiple availability zones to ensure high availability for your application.
- If you're using specialized hardware, such as GPU-enabled nodes, ensure that only workloads that need GPUs are scheduled to those nodes by utilizing taints.
- Use `NodeCondition` taints to proactively avoid failing or degraded nodes.
- Apply nodeSelectors to your pod specifications to schedule pods to specialized hardware that you have deployed in the cluster.
- Before going to production, experiment with different node sizes to find a good mix of cost and performance for node types.
- If you're deploying a mix of workloads with different performance characteristics, utilize node pools to have mixed node types in a single cluster.
- Ensure that you set memory and CPU limits for all pods deployed to your cluster.
- Utilize `ResourceQuotas` to ensure that multiple teams or applications are allotted their fair share of resources in the cluster.
- Implement `LimitRange` to set default limits and requests for pod specifications that don't set limits or requests.
- Start with manual cluster scaling until you understand your workload profiles on Kubernetes. You can use autoscaling, but it comes with additional considerations around node spin-up time and cluster scale down.
- Use the HPA for workloads that are variable and that have unexpected spikes in their usage.

Summary

In this chapter, we discussed how you can optimally manage Kubernetes and application resources. Kubernetes provides many built-in features to manage resources that you can use to maintain a reliable, highly utilized, and efficient cluster. Cluster and pod sizing can be difficult at first, but through monitoring your applications in production you can discover ways to optimize your resources.

## CHAPTER 9

Networking, Network Security, and Service Mesh

Kubernetes is effectively a manager of distributed systems across a cluster of connected systems. This immediately puts critical importance on how the connected systems communicate with one another, and networking is the key to this. Understanding how Kubernetes facilitates communication among the distributed services it manages is important for the effective application of interservice communication.

This chapter focuses on the principles that Kubernetes places on the network and best practices around applying these concepts in different situations. With any discussion of networking, security is usually brought along for the ride. The traditional models of network security boundaries being controlled at the network layer are not absent in this new world of distributed systems in Kubernetes, but how they are implemented and the capabilities offered change slightly. Kubernetes brings along a native API for network security policies that will sound eerily similar to firewall rules of old.

The last section of this chapter delves into the new and scary world of service meshes. The term "scary" is used in jest, but it is quite the Wild West when it comes to service mesh technology in Kubernetes.

Kubernetes Network Principles

Understanding how Kubernetes uses the underlying network to facilitate communication among services is critical to understanding how to effectively plan application architectures. Usually, networking topics start to give most people major headaches. We are going to keep this rather simple because this is more of a best practice guidance than a lesson on container networking. Luckily for us, Kubernetes has laid down some rules of the road for networking that give us a start. The rules outline how communication is expected to behave between different components. Let's take a closer look at each of these rules:

Container-to-container communication in the same pod

All containers in the same pod share the same network space. This effectively allows localhost communication between the containers. It also means that containers in the same pod need to expose different ports. This is done using the power of Linux namespaces and Docker networking to allow these containers to be on the same local network through the use of a paused container in every pod that does nothing but host the networking for the pod. Figure 9-1 shows how Container A can communicate directly with Container B using localhost and the port number that the container is listening on.

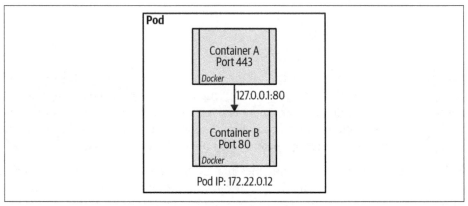

Figure 9-1. Intrapod communication between containers

Pod-to-pod communication

All pods need to communicate with one another without any network address translation (NAT). This means that the pod's IP address that is seen by the receiving pod is the sender's actual IP address. This is handled in different ways, depending on the network plug-in used, which we discuss in more detail later in the chapter. This rule is true between pods on the same node and pods that are on different nodes in the same cluster. This also extends to the node being able to communicate directly to the pod with no NAT involved. This allows host-based agents or system daemons to communicate to the pods as needed. Figure 9-2 is a representation of the communication processes between pods in the same node and pods in different nodes of the cluster.

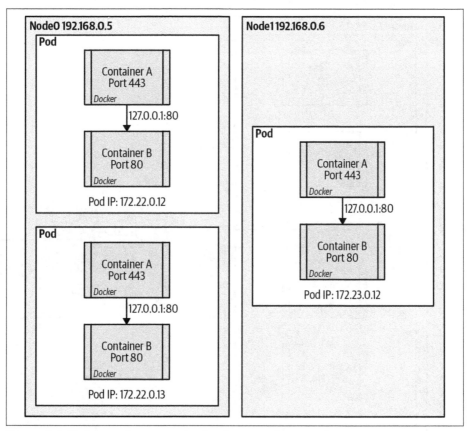

Figure 9-2. Pod-to-pod communication intra- and internode

Service-to-pod communication

Services in Kubernetes represent a durable IP address and port that is found on each node that will forward all traffic to the endpoints that are mapped to the service. Over the different iterations of Kubernetes, the method in favor of enabling this has changed, but the two main methods are via the use of iptables or the newer IP Virtual Server (IPVS). Some cloud providers and more advanced implementations allow for a new eBPF-based dataplane. Most implementations today use the iptables implementation to enable a pseudo–Layer 4 load balancer on each node. Figure 9-3 is a visual representation of how the service is tied to the pods via label selectors.

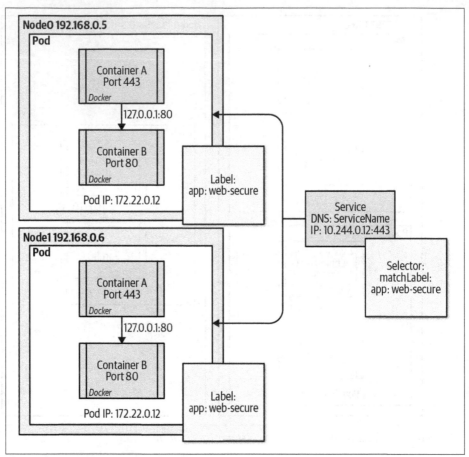

Figure 9-3. Service-to-pod communication

Network Plug-ins

Early on, the Special Interest Group (SIG) guided the networking standards to more of a pluggable architecture, opening the door for numerous third-party networking projects, which in many cases injected value-added capabilities into Kubernetes workloads. These network plug-ins come in two flavors. The most basic is called Kubenet and is the default plug-in provided by Kubernetes natively. The second type of plug-in follows the Container Network Interface (CNI) specification, which is a generic plug-in network solution for containers.

Kubenet

Kubenet is the most basic network plug-in that comes out of the box in Kubernetes. It is the simplest of the plug-ins and provides a Linux bridge, cbr0, that's a virtual Ethernet pair for the pods connected to it. The pod then gets an IP address from a Classless Inter-Domain Routing (CIDR) range that is distributed across the nodes of the cluster. There is also an IP masquerade flag that should be set to allow traffic destined to IPs outside the pod CIDR range to be masqueraded. This obeys the rules of pod-to-pod communication because only traffic destined outside the pod CIDR undergoes network address translation (NAT). After the packet leaves a node to go to another node, some kind of routing is put in place to facilitate the process to forward the traffic to the correct node.

Kubenet Best Practices

- Kubenet allows for a simple network stack and does not consume precious IP addresses on already crowded networks. This is especially true of cloud networks that are extended to on-premises datacenters.

- Ensure that the pod CIDR range is large enough to handle the potential size of the cluster and the pods in each cluster. The default pods per node set in kubelet is 110, but you can adjust this.

- Understand and plan accordingly for the route rules to properly allow traffic to find pods in the proper nodes. In cloud providers, this is usually automated, but on-premises or edge cases will require automation and solid network management.

The CNI Plug-in

The CNI plug-in has basic requirements set aside by the specification. These specifications dictate the interfaces and minimal API actions that the CNI offers and how it will interface with the container runtime that is used in the cluster. The network management components are defined by the CNI, but they all must include some type of IP address management and minimally allow for the addition and deletion of a container to a network. The full original specification originally derived from the rkt networking proposal is available on GitHub (*https://oreil.ly/wGvF7*).

The Core CNI project provides libraries that you can use to write plug-ins that provide the basic requirements and can call other plug-ins to perform various functions. This adaptability led to numerous CNI plug-ins that you can use in container networking from cloud providers, like the Microsoft Azure native CNI and the Amazon Web Services (AWS) VPC CNI plug-in, as well as plug-ins from traditional network providers such as Nuage CNI, Juniper Networks Contrail/Tunsten Fabric, and VMware NSX.

CNI Best Practices

Networking is a critical component of a functioning Kubernetes environment. The interaction between the virtual components within Kubernetes and the physical network environment should be carefully designed to ensure dependable application communication:

1. Evaluate the feature set needed to accomplish the overall networking goals of the infrastructure. Some CNI plug-ins provide native high availability, multicloud connectivity, Kubernetes network policy support, and various other features.

2. If you are running clusters via public cloud providers, verify that any CNI plug-ins that are not native to the cloud provider's Software-Defined Network (SDN) are actually supported.

3. Verify that any network security tools, network observability, and management tools are compatible with the CNI plug-in of choice. If not, research which tools can replace the existing ones. It is important to not lose either observability or security capabilities because the needs will be expanded when moving to a large-scale distributed system such as Kubernetes. You can add tools like Weaveworks Weave Scope, Dynatrace, and Sysdig to any Kubernetes environment, and each offers its own benefits. If you're running in a cloud provider's managed service, such as Azure AKS, Google GCE, or AWS EKS, look for native tools like Azure Container Insights and Network Watcher, Google Logging and Monitoring, and AWS CloudWatch. Whatever tool you use, it should provide insight into the network stack and the Four Golden signals, made popular by the amazing Google SRE team and Rob Ewashuck: Latency, Traffic, Errors, and Saturation.

4. If you're using CNIs that do not provide an overlay network separate from the SDN space, ensure that you have proper network address space to handle node IPs, pod IPs, internal load balancers, and overhead for cluster upgrade and scale out processes.

Services in Kubernetes

When pods are deployed into a Kubernetes cluster, because of the basic rules of Kubernetes networking and the network plug-in used to facilitate these rules, pods can directly communicate only with other pods within the same cluster. Some CNI plug-ins give the pods IPs on the same network space as the nodes, so technically, after the IP of a pod is known, it can be accessed directly from outside the cluster. This, however, is not an efficient way to access services being served by a pod, because of the ephemeral nature of pods in Kubernetes. Imagine that you have a function or system that needs to access an API that is running in a pod in Kubernetes. For a while, that might work with no issue, but at some point there might be a voluntary or involuntary disruption that will cause that pod to disappear. Kubernetes will potentially create a replacement pod with a new name and IP address, so naturally there needs to be some mechanism to find the replacement pod. This is where the service API comes to the rescue.

The service API allows for a durable IP and port to be assigned within the Kubernetes cluster and automatically mapped to the proper pods as endpoints to the service. This magic happens through the iptables or IPVS on Linux nodes to create a mapping of the assigned service IP and port to the endpoint's or pod's actual IPs. The controller that manages this is called the kube-proxy service, which actually runs on each node in the cluster. It is responsible for manipulating the iptables rules on each node.

When a service object is defined, the type of service needs to be defined. The service type will dictate whether the endpoints are exposed only within the cluster or outside of the cluster. We will briefly discuss four basic service types in the following sections.

Service Type ClusterIP

ClusterIP is the default service type if one is not declared in the specification. ClusterIP means that the service is assigned an IP from a designated service CIDR range. This IP is as long-lasting as the service object, so it provides an IP and port and protocol mapping to backend pods using the selector field; however, as we will see, there are cases for which you can have no selector. The declaration of the service also provides for a Domain Name System (DNS) name for the service. This facilitates service discovery within the cluster and allows for workloads to easily communicate with other services within the cluster by using DNS lookup based on the service name. As an example, if you have the service definition shown in the following example and need to access that service from another pod inside the cluster via an HTTP call, the call can simply use http://web1-svc if the client is in the same namespace as the service:

```
apiVersion: v1
kind: Service
metadata:
  name: web1-svc
spec:
  selector:
    app: web1
  ports:
  - port: 80
    targetPort: 8081
```

If it is required to find services in other namespaces, the DNS pattern would be *<service_name>*.*<namespace_name>*.svc.cluster.local.

If no selector is given in a service definition, the endpoints can be explicitly defined for the service by using an endpoint API definition. This will basically add an IP and port as a specific endpoint to a service instead of relying on the selector attribute to automatically update the endpoints from the pods that are in scope by the selector match. This can be useful in a few scenarios in which you have a specific database that is not in a cluster that is to be used for testing, but you will change the service later to a Kubernetes-deployed database. This is sometimes called a *headless service* because it is not managed by kube-proxy as other services are, but you can directly manage the endpoints, as shown in Figure 9-4.

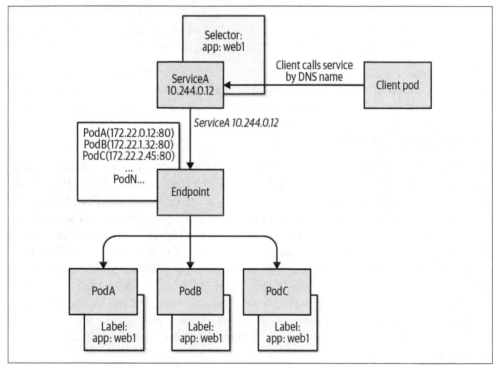

Figure 9-4. ClusterIP-pod and service visualization

Service Type NodePort

The NodePort service type assigns a high-level port on each node of the cluster to the service IP and port on each node. The high-level NodePorts fall within the 30,000 through 32,767 ranges and can either be statically assigned or explicitly defined in the service specification. NodePorts are typically used for on-premises clusters or bespoke solutions that do not offer automatic load-balancing configuration. To directly access the service from outside the cluster, use NodeIP:NodePort, as depicted in Figure 9-5.

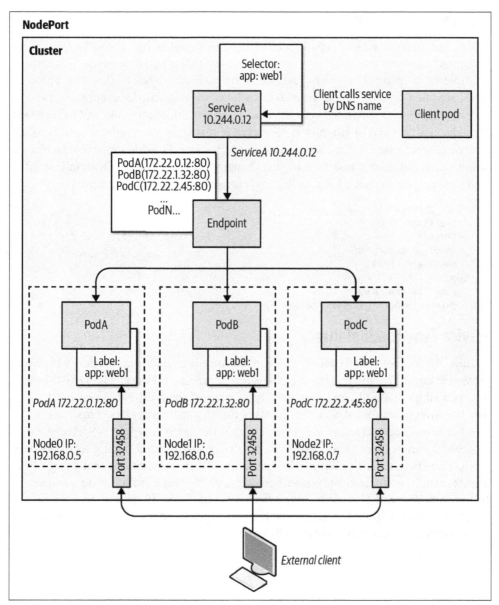

Figure 9-5. NodePort–pod, service and host network visualization

Service Type ExternalName

The ExternalName service type is seldom used in practice, but it can be helpful for passing cluster-durable DNS names to external DNS named services. A common example is an external database service from a cloud provider that has a unique DNS supplied by the cloud provider, such as `mymongodb.documents.azure.com`. Technically, this can be added very easily to a pod specification using an `Environment` variable, as discussed in Chapter 6. However, it might be more advantageous to use a more generic name in the cluster, such as `prod-mongodb`, which enables the change of the actual database it points to by just changing the service specification instead of having to recycle the pods because the `Environment` variable has changed:

```
kind: Service
apiVersion: v1
metadata:
  name: prod-mongodb
  namespace: prod
spec:
  type: ExternalName
  externalName: mymongodb.documents.azure.com
```

Service Type LoadBalancer

LoadBalancer is a very special service type because it enables automation with cloud providers and other programmable cloud infrastructure services. The `LoadBalancer` type is a single method to ensure the deployment of the load-balancing mechanism that the infrastructure provider of the Kubernetes cluster supplies. This means that in most cases, `LoadBalancer` will work roughly the same way in AWS, Azure, GCE, OpenStack, and others. This entry will usually create a public-facing load-balanced service; however, each cloud provider has some specific annotations that enable other features, such as internal-only load balancers, AWS ELB configuration parameters, and so on. You can also define the actual load-balancer IP to use and the source ranges to allow within the service specification, as seen in the code sample that follows and the visual representation in Figure 9-6:

```
kind: Service
apiVersion: v1
metadata:
  name: web-svc
spec:
  type: LoadBalancer
  selector:
    app: web
  ports:
  - protocol: TCP
    port: 80
    targetPort: 8081
  loadBalancerIP: 13.12.21.31
```

```
loadBalancerSourceRanges:
- "142.43.0.0/16"
```

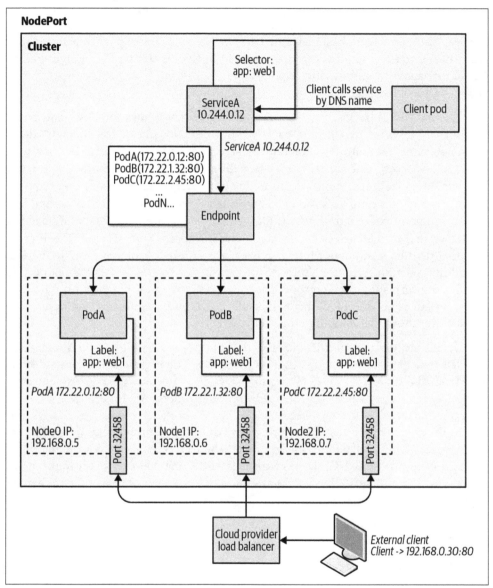

Figure 9-6. LoadBalancer–pod, service, node, and cloud provider network visualization

Ingress and Ingress Controllers

Although not technically a service type in Kubernetes, the Ingress specification is an important concept for ingress to workloads in Kubernetes. Services, as defined by the Service API, allow for a basic level of Layer 3/4 load balancing. The reality is that many of the stateless services that are deployed in Kubernetes require a high level of traffic management and usually require application-level control: more specifically, HTTP protocol management.

The Ingress API is basically an HTTP-level router that allows for host- and path-based rules to direct to specific backend services. Imagine a website hosted on www.evillgenius.com and two different paths that are hosted on that site, */registration* and */labaccess*, that are served by two different services hosted in Kubernetes, reg-svc and labaccess-svc. You can define an ingress rule to ensure that requests to www.evillgenius.com/registration are forwarded to the reg-svc service and the correct endpoint pods, and, similarly, that requests to www.evillgenius.com/labaccess are forwarded to the correct endpoints of the labaccess-svc service. The Ingress API also permits host-based routing to allow for different hosts on a single ingress. An additional feature is the ability to declare a Kubernetes secret that holds the certificate information for Transport Layer Security (TLS) termination on port 443. When a path is not specified, there is usually a default backend that can be used to give a better user experience than the standard 404 error.

The details around the specific TLS and default backend configuration are actually handled by what is known as the Ingress controller. The Ingress controller is decoupled from the Ingress API and allows for operators to deploy an Ingress controller of choice, such as NGINX, Traefik, HAProxy, and others. An Ingress controller, as the name suggests, is a controller just like any Kubernetes controller, but it's not part of the system and is instead a third-party controller that understands the Kubernetes Ingress API for dynamic configuration. The most common implementation of an Ingress controller is NGINX because it is partly maintained by the Kubernetes project; however, there are numerous examples of both open source and commercial Ingress controllers:

```
apiVersion: networking.k8s.io/v1
kind: Ingress
metadata:
  name: labs-ingress
  annotations:
    nginx.ingress.kubernetes.io/rewrite-target: /
spec:
  tls:
  - hosts:
    - www.evillgenius.com
    secretName: secret-tls
  rules:
  - host: www.evillgenius.com
```

```
http:
  paths:
  - path: /registration
    pathType: ImplementationSpecific
    backend:
      service:
        name: reg-svc
        port:
          number: 8088
  - path: /labaccess
    pathType: ImplementationSpecific
    backend:
      service:
        name: labaccess-svc
        port:
          number: 8089
```

Gateway API

The Ingress API had some challenges over the years that it was in beta and following its v1 promotion. These challenges have led to other network services offering different abstractions through the use of Custom Resource Definitions and controllers to create their own APIs that fill some of the gaps Ingress has had. Some of the most common challenges with the Ingress API have been:

- The lack of expressiveness in the definition as it represents the lowest common denominator for the capabilities of the particular Ingress implementation.

- A general lack of extensibility in the architecture. Vendors have used countless annotations to expose specific implementation capabilities; however, this has some limitations.

- The use of vendor-specific annotations has removed some of the portability promised by the API. An annotation to expose a capability in an NGINX-based Ingress controller may be different or expressed differently from a Kong-based controller implementation.

- There is no formal way to do multi-tenancy with the current Ingress API, and DevOps teams have to create very tight controls to prevent path conflicts between Ingress definitions that could impact other tenants in the same cluster.

Introduced in 2019, the Gateway API is currently managed as a project by the SIG Network team under the Kubernetes Project. The Gateway API does not intend to replace the Ingress API as it primarily targets exposing HTTP applications with a declarative syntax. This API exposes a more general API for proxying for many types of protocols, and fits a more role-based management process because it models more closely the infrastructure components in the environment.

The role-based paradigm, as shown in Figure 9-7, is important in answering some of the shortcomings of the existing Ingress API. The separate components allow for infrastructure providers, such as cloud providers and proxy ISVs, to define the infrastructure and platform operators to define through policy what infrastructure can be used. Developers can then worry about how they want to expose their services within the constraints they are given. Figure 9-8 shows a practical example of how Gateway API structure abstracts the infrastructure services and capabilities away from the developer and allows them to focus on their specific service needs.

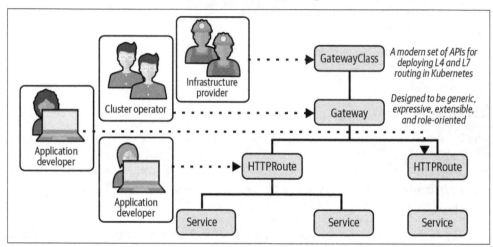

Figure 9-7. Gateway API structure

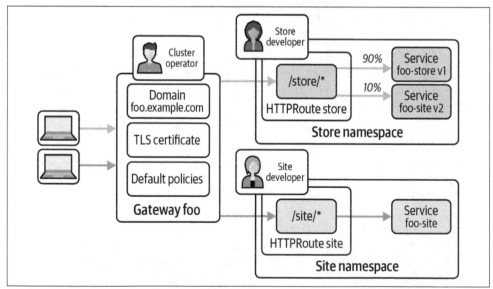

Figure 9-8. Gateway API structure, continued

The specification is very promising, and many of the leading providers of proxies and services meshes, as well as cloud providers, have begun to implement the Gateway API into their stack. Google's GKE, Acnodeal EPIC, Contour, Apache APISIX, and others have begun to offer limited preview or alpha support. As of this writing, the API itself is in beta for the GatewayClass, Gateway, and HTTPRoute resources, and others are in Alpha support. Unlike the Ingress API, this is a custom resource that can be added to any cluster and therefore does not follow the Kubernetes alpha or beta release process.

Services and Ingress Controllers Best Practices

Creating a complex virtual network environment with interconnected applications requires careful planning. Effectively managing how the different services of the application communicate with one another and the outside world requires constant attention as the application changes. These best practices will help make management easier:

- Limit the number of services that need to be accessed from outside the cluster. Ideally, most services will be ClusterIP, and only external-facing services will be exposed externally to the cluster.

- If the services that need to be exposed are primarily HTTP/HTTPS-based services, it is best to use an Ingress API and Ingress controller to route traffic to backing services with TLS termination. Depending on the type of Ingress controller used, features such as rate limiting, header rewrites, OAuth authentication, observability, and other services can be made available without having to build them into the applications themselves.

- Choose an Ingress controller that has the needed functionality for secure ingress of your web-based workloads. Standardize on one and use it across the enterprise because many of the specific configuration annotations vary between implementations and prevent the deployment code from being portable across enterprise Kubernetes implementations.

- Evaluate cloud service provider–specific Ingress controller options to move the infrastructure management and load of the ingress out of the cluster, but still allow for Kubernetes API configuration.

- When serving mostly APIs externally, evaluate API-specific Ingress controllers, such as Kong or Ambassador, that have more fine-tuning for API-based workloads. Although NGINX, Traefik, and others might offer some API tuning, it will not be as fine-grained as specific API proxy systems.

- When deploying Ingress controllers as pod-based workloads in Kubernetes, ensure that the deployments are designed for high availability and aggregate performance throughput. Use metrics observability to properly scale the ingress, but include enough cushion to prevent client disruptions while the workload scales.

Network Security Policy

The NetworkPolicy API built into Kubernetes allows for network-level ingress and egress access control defined with your workload. Network policies allow you to control how groups of pods are allowed to communicate with one another and with other endpoints. If you want to dig deeper into the NetworkPolicy specification, it might sound confusing, especially given that it is defined as a Kubernetes API, but it requires a network plug-in that supports the NetworkPolicy API.

Network policies have a simple YAML structure that can look complicated, but if you think of it as a simple East-West traffic firewall, it might help you to understand it a little better. Each policy specification has `podSelector`, `ingress`, `egress`, and `policyType` fields. The only required field is `podSelector`, which follows the same convention as any Kubernetes selector with a `matchLabels`. You can create multiple NetworkPolicy definitions that can target the same pods, and the effect is additive. Because NetworkPolicy objects are namespaced objects, if no selector is given for a `podSelector`, all pods in the namespace fall into the scope of the policy. If any ingress or egress rules are defined, this creates an allow list for what can ingress or egress from the pod. There is an important distinction here: if a pod falls into the scope of a policy because of a selector match, all traffic, unless explicitly defined in an ingress or egress rule, is blocked. This little, nuanced detail means that if a pod does not fall into any policy because of a selector match, all ingress and egress is allowed to the pod. This was done on purpose to allow for ease of deploying new workloads into Kubernetes without any blockers.

The `ingress` and `egress` fields are basically a list of rules based on source or destination and can be specific CIDR ranges, `podSelectors`, or `namespaceSelectors`. If you leave the ingress field empty, it is like a deny-all inbound. Similarly, if you leave the egress empty, it is deny-all outbound. Port and protocol lists are also supported to further tighten down the type of communications allowed.

The `policyTypes` field specifies to which network policy rule types the policy object is associated. If the field is not present, it will just look at the `ingress` and `egress` lists fields. The difference again is that you must explicitly call out egress in `policyTypes` and also have an egress rule list for this policy to work. Ingress is assumed, and defining it explicitly is not needed.

Let's use a prototypical example of a three-tier application deployed to a single namespace where the tiers are labeled as `tier: "web"`, `tier: "db"`, and `tier: "api"`. If you want to ensure that traffic is properly limited to each tier, create a NetworkPolicy manifest like the following.

Default deny rule:

```
apiVersion: networking.k8s.io/v1
kind: NetworkPolicy
metadata:
  name: default-deny-all
spec:
  podSelector: {}
  policyTypes:
  - Ingress
```

Web layer network policy:

```
apiVersion: networking.k8s.io/v1
kind: NetworkPolicy
metadata:
  name: webaccess
spec:
  podSelector:
    matchLabels:
      tier: "web"
  policyTypes:
  - Ingress
  ingress:
  - {}
```

API layer network policy:

```
apiVersion: networking.k8s.io/v1
kind: NetworkPolicy
metadata:
  name: allow-api-access
spec:
  podSelector:
    matchLabels:
      tier: "api"
  policyTypes:
  - Ingress
  ingress:
  - from:
    - podSelector:
        matchLabels:
          tier: "web"
```

Database layer network policy:

```
apiVersion: networking.k8s.io/v1
kind: NetworkPolicy
metadata:
  name: allow-db-access
spec:
  podSelector:
    matchLabels:
      tier: "db"
```

```
policyTypes:
- Ingress
ingress:
- from:
  - podSelector:
      matchLabels:
        tier: "api"
```

Network Policy Best Practices

Securing network traffic in an enterprise system was once the domain of physical hardware devices with complex networking rule sets. Now, with Kubernetes network policy, a more application-centric approach can be taken to segment and control the traffic of the applications hosted in Kubernetes. Some common best practices apply no matter which policy plug-in is used:

- Start off slow and focus on traffic ingress to pods. Complicating matters with ingress and egress rules can make network tracing a nightmare. As soon as traffic is flowing as expected, you can begin to look at egress rules to further control flow to sensitive workloads. The specification also favors ingress because it defaults many options even if nothing is entered into the ingress rules list.

- Ensure that the network plug-in used either has some of its own interface to the NetworkPolicy API or supports other well-known plug-ins. Example plug-ins include Calico, Cilium, Kube-router, Romana, and Weave Net.

- If the network team is used to having a "default-deny" policy in place, create a network policy such as the following for each namespace in the cluster that will contain workloads to be protected. This ensures that even if another network policy is deleted, no pods are accidentally "exposed":

```
apiVersion: networking.k8s.io/v1
kind: NetworkPolicy
metadata:
  name: default-deny-all
spec:
  podSelector: {}
  policyTypes:
  - Ingress
```

- If pods need to be accessed from the internet, use a label to explicitly apply a network policy that allows ingress. Be aware of the entire flow in case the actual IP that a packet is coming from is not the internet but rather the internal IP of a load balancer, firewall, or other network device. For example, to allow traffic from all (including external) sources for pods having the `allow-internet=true` label, do this:

```
apiVersion: networking.k8s.io/v1
kind: NetworkPolicy
metadata:
  name: internet-access
spec:
  podSelector:
    matchLabels:
      allow-internet: "true"
  policyTypes:
  - Ingress
  ingress:
  - {}
```

- Try to align application workloads to single namespaces for ease of creating rules because the rules themselves are namespace specific. If cross-namespace communication is needed, try to be as explicit as possible and perhaps use specific labels to identify the flow pattern:

```
apiVersion: networking.k8s.io/v1
kind: NetworkPolicy
metadata:
  name: namespace-foo-2-namespace-bar
  namespace: bar
spec:
  podSelector:
    matchLabels:
      app: bar-app
  policyTypes:
  - Ingress
  ingress:
  - from:
    - namespaceSelector:
        matchLabels:
          networking/namespace: foo
      podSelector:
        matchLabels:
          app: foo-app
```

- Have a test bed namespace that has fewer restrictive policies, if any at all, to allow time to investigate the correct traffic patterns needed.

Service Meshes

It is easy to imagine a single cluster hosting hundreds of services that load-balance across thousands of endpoints that communicate with one another, access external resources, and are potentially being accessed from external sources. This can be quite daunting when trying to manage, secure, observe, and trace all the connections among these services, especially with the dynamic nature of the endpoints coming and going from the overall system. The concept of a *service mesh*, which is not unique to Kubernetes, allows for control over how these services are connected and secured with a dedicated date plane and control plane. Service meshes all have different capabilities, but usually they all offer some of the following:

- Load balancing of traffic with potentially fine-grained traffic-shaping policies that are distributed across the mesh.

- Service discovery of services that are members of the mesh, which might include services within a cluster or in another cluster, or an outside system that is a member of the mesh.

- Observability of the traffic and services, including tracing across the distributed services using tracing systems like Jaeger or Zipkin that follow the OpenTracing standards.

- Security of the traffic in the mesh using mutual authentication. In some cases, not only pod-to-pod or East-West traffic is secured, but an Ingress controller is also provided that offers North-South security and control.

- Resiliency, health, and failure-prevention capabilities that allow for patterns such as circuit breaker, retries, deadlines, and so on.

The key here is that all these features are integrated into the applications that take part in the mesh with little or no application changes. How can all these amazing features come for free? Sidecar proxies are usually the way this is done. The majority of service meshes available today inject a proxy that is part of the data plane into each pod that is a member of the mesh. This allows for policies and security to be synchronized across the mesh by the control-plane components. This hides the network details from the container that holds the workload and leaves it to the proxy to handle the complexity of the distributed network. In the application's perspective, it only communicates via localhost to its proxy. In many cases, the control plane and data plane might be different technologies but complementary to each other.

In many cases, the first service mesh that comes to mind is Istio, a project by Google, Lyft, and IBM that uses Envoy as its data-plane proxy and uses proprietary control-plane components Mixer, Pilot, Galley, and Citadel. Other service meshes offer varying levels of capabilities, such as Linkerd2, which uses its own data-plane proxy built using Rust. HashiCorp has recently added more Kubernetes-centric service mesh capabilities to Consul, which allows you to choose between Consul's own proxy or Envoy, and offers commercial support for its service mesh.

The topic of service meshes in Kubernetes is a fluid one—if not overly emotional in many social media tech circles—so a detailed explanation of each mesh has no value here. We would be remiss if we did not mention the promising efforts led by Microsoft, Linkerd, HashiCorp, Solo.io, Kinvolk, and Weaveworks around the Service Mesh Interface (SMI). The SMI hopes to set a standard interface for basic feature sets that are expected of all service meshes. The specification as of this writing covers traffic policy such as identity and transport-level encryption, traffic telemetry that captures key metrics between services in the mesh, and traffic management to allow for traffic shifting and weighting between different services. This project hopes to take some of the variability out of the service meshes yet allow for service mesh vendors to extend and build value-added capabilities into their products to differentiate themselves.

Service Mesh Best Practices

The service mesh community continues to grow every day, and as more enterprises help define their needs, the service mesh ecosystem will change dramatically. These best practices are, as of this writing, based on common problems that service meshes try to solve today:

- Rate the importance of the key features service meshes offer and determine which current offerings provide the most important features with the least amount of overhead. Overhead here means both human technical debt and infrastructure resource debt. If all that is really required is mutual TLS between certain pods, would it be easier to perhaps find a CNI that offers that capability integrated into the plug-in?

- Is the need for a cross-system mesh, such as multicloud or hybrid scenarios, a key requirement? Not all service meshes offer this capability, and if they do, it is a complicated process that often introduces fragility into the environment.

- Many of the service mesh offerings are open source community-based projects, and if the team that will be managing the environment is new to service meshes, commercially supported offerings might be a better option. Some companies are beginning to offer commercially supported and managed service meshes based on Istio, which can be helpful because it is almost universally agreed upon that Istio is a complicated system to manage.

Summary

In addition to application management, one of the most important things that Kubernetes provides is the ability to link different pieces of your application. In this chapter, we looked at the details of how Kubernetes works, including how pods get their IP addresses through CNI plug-ins, how those IPs are grouped to form services, and how more application or Layer 7 routing can be implemented via Ingress resources (which in turn use services). You also saw how to limit traffic and secure your network using networking policies, and, finally, how service mesh technologies are transforming the ways in which people connect and monitor the connections between their services. In addition to setting up your application to run and be deployed reliably, setting up the networking for your application is a crucial piece of using Kubernetes successfully. Understanding how Kubernetes approaches networking and how that intersects optimally with your application is critical to its ultimate success.

## CHAPTER 10

Pod and Container Security

When it comes to pod security via the Kubernetes API, you have two main options at your disposal: Pod Security Admission and RuntimeClass. In this chapter, we review the purpose and use of each API and provide best practices for their use.

Pod Security Admission Controller

This cluster-wide resource creates a single place to define and manage all the security-sensitive fields found in pod specifications. Prior to the creation of the Pod Security Admission resource, cluster administrators and/or users used PodSecurityPolicy, which was complex and could be challenging to set up correctly. Before PodSecurityPolicy, users would need to independently define individual `SecurityContext` settings for each pod or Deployment in their workloads or enable bespoke admission controllers on the cluster to enforce some aspects of pod security.

> The Pod Security Admission controller replaced the beta PodSecurityPolicy API starting with Kubernetes 1.22. PodSecurityPolicy was removed in Kubernetes 1.25. Pod Security Admission provides a simplified API for securing pods, but it does not provide complete feature parity with PodSecurityPolicy. For that you will need to install a more complete policy solution like the Gatekeeper (*https://oreil.ly/0lVJP*) project.

Pod Security Admission was developed to address this complexity and make it fairly straightforward for a cluster administrator to secure pods on their cluster. While it is markedly less complicated than other solutions, Pod Security Admission also has significant limitations in that it has coarse-grained permissions that are applied at the namespace level. Though you can exempt specific users or runtime classes from policy enforcement, you cannot enable different levels of security for different pods or users within a namespace.

Because of these limitations, many enterprises or administrators running multitenant clusters will likely need to implement a policy solution like the Gatekeeper (*https:// oreil.ly/0lVJP*) project. But especially for many smaller single-tenant clusters, Pod Security Admission control may be appropriate.

Enabling Pod Security Admission

If your cluster is Kubernetes 1.22 or newer, Pod Security Admission is likely to be enabled. You can check the version of your cluster using the `kubectl version` command. If you are running on an older version of Kubernetes, we recommend updating since such older versions are no longer actively supported by the Kubernetes project, which puts you at risk for unpatched security vulnerabilities.

 Proceed with caution when enabling Pod Security Admission control on existing clusters because it's potentially workload blocking if adequate preparation isn't done at the outset. Consider starting with the `warn` and `audit` enforcement modes to ensure that your policy works as expected.

Pod Security levels

The Pod Security Admission controller simplifies security configuration by implementing three different policy levels for administrators to choose from. Each security level contains a collection of different rules for restricting pod configurations. The details of the security levels can be found in the Kubernetes documentation (*https:// oreil.ly/3bKXr*).

The three Pod Security Standard levels are:

`privileged`
　　Effectively no restrictions. It matches the default behavior of a Kubernetes cluster with no pod security enabled.

`baseline`
　　Protects against known privilege escalations and other security issues.

`restricted`
　　The current community best practice for pod security.

When starting out with policy, it may be tempting to immediately start enforcing the `restricted` level for all namespaces, but it is important to note that preexisting configurations in the cluster may break, and community solutions or software provided by other third parties may not work correctly.

In addition to the security levels, the Pod Security Admission controller provides three levels of activation for the policy. The enforce level actively blocks pods from being created if they don't match the security level. The warn level provides a warning to a user that their pod violates policy but doesn't block it from being created. The audit level logs policy violations but doesn't provide user feedback.

Finally, each security level is versioned to match a particular Kubernetes version (e.g., v1.25). It's important to note that while the security level is associated with a Kubernetes version, it is available in other Kubernetes versions: you can use the v1.25 security level in a Kubernetes 1.26 cluster. The versions follow the same three-version deprecation policy as any other Kubernetes component. There is also a latest version that tracks whatever is the most up-to-date policy. However, as with using latest in container images, this is discouraged because your security policy will change when the cluster is upgraded, which means that you could break your cluster by adopting a new policy unexpectedly. Instead, incremental upgrading of security policy after a cluster upgrade is a best practice.

 It's important to note that the warn level provides warnings only in tools that support warnings, like kubectl. If you are using other tools for deployment, especially CI/CD automation, the warnings may not be surfaced to your users. In such situations, you may want to combine some sort of linter that examines the configurations before they are checked in along with pod security audit.

Activating Pod Security Using Namespace Labels

The activation of Pod Security is done on a per-namespace basis by adding labels to the namespaces. You can do this in your namespace YAML by adding labels as shown in the following example. We will start with a configuration that simply audits existing usage at the baseline security level:

```
...
metadata:
  labels:
    # Start with enforce and warn unrestricted so as not to
    # interfere with existing users
    pod-security.kubernetes.io/enforce: privileged
    pod-security.kubernetes.io/enforce-version: v1.25
    pod-security.kubernetes.io/warn: privileged
    pod-security.kubernetes.io/warn-version: v1.25

    # Turn on baseline auditing
    pod-security.kubernetes.io/audit: baseline
    pod-security.kubernetes.io/audit-version: v1.25
```

Once this configuration is applied to all namespaces, you will start seeing audit information in the cluster audit logs. This will give you a sense of your cluster's level of compliance. If your cluster is very far out of compliance, you will likely need to identify the owners of various workloads and work with them to bring their workloads into compliance. Because the enforcement is per-namespace, you can work with teams individually and move to enforcement as their workloads become compliant.

Ultimately, your final security posture is a function of your teams and their workloads, so it is difficult to identify a single best practice for pod security configuration. However, for most users, setting `audit` and `warn` to `restricted` and `enforce` to `baseline` is a pretty good place to start. It will give you visibility into potentially vulnerable configurations while enabling enforcement to prevent the most egregious violations.

Workload Isolation and RuntimeClass

Container runtimes are still largely considered an insecure workload isolation boundary. There is no clear path to whether the most common runtimes of today will ever be recognized as secure. The momentum and interest among those in the industry toward Kubernetes has led to the development of different container runtimes that offer varying levels of isolation. Some are based on familiar and trusted technology stacks, whereas others are a completely new attempt to tackle the problem. Open source projects like Kata containers, gVisor, and Firecracker tout the promise of stronger workload isolation. These specific projects are either based on nested virtualization (running a super lightweight virtual machine within a virtual machine) or system call filtering and servicing. There has also been recent interest in the sandbox provided by the WebAssembly virtual machine, which was originally built for running in the browser but is seeing increased usage on the server side. The `containerd` project, one of the most popular container runtimes, now supports WebAssembly (WASM) based containers. Additionally RuntimeClass may be needed to choose a container runtime based on specific hardware capabilities like interacting with a GPU for artificial intelligence and machine learning workloads.

The introduction of these container runtimes that offer different workload isolation allows users to choose different runtimes based on their isolation guarantees in the same cluster. For example, you could have trusted and untrusted workloads running in the same cluster in different container runtimes.

RuntimeClass was introduced into Kubernetes as an API to allow container runtime selection. It is used to represent one of the supported container runtimes on the cluster when it has been configured by the cluster administrator. As a Kubernetes user, you can define specific runtime classes for your workloads by using the RuntimeClassName in the pod specification. How this is implemented under the hood is that the RuntimeClass designates a `RuntimeHandler` that is passed to the Container Runtime Interface (CRI) to implement. Node labeling or node taints can then be used in conjunction with nodeSelectors or tolerations to ensure that the workload lands on a node capable of supporting the desired RuntimeClass. Figure 10-1 demonstrates how a kubelet uses RuntimeClass when launching pods.

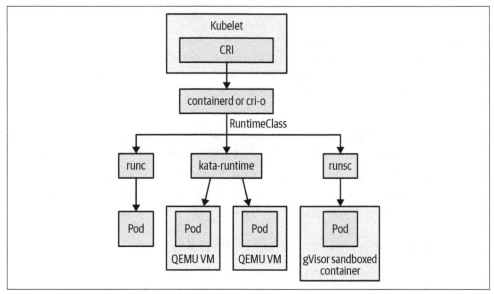

Figure 10-1. RuntimeClass flow diagram

Using RuntimeClass

If a cluster administrator has set up different RuntimeClasses, you can use them by specifying `runtimeClassName` in the pod specification; for example:

```
apiVersion: v1
kind: Pod
metadata:
  name: nginx
spec:
  runtimeClassName: firecracker
```

Runtime Implementations

Following are some open source container runtime implementations that offer differ-ent levels of security and isolation for your consideration. This list is intended as a guide and is by no means exhaustive:

CRI containerd (https://oreil.ly/1wxU1)
An API facade for container runtimes with an emphasis on simplicity, robustness, and portability.

cri-o (https://oreil.ly/OiXpP)
A purpose-built, lightweight Open Container Initiative (OCI)-based implementation of a container runtime for Kubernetes.

Firecracker (https://oreil.ly/on3Ge)
Built on top of the Kernel-based Virtual Machine (KVM), this virtualization technology allows you to launch microVMs in nonvirtualized environments very quickly using the security and isolation of traditional VMs.

gVisor (https://oreil.ly/ZZt3n)
An OCI-compatible sandbox runtime that runs containers with a new user-space kernel, which provides a low overhead and secure, isolated container runtime.

Kata Containers (https://oreil.ly/giOxk)
A secure container runtime that provides VM-like security and isolation by running lightweight VMs that feel and operate like containers.

Workload Isolation and RuntimeClass Best Practices

The following best practices will help you to avoid common workload isolation and RuntimeClass pitfalls:

- Implementing different workload isolation environments via RuntimeClass will complicate your operational environment. This means that workloads might not be portable across different container runtimes given the nature of the isolation they provide. Understanding the matrix of supported features across different runtimes can be complicated and will lead to poor user experience. We recommend having separate clusters, each with a single runtime, to avoid confusion, if possible.

- Workload isolation doesn't mean secure multitenancy. Even though you might have implemented a secure container runtime, this doesn't mean that the Kubernetes cluster and APIs have been secured in the same fashion. You must consider the total surface area of Kubernetes end to end. Just because you have an isolated workload doesn't mean that it cannot be modified by a bad actor via the Kubernetes API.

- Tooling across different runtimes is inconsistent. You might have users who rely on container runtime tooling for debugging and introspection. Having different runtimes means that you might no longer be able to run docker ps to list running containers. This leads to confusion and complications when troubleshooting.

Other Pod and Container Security Considerations

In addition to Pod Security Admission control and workload isolation, here are some other tools you may consider when determining how to handle pod and container security.

Admission Controllers

The previous discussion of pod security was powered by the Pod Security Admission controller, but there are many other admission controllers that you can choose from in the cloud native ecosystem. If you find the Pod Security Admission controller to be too restrictive, many other options provide more sophisticated policy solutions. For more information on admission control, refer to Chapter 17.

Intrusion and Anomaly Detection Tooling

We've covered security policies and container runtimes, but what happens when you want to introspect and enforce policy within the container runtime? There are open source tools that can do this and more. They operate by either listening and filtering Linux system calls or by utilizing a Berkeley Packet Filter (BPF). One such tool is Falco (*https://oreil.ly/9KOeg*), a Cloud Native Computing Foundation (CNCF) project that installs as a DaemonSet and allows you to configure and enforce policy during execution. Falco is just one approach. We encourage you to explore the tooling in this space to see what works for you.

Summary

In this chapter, we covered in depth both the Pod Security Admission control and the RuntimeClass APIs with which you can configure a granular level of security for your workloads. We have also taken a look at some open source ecosystem tooling that you can use to monitor and enforce policy within the container runtime. We have provided a thorough overview for you to make an informed decision about providing the level of security best suited for your workload needs.

## CHAPTER 11

Policy and Governance for Your Cluster

Have you ever wondered how you might ensure that all containers running on a cluster come only from an approved container registry? Or maybe you've been asked by the security team to enforce a policy that services are never exposed to the internet. These are precisely the challenges that policy and governance for your cluster set out to address. As Kubernetes continues to mature and becomes adopted by more enterprises, the question of how to apply policy and governance to Kubernetes resources is increasing in frequency. In this chapter we share what you can do and the tools to use to make sure that your cluster is in compliance with the defined policies, whether you work at a startup or an enterprise.

Why Policy and Governance Are Important

Whether you operate in a highly regulated environment—for example, health care or financial services—or you simply want to make sure that you maintain a level of control over what's running on your clusters, you're going to need a way to implement the company-specific policies. Once your policy is defined, you will need to determine how to implement it and maintain clusters that are compliant to these policies. These policies may be required to meet regulatory compliance or simply to enforce best practices. Whatever the reason, you must be sure that you do not sacrifice developer agility and self-service when implementing these policies.

How Is This Policy Different?

In Kubernetes, policy is everywhere. Whether it be network policy or pod security, we've all come to understand what policy is and when to use it. We trust that whatever is declared in Kubernetes resource specifications is implemented as per the policy definition. Both network policy and pod security are implemented at runtime. However, what policy restricts the field values in these Kubernetes resource specifications? That's the job of policy and governance. Rather than implementing policy at runtime, when we talk about policy in the context of governance, what we mean (or at least what we are trying to achieve) is the ability to limit the way fields are configured in Kubernetes resources. Only Kubernetes resource specifications that are compliant when evaluated by policies are allowed and committed to the cluster state.

Cloud Native Policy Engine

To be able to evaluate which resources are compliant, we need a policy engine that is flexible enough to meet a variety of needs. The Open Policy Agent (OPA) (*https://oreil.ly/xzN2p*) is an open source, flexible, lightweight policy engine that has become increasingly popular in the cloud native ecosystem. Having OPA in the ecosystem has allowed many implementations of different Kubernetes governance tools to appear. One such Kubernetes policy and governance project the community is rallying around is called Gatekeeper (*https://oreil.ly/RvKUw*). For the rest of this chapter, we use Gatekeeper as the canonical example to illustrate how you might achieve policy and governance for your cluster. Although there are other implementations of policy and governance tools in the ecosystem, they all seek to provide the same user experience (UX) by allowing only compliant Kubernetes resource specifications to be committed to the cluster.

Introducing Gatekeeper

Gatekeeper is an open source, customizable Kubernetes admission webhook for cluster policy and governance. Gatekeeper takes advantage of the OPA constraint framework to enforce custom resource definition (CRD)-based policies. Using CRDs allows for an integrated Kubernetes experience that decouples policy authoring from implementation. Policy templates are referred to as *constraint templates*, which can be shared and reused across clusters. Gatekeeper enables resource validation and audit functionality. One of the great things about Gatekeeper is that it's portable, which means that you can implement it on any Kubernetes clusters, and if you are already using OPA, you might be able to port that policy over to Gatekeeper.

Gatekeeper is a production-ready open source project. For the latest stable version, please visit the official upstream repository (*https://oreil.ly/Rk8dc*).

Example Policies

Before diving into how to configure Gatekeeper, it's important to keep the problem we are trying to solve in focus. While every organization/team will need to optimize their policies for their needs, some fairly universal policies serve as best practices. Let's look at some policies that solve the most common compliance issues for context:

- Services must not be exposed publicly on the internet.
- Allow containers only from trusted container registries.
- All containers must have resource limits.
- Ingress hostnames must not overlap.
- Ingresses must use only HTTPS.

Gatekeeper Terminology

Gatekeeper has adopted much of the same terminology as OPA. It's important that we cover that terminology so you can understand how Gatekeeper operates. Gatekeeper uses the OPA constraint framework, which introduces three new terms:

- Constraint
- Rego
- Constraint template

Constraint

The best way to think about constraints is as restrictions that you apply to specific fields and values of Kubernetes resource specifications. This is really just a long way of saying policy. When constraints are defined, you are effectively stating that you *DO NOT* want to allow this. The implications of this approach mean that resources are implicitly allowed without a constraint that issues a deny. This is an important nuance because rather then allowing the Kubernetes resources specification fields and values you want, you are denying only the ones you *DO NOT* want. This architectural decision suits Kubernetes resource specifications nicely because they are ever changing.

Rego

Rego is an OPA-native query language. Rego queries are assertions on the data stored in OPA. Gatekeeper stores rego in the constraint template.

Constraint template

Think of this as a policy template. It's portable and reusable. Constraint templates consist of typed parameters and the target rego that is parameterized for reuse.

Defining Constraint Templates

Constraint templates are a custom resource definition (*https://oreil.ly/LQSAH*) (CRD) that provide a means of templating policy so that it can be shared or reused. In addition, parameters for the policy can be validated. Let's look at a constraint template, from the upstream Gatekeeper policy library (*https://oreil.ly/HksnE*), in the context of the earlier examples. In the following example, we share a constraint template that provides the policy "Only allow containers from trusted container registries":

```
apiVersion: templates.gatekeeper.sh/v1
kind: ConstraintTemplate
metadata:
  name: k8sallowedrepos
  annotations:
    metadata.gatekeeper.sh/title: "Allowed Repositories"
    metadata.gatekeeper.sh/version: 1.0.0
    description: >-
      Requires container images to begin with a string from the specified list.
spec:
  crd:
    spec:
      names:
        kind: K8sAllowedRepos
      validation:
        # Schema for the `parameters` field
        openAPIV3Schema:
          type: object
          properties:
            repos:
              description: The list of prefixes a container image is allowed to
                have.
              type: array
              items:
                type: string
  targets:
    - target: admission.k8s.gatekeeper.sh
      rego: |
        package k8sallowedrepos

        violation[{"msg": msg}] {
          container := input.review.object.spec.containers[_]
          satisfied := [good | repo = input.parameters.repos[_] ;
            good = startswith(container.image, repo)]
          not any(satisfied)
          msg := sprintf("container <%v> has an invalid image repo <%v>,
            allowed repos are %v",
              [container.name, container.image, input.parameters.repos])
        }

        violation[{"msg": msg}] {
          container := input.review.object.spec.initContainers[_]
```

```
        satisfied := [good | repo = input.parameters.repos[_] ;
          good = startswith(container.image, repo)]
      not any(satisfied)
      msg := sprintf("initContainer <%v> has an invalid image repo <%v>,
        allowed repos are %v",
          [container.name, container.image, input.parameters.repos])
    }

    violation[{"msg": msg}] {
      container := input.review.object.spec.ephemeralContainers[_]
      satisfied := [good | repo = input.parameters.repos[_] ;
        good = startswith(container.image, repo)]
      not any(satisfied)
      msg := sprintf("ephemeralContainer <%v> has an invalid image repo <%v>,
        allowed repos are %v",
          [container.name, container.image, input.parameters.repos])
    }
```

The constraint template consists of three main components:

Kubernetes-required CRD metadata
> The name is the most important part. It's best practice to make it descriptive
> enough to easily identify the purpose of the policy. We reference this later.

Schema for input parameters
> Indicated by the validation field, this section defines the input parameters and
> their associated types. In this example, we have a single parameter called repos
> that is an array of strings.

Policy definition
> Indicated by the target field, this section contains templated rego (the language
> to define policy in OPA). Using a constraint template allows the templated rego
> to be reused and means that generic policy can be shared. If the rule matches, the
> constraint is violated.

Defining Constraints

To use the previous constraint template, we must create a constraint resource. The
purpose of the constraint resource is to provide the necessary parameters to the
constraint template that we created earlier. You can see that the kind of the resource
defined in the following example is K8sAllowedRepos, which maps to the constraint
template defined in the previous section:

```
apiVersion: constraints.gatekeeper.sh/v1beta1
kind: K8sAllowedRepos
metadata:
  name: prod-repo-is-openpolicyagent
spec:
  enforcementAction: deny
```

```
    match:
      kinds:
        - apiGroups: [""]
          kinds: ["Pod"]
      namespaces:
        - "production"
    parameters:
      repos:
        - "openpolicyagent/"
```

The constraint consists of two main sections:

Kubernetes metadata
> Notice that this constraint is of kind `K8sAllowedRepos`, which matches the name of the constraint template.

The spec
> The `match` field defines the scope of intent for the policy. In this example, we are matching pods only in the production namespace.
>
> The parameters define the intent for the policy. Notice that they match the type from the constraint template schema from the previous section. In this case, we allow only container images that start with `openpolicyagent/`.

Constraints have the following operational characteristics:

- Logical AND
  - When multiple policies validate the same field, if one violates then the whole request is rejected
- Schema validation that allows early error detection
- Selection criteria
  - Can use label selectors
  - Constrain only certain kinds
  - Constrain only in certain namespaces

Data Replication

In some cases, you might want to compare the current resource against other resources that are in the cluster, for example, in the case of "Ingress hostnames must not overlap." OPA needs to have all the other Ingress resources in its cache in order to evaluate the rule. Gatekeeper uses a `config` resource to manage which data is cached in OPA in order to perform evaluations such as the one previously mentioned. In addition, `config` resources are also used in the audit functionality, which we explore a bit later on.

The following example `config` resource caches v1 service, pods, and namespaces:

```
apiVersion: config.gatekeeper.sh/v1alpha1
kind: Config
metadata:
name: config
  namespace: gatekeeper-system
spec:
  sync:
    syncOnly:
    - kind: Service
      version: v1
    - kind: Pod
      version: v1
    - kind: Namespace
      version: v1
```

UX

Gatekeeper enables real-time feedback to cluster users for resources that violate defined policy. If we consider the example from the previous sections, we allow containers only from repositories that start with openpolicyagent/.

Let's try to create the following resource; it is not compliant given the current policy:

```
apiVersion: v1
kind: Pod
metadata:
  name: opa
  namespace: production
spec:
  containers:
    - name: opa
      image: quay.io/opa:0.9.2
```

This gives you the violation message that's defined in the constraint template:

```
$ kubectl create -f bad_resources/opa_wrong_repo.yaml
Error from server (Forbidden): error when creating "STDIN": admission webhook
  "validation.gatekeeper.sh" denied the request: [repo-is-openpolicyagent]
    container <opa> has an invalid image repo <quay.io/opa:0.9.2>, allowed
      repos are ["openpolicyagent/"]
```

Using Enforcement Action and Audit

Thus far, we have discussed only how to define policy and have it enforced as part of the request admission process. Constraints include the ability to configure an enfor cementAction, which by default is set to deny. In addition to deny, enforcementAc tion also allows accepted values of warn and dryrun. When we think about rolling out policy, it's not always the case that you are applying to a cluster or namespace without resources already deployed. It's therefore important to understand how to deploy policy to a cluster that already has resources deployed with the confidence that you can identify and remediate policy violations without necessarily breaking deployed workloads. The `enforcementAction` field allows you to define the behavior. When set to `deny`, a resource that violates policy will not be created and an error message will both be audit logged and sent back to the user. If set to `warn`, the resource will be created; however, a warning message will be audit logged and sent back to the user. Finally, if `dryrun` is set, the resource will be created and resources that violate the policy will be available in the audit log.

Whatever `enforcementAction` you decide to use, Gatekeeper will periodically evaluate resources against any configured policy and provide an audit log. This helps with the detection of misconfigured resources according to policy and allows for remediation. The audit results are stored in the status field of the constraint, making them easy to find by simply using `kubectl`. To use audit, the resources to be audited must be replicated. For more details, refer to "Data Replication" on page 160.

Let's look at the constraint called `prod-repo-is-openpolicyagent` that you defined in the previous section. In this case, imagine we already had a pod called nginx running in the production namespace and we would like to check its compliance to the policy using audit:

```
$ kubectl get k8sallowedrepos
NAME                            ENFORCEMENT-ACTION   TOTAL-VIOLATIONS
prod-repo-is-openpolicyagent    deny                 1

$ kubectl get k8sallowedrepos prod-repo-is-openpolicyagent -o yaml
apiVersion: constraints.gatekeeper.sh/v1beta1
kind: K8sAllowedRepos
metadata:
  annotations:
    kubectl.kubernetes.io/last-applied-configuration: ...
  creationTimestamp: "..."
  generation: 1
  name: prod-repo-is-openpolicyagent
  resourceVersion: "..."
  uid: ...
spec:
  match:
    kinds:
    - apiGroups:
      - ""
      kinds:
      - Pod
    namespaces:
    - production
  parameters:
    repos:
    - openpolicyagent/
```

```
status:
  auditTimestamp: "2022-11-27T23:37:42Z"
  totalViolations: 1
  violations:
  - enforcementAction: deny
    group: ""
    kind: Pod
    message: container <nginx> has an invalid image repo <nginx>, allowed repos
      are ["openpolicyagent/"]
    name: nginx
    namespace: production
    version: v1
```

Upon inspection, you can see the last time the audit ran in the `auditTimestamp` field. We also see all the resources that violate this constraint, only the nginx pod in this case, under the `violations` along with the `enforcementAction`.

Mutation

In addition to resource validation, Gatekeeper also allows you to configure mutation policies. Mutation policies allow you to modify Kubernetes resources at admission time. Generally, mutating resources at admission time is not considered best practice. Having resources "magically" modified by Gatekeeper is a cloud native antipattern as this is counter to the declarative nature of Kubernetes. Mutation policies are simply mentioned here to provide guidance to avoid them unless you feel your use case absolutely requires them and that you have exhausted other best practices. Refer to Chapter 18 for more details on how to implement declarative best practices for Kubernetes resources.

Testing Policies

As the GitOps philosophy has become widely adopted, testing policy and evaluation as part of local testing or CI/CD pipelines has become a must have. Gatekeeper ships with a `gator` CLI that enables you to take the constraint templates and constraints and run a local evaluation. This is a great tool for building new policies, testing them against your resources, and remediating any issues prior to deploying them to your production clusters. The Gatekeeper documentation (*https://oreil.ly/Qj4p8*) provides a practical guide to using the `gator` CLI to test policy.

Becoming Familiar with Gatekeeper

If you'd like to explore Gatekeeper further, the repository ships with fantastic demonstration content that walks you through a detailed example of building policies to meet compliance for a bank. We would strongly recommend walking through the demonstration for a hands-on approach to how Gatekeeper operates. You can find the demonstration in this Git repository (*https://oreil.ly/GcR3i*). Gatekeeper also maintains a public library (*https://oreil.ly/e8ESD*) of policies that you can apply to your cluster with easy installation guidance via ArtifactHub (*https://oreil.ly/uEcfn*).

Policy and Governance Best Practices

You should consider the following best practices when implementing policy and governance on your clusters:

- If you want to enforce a specific field in a pod, you need to determine which Kubernetes resource specification you want to inspect and enforce. Let's consider the case of Deployments, for example. Deployments manage ReplicaSets, which manage pods. We could enforce at all three levels, but the best choice is the one that is the lowest handoff point before the runtime, which in this case is the pod. This decision, however, has implications. The user-friendly error message when we try to deploy a noncompliant pod, as seen in "UX" on page 161, is not going to be displayed. This is because the user is not creating the noncompliant resource, the ReplicaSet is. This experience means that the user would need to determine that the resource is not compliant by running a kubectl describe on the current ReplicaSet associated with the Deployment. Although this might seem cumbersome, this is consistent behavior with other Kubernetes features, such as pod security.

- Constraints can be applied to Kubernetes resources on the following criteria: kinds, namespaces, and label selectors. We would strongly recommend scoping the constraint to the resources to which you want it to be applied as tightly as possible. This ensures consistent policy behavior as the resources on the cluster grow, and means that resources that don't need to be evaluated aren't being passed to OPA, which can result in other inefficiencies.

- On clusters with resources that are already deployed, utilize warn and dryrun along with audit to remediate resources that violate policy before setting the enforcementAction to deny.

- Don't use mutation policies; instead consider other declarative approaches, including GitOps.

- Synchronizing and enforcing on potentially sensitive data such as Kubernetes secrets is *not* recommended. Given that OPA will hold this in its cache (if it is configured to replicate that data) and resources will be passed to Gatekeeper, it leaves surface area for a potential attack vector.

- If you have many constraints defined, a deny of constraint means that the entire request is denied. There is no way to make this function as a logical OR.

Summary

In this chapter, we covered why policy and governance are important and walked through a project that's built upon OPA, a cloud native ecosystem policy engine, to provide a Kubernetes-native approach to policy and governance. You should now be prepared and confident the next time the security teams asks, "Are our clusters in compliance with our defined policy?"

## CHAPTER 12

Managing Multiple Clusters

In this chapter, we discuss best practices for managing multiple Kubernetes clusters. We dive into the details of the differences between multicluster management and federation, tools to manage multiple clusters, and operational patterns for managing multiple clusters.

You might wonder why you would need multiple Kubernetes clusters. Kubernetes was built to consolidate many workloads to a single cluster, correct? This is true, but there are scenarios that might require multiple clusters, such as workloads across regions, concerns of blast radius, regulatory compliance, and specialized workloads.

We discuss these scenarios and explore the tools and techniques for managing multiple clusters in Kubernetes.

Why Multiple Clusters?

When adopting Kubernetes, you will likely have more than one cluster, and you might even start with more than one cluster to break out production from staging, user acceptance testing (UAT), or development. Kubernetes provides some multitenancy features with namespaces, which are a logical way to break up a cluster into smaller logical constructs. Namespaces allow you to define Role-Based Access Control (RBAC), quotas, pod security policies, and network policies to allow separation of workloads. This is a great way to separate multiple teams and projects, but there are other concerns that might require you to build a multicluster architecture. Concerns to think about when deciding to use multicluster versus a single-cluster architecture:

- Blast radius
- Compliance
- Security

- Hard multitenancy
- Regional-based workloads
- Specialized workloads

When thinking through your architecture, *blast radius* should come front and center. This is one of the main concerns that we see with users designing for multicluster architectures. With microservice architectures we employ circuit breakers, retries, bulkheads, and rate limiting to constrain the extent of damage to our systems. You should design the same into your infrastructure layer, and multiple clusters can help with preventing the impact of cascading failures due to software issues. For example, if you have one cluster that serves 500 applications and you have a platform issue, it takes out 100% of the 500 applications. If you had a platform layer issue with five clusters serving those 500 applications, you affect only 20% of the applications. The downside to this is that now you need to manage five clusters, and your consolidation ratios will not be as good as with a single cluster. Dan Woods wrote a great article (*https://oreil.ly/YnGUD*) about an actual cascading failure in a production Kubernetes environment. It is a great example of why you will want to consider multicluster architectures for larger environments.

Compliance is another area of concern for multicluster design because there are special considerations for Payment Card Industry (PCI), Health Insurance Portability and Accountability (HIPAA), and other workloads. It's not that Kubernetes doesn't provide some multitenant features, but these workloads might be easier to manage if they are segregated from general purpose workloads. These compliant workloads might have specific requirements with respect to security hardening, nonshared components, or dedicated workload requirements. It's just much easier to separate these workloads than to have to treat the cluster in such a specialized fashion.

Security in large Kubernetes clusters can become difficult to manage. As you start onboarding more and more teams to a Kubernetes cluster, each team may have different security requirements, and it can become very difficult to meet those needs in a large multitenant cluster. Even just managing RBAC, network policies, and pod security policies can become difficult at scale in a single cluster. A small change to a network policy can inadvertently open up security risk to other users of the cluster. With multiple clusters you can limit the security impact with a misconfiguration. If you decide that a larger Kubernetes cluster fits your requirements, then ensure that you have a very good operational process for making security changes and that you understand the blast radius of making a change to RBAC, network policy, and pod security policies.

Kubernetes doesn't provide *hard multitenancy* because it shares the same API boundary with all workloads running within the cluster. With namespacing this gives us good soft multitenancy, but not enough to protect against hostile workloads within the cluster. Hard multitenancy is not a requirement for a lot of users; they trust the workloads that will be running within the cluster. Hard multitenancy is typically a requirement if you are a cloud provider, hosting software as a service (SaaS)-based software, or hosting untrusted workloads with untrusted user control.

 The Kubernetes project does address hard multitenancy concerns with Virtual Clusters, outside the scope of the book. Find more information on the project's GitHub (*https://oreil.ly/KlFlK*).

When running workloads that need to serve traffic from in-region endpoints, your design will include multiple clusters that are based per region. When you have a globally distributed application, it becomes a requirement at that point to run multiple clusters. When you have workloads that need to be *regionally distributed*, it's a great use case for cluster federation of multiple clusters, which we dig into further later in this chapter.

Specialized workloads, such as high-performance computing (HPC), machine learning (ML), and grid computing, also need to be addressed in the multicluster architecture. These types of specialized workloads might require specific types of hardware, have unique performance profiles, and have specialized users of the clusters. We've seen this use case to be less prevalent in the design decision because having multiple Kubernetes node pools can help address specialized hardware and performance profiles. When you need a very large cluster for an HPC or machine learning workload, you should consider just dedicating clusters for these workloads.

With multicluster, you get isolation for "free," but it also has design concerns that you need to address at the outset.

Multicluster Design Concerns

When choosing a multicluster design there are some challenges that you'll run into. Some of these challenges might deter you from attempting a multicluster design given that the design might overcomplicate your architecture. Some of the common challenges we find users running into are:

- Data replication
- Service discovery
- Network routing
- Operational management
- Continuous deployment

Data replication and consistency have always been the crux of deploying workloads across geographical regions and multiple clusters. When running these services, you need to decide what runs where and develop a replication strategy. Most databases have built-in tools to perform the replication, but you need to design the application to be able to handle the replication strategy. For NoSQL-type database services this can be easier because they can handle scaling across multiple instances, but you still need to ensure that your application can handle eventual consistency across geographic regions or at least the latency across regions. Some cloud services, such as Google Cloud Spanner and Microsoft Azure CosmosDB, have built database services to help with the complications of handling data across multiple geographic regions.

Each Kubernetes cluster deploys its own *service discovery* registry, and registries are not synchronized across multiple clusters. This complicates applications being able to easily identify and discover one another. Tools such as HashiCorp's Consul can transparently synchronize services from multiple clusters and even services that reside outside of Kubernetes. Other tools like Istio, Linkerd, and Cilium are building on multiple cluster architectures to extend service discovery between clusters.

Kubernetes makes networking from within the cluster very easy, as it's a flat network and avoids using network address translation (NAT). If you need to route traffic in and out of the cluster, this becomes more complicated. Ingress into the cluster is implemented as a 1:1 mapping of ingress to the cluster because it doesn't support multicluster topologies with the Ingress resource. You'll also need to consider the egress traffic between clusters and how to route that traffic. When your applications reside within a single cluster this is easy, but when introducing multicluster, you need to think about the latency of extra hops for services that have application dependencies in another cluster. For applications that have tightly coupled dependencies, you should consider running these services within the same cluster to remove latency and extra complexity.

One of the biggest overheads to managing multiclusters is the *operational management*. Instead of one or a couple of clusters to manage and keep consistent, you might now have many clusters to manage in your environment. One of the most important aspects to managing multiclusters is ensuring that you have good automation practices in place because this will help to reduce the operational burden. When automating your clusters, you need to take into account the infrastructure deployment and managing add-on features to your clusters. For managing the infrastructure, using a tool like HashiCorp's Terraform can help with deploying and managing a consistent state across your fleet of clusters.

Using an *Infrastructure as Code* (IaC) tool like Terraform will give you the benefit of providing a reproducible way to deploy your clusters. On the other hand, you also need to be able to consistently manage add-ons to the cluster, such as monitoring, logging, ingress, security, and other tools. Security is another important aspect of operational management, and you must be able to maintain security policies, RBAC, and network policies across clusters. Later in this chapter, we dive deeper into the topic of maintaining consistent clusters with automation.

With multiple clusters and continuous delivery (CD), you now need to deal with multiple Kubernetes API endpoints versus a single API endpoint. This can cause challenges in the distribution of applications. You can easily manage multiple pipelines, but suppose that you have a hundred different pipelines to manage, which can make application distribution very difficult. With this in mind, you need to look at different approaches to managing this situation. We take a look at solutions to help manage this later in the chapter.

Managing Multiple Cluster Deployments

One of the first steps you want to take when managing multicluster deployments is to use an IaC tool like Terraform to set up deployments. Other deployment tools, such as kubespray, kops, or other cloud provider–specific tools, are all valid choices, but, most importantly, use a tool that allows you to source control your cluster deployment for repeatability.

Automation is key to successfully managing multiple clusters in your environment. You might not have everything automated on day one, but you should make it a priority to automate all aspects of your cluster deployments and operations.

An interesting project is the Kubernetes Cluster API (*https://oreil.ly/edzIa*), a Kubernetes project to bring declarative, Kubernetes-style APIs to cluster creation, configuration, and management. It provides optional additive functionality on top of core Kubernetes. The Cluster API provides a cluster-level configuration declared through a common API, which will give you the ability to easily automate and build tooling around cluster automation. The Cluster API is still in its early stages, but it's a project to keep an eye on.

Deployment and Management Patterns

Kubernetes operators were introduced as an implementation of the *Infrastructure as Software* concept. Using them allows you to abstract the deployment of applications and services in a Kubernetes cluster. For example, suppose that you want to standardize on Prometheus for monitoring your Kubernetes clusters. You would need to create and manage various objects (deployment, service, ingress, etc.) for each cluster and team. You would also need to maintain the fundamental configurations of Prometheus, such as versions, persistence, retention policies, and replicas. As you can imagine, the maintenance of such a solution could be difficult across a large number of clusters and teams.

Instead of dealing with so many objects and configurations, you could install the `prometheus-operator`. This extends the Kubernetes API, exposing multiple new object kinds called `Prometheus`, `ServiceMonitor`, `PrometheusRule`, and `AlertMan ager`, which allow you to specify all the details of a Prometheus deployment using just a few objects. You can use the `kubectl` tool to manage such objects, just as it manages any other Kubernetes API object.

Figure 12-1 shows the architecture of the `prometheus-operator`.

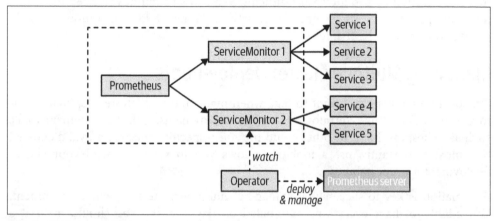

Figure 12-1. `prometheus-operator` architecture

Utilizing the *Operator* pattern for automating key operational tasks can help improve your overall cluster management capabilities. The Operator pattern was introduced by the CoreOS team in 2016 with the etcd operator and `prometheus-operator`. The Operator pattern builds on two concepts:

- Custom resource definitions
- Custom controllers

Custom resource definitions (CRDs) are objects that allow you to extend the Kubernetes API, based on your own API that you define.

Custom controllers are built on the core Kubernetes concepts of resources and controllers. Custom controllers allow you to build your own logic by watching events from Kubernetes API objects such as namespaces, Deployments, pods, or your own CRD. With custom controllers, you can build your CRDs in a declarative way. If you consider how the Kubernetes Deployment controller works in a reconciliation loop to always maintain the state of the Deployment object to maintain its declarative state, this brings the same advantages of controllers to your CRDs.

When utilizing the Operator pattern, you can build in automation to operational tasks that need to be performed on operational tooling in multiclusters. Let's take the following Elasticsearch operator (*https://oreil.ly/9WvJQ*) as an example. The Elasticsearch operator can perform the following operations:

- Replicas for master, client, and data nodes
- Zones for highly available deployments
- Volume sizes for master and data nodes
- Resizing of cluster
- Snapshot for backups of the Elasticsearch cluster

As you can see, the operator provides automation for many tasks that you would need to perform when managing Elasticsearch, such as automating snapshots for backup and resizing the cluster. The beauty of this is that you manage everything through familiar Kubernetes objects.

Think about how you can take advantage of different operators like the `prometheus-operator` in your environment and also how you can build your own custom operator to offload common operational tasks.

The GitOps Approach to Managing Clusters

GitOps was popularized by the folks at Weaveworks, and the idea and fundamentals were based on their experience of running Kubernetes in production. GitOps takes the concepts of the software development life cycle and applies them to operations. With GitOps, your Git repository becomes your source of truth, and your cluster is synchronized to the configured Git repository. For example, if you update a Kubernetes Deployment manifest, those configuration changes are automatically reflected in the cluster state.

By using this method, you can make it easier to maintain multiclusters that are consistent and avoid configuration drift across the fleet. GitOps allows you to declaratively describe your clusters for multiple environments and drives to maintain that state for the cluster. The practice of GitOps can apply to both application delivery and operations, but in this chapter, we focus on using it to manage clusters and operational tooling.

Weaveworks Flux was one of the first tools to enable the GitOps approach, and it's the tool we will use throughout the rest of the chapter. There are many new tools that have been released into the cloud native ecosystem that are worth a look, such as Argo CD, from the folks at Intuit, which has also been widely adopted for the GitOps approach.

We'll get into a deeper dive of utilizing a GitOps model in Chapter 18, but the following provides a quick glance at the benefit of utilizing GitOps for cluster management.

Figure 12-2 presents a representation of a GitOps workflow.

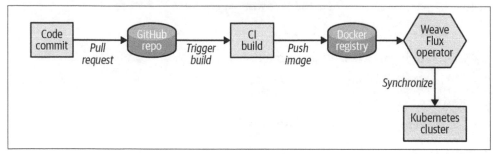

Figure 12-2. GitOps workflow

So, let's get Flux set up in your cluster and get a repository synchronized to the cluster:

```
git clone https://github.com/weaveworks/flux
cd flux
```

You now need to change the Deployment manifest to configure it with your forked repo from Chapter 5. Modify the following line in the Deployment file to match your forked GitHub repository:

```
vim deploy/flux-deployment.yaml
```

Modify the following line with your Git repository:

```
--git-url=git@github.com:weaveworks/flux-get-started
  (ex. --git-url=git@github.com:your_repo/kbp )
```

Now, go ahead and deploy Flux to your cluster:

```
kubectl apply -f deploy
```

When Flux installs, it creates an SSH key so that it can authenticate with the Git repository. Use the Flux command-line tool to retrieve the SSH key so that you can configure access to your forked repository; first, you need to install `fluxctl`.

For macOS:

```
brew install fluxctl
```

For Linux Snap Packages:

```
snap install fluxctl
```

For all other packages, you can find the latest binaries here (*https://oreil.ly/4TAx5*):

```
fluxctl identity
```

Open GitHub, navigate to your fork, go to Setting > "Deploy keys," click "Add deploy key," give it a Title, select the "Allow write access" checkbox, paste the Flux public key, and then click "Add key." See the GitHub documentation (*https://oreil.ly/Oet57*) for more information on how to manage deploy keys.

Now if you view the Flux logs, you should see that it is synchronizing with your GitHub repository:

```
kubectl -n default logs deployment/flux -f
```

After you see that it's synchronizing with your GitHub repository, you should see that the Elasticsearch, Prometheus, Redis, and frontend pods are created:

```
kubectl get pods -w
```

With this example complete, you should be able to see how easy it is for you to synchronize your GitHub repository state with your Kubernetes cluster. This makes managing the multiple operational tools in your cluster much easier, because multiple clusters can synchronize with a single repository and you avoid the situation of having snowflake clusters.

Multicluster Management Tools

When working with multiple clusters, using kubectl can immediately become confusing because you need to set different contexts to manage the different clusters. Two tools that you will want to install right away when dealing with multiple clusters are *kubectx* and *kubens*, which allow you to easily change between multiple contexts and namespaces.

When you need a full-fledged multicluster management tool, there are a few within the Kubernetes ecosystem to look at for managing multiple clusters. Following is a summary of some of the more popular tools:

Rancher (https://oreil.ly/8qGNh)
> Rancher centrally manages multiple Kubernetes clusters in a centrally managed UI. It monitors, manages, backs up, and restores Kubernetes clusters across on-premises, cloud, and hosted Kubernetes setups. It also has tools for controlling applications deployed across multiple clusters and provides operational tooling.

Open Cluster Management (https://oreil.ly/HUv5k) (OCM)
> OCM is a community-driven project focused on multicluster and multicloud scenarios for Kubernetes apps. It provides cluster registration, workload distribution, and dynamic placement of policies and workloads.

Gardener (https://oreil.ly/fElD5)
> Gardener takes a different approach to multicluster management in that it utilizes Kubernetes primitives to provide Kubernetes as a Service to your end users. It provides support for all major cloud vendors and was developed by the folks at

SAP. This solution is geared to users who are building a Kubernetes as a Service offering.

Kubernetes Federation

Kubernetes first introduced Federation v1 in Kubernetes 1.3, and it has since been deprecated in lieu of Federation v2. Federation v1 set out to help with the distribution of applications to multiple clusters. Federation v1 was built utilizing the Kubernetes API and heavily relied on Kubernetes annotations, which imposed some problems in its design. The design was tightly coupled to the core Kubernetes API, which made Federation v1 quite monolithic. At the time, the design decisions were probably not bad choices, but they were built on the primitives that were available. The introduction of Kubernetes CRDs allowed a different way of thinking about how Federation could be designed.

Managing Multiple Clusters Best Practices

Consider the following best practices when managing multiple Kubernetes clusters:

- Limit the blast radius of your clusters to ensure cascading failures don't have a bigger impact on your applications.
- If you have regulatory concerns such as PCI, HIPPA, or HiTrust, think about utilizing multiclusters to ease the complexity of mixing these workloads with general workloads.
- If hard multitenancy is a business requirement, workloads should be deployed to a dedicated cluster.
- If multiple regions are needed for your applications, utilize a Global Load Balancer to manage traffic between clusters.
- You can break out specialized workloads such as HPC into their own individual clusters to ensure that the specialized needs for the workloads are met.
- If you're deploying workloads that will be spread across multiple regional data-centers, first ensure there is a data replication strategy for the workload. Multiple clusters across regions can be easy, but replicating data across regions can be complicated, so ensure there is a sound strategy to handle asynchronous and synchronous workloads.
- Utilize Kubernetes operators like the `prometheus-operator` or Elasticsearch operator to handle automated operational tasks.
- When designing your multicluster strategy, also consider how you will implement service discovery and networking between clusters. Service mesh tools like HashiCorp's Consul or Istio can help with networking across clusters.

- Be sure that your CD strategy can handle multiple rollouts between regions or multiple clusters.

- Investigate utilizing a GitOps approach to managing multiple cluster operational components to ensure consistency between all clusters in your fleet. The GitOps approach doesn't work for everyone's environment, but you should at least investigate it to ease the operational burden of multicluster environments.

Summary

In this chapter, we discussed different strategies for managing multiple Kubernetes clusters. It's important to think about your needs at the outset and whether those needs match a multicluster topology. The first scenario to think about is whether you truly need *hard* multitenancy because this will automatically require a multicluster strategy. If you don't, consider your compliance needs and whether you have the operational capacity to consume the overhead of multicluster architectures. Finally, if you're going with more, smaller clusters, ensure that you automate their delivery and management to reduce the operational burden.

## CHAPTER 13

Integrating External Services with Kubernetes

In many of the chapters in this book, we've discussed how to build, deploy, and manage services in Kubernetes. However, the truth is that systems don't exist in a vacuum, and most of the services that we build will need to interact with systems and services that exist outside of the Kubernetes cluster in which they're running. This might be necessary because we are building new services being accessed by legacy infrastructure running in virtual or physical machines. Additionally, it might be because the services we are building need to access preexisting databases or other services that are running on physical infrastructure in an on-premises datacenter. Finally, you might have multiple Kubernetes clusters with services you need to interconnect. For all these reasons, the ability to expose, share, and build services that span the boundary of your Kubernetes cluster is an important part of building real-world applications.

Importing Services into Kubernetes

The most common pattern for connecting Kubernetes with external services consists of a Kubernetes Service that is consuming a service that exists outside of the Kubernetes cluster. Often, this is because Kubernetes is being used for new application development or is serving as an interface for a legacy resource like an on-premises database. In many existing applications, parts of the application are easier to move than others. For example, a database with mission-critical data may be required to stay on premises for reasons of data governance, compliance, or business continuity. At the same time, there are significant benefits to building new interfaces to these legacy databases in Kubernetes. If every migration to Kubernetes required a lift and shift of the entire application, then many applications would be required to stay with their legacy implementations forever. Instead, this chapter shows how you can integrate cloud native development of new applications with existing services such as databases that may be running on traditional virtual machines, bare metal servers, or even mainframes.

When we consider the task of making an external service accessible from Kubernetes, the first challenge is simply to get the networking to work correctly. The details of making networking operational are specific to both the location of the database and the location of the Kubernetes cluster. As a result, they are beyond the scope of this book, but generally, cloud-based Kubernetes providers enable the deployment of a cluster into a user-provided virtual network (VNET), and those virtual networks can then be peered up with an on-premises network.

After you've established network connectivity between pods in the Kubernetes cluster and the on-premises resource, the next challenge is to make the external service look and feel like a Kubernetes Service. In Kubernetes, service discovery occurs via Domain Name System (DNS) lookups, so, to make our external database feel like it is a native part of Kubernetes, we need to make the database discoverable in the same DNS. We'll get into the details of how to do this next.

Selector-Less Services for Stable IP Addresses

The first way to achieve this is with a *selector-less* Kubernetes Service. When you create a Kubernetes Service without a selector, there are no pods whose labels match the nonexistent service selector; thus, no load balancing is performed. Instead, you can program this selector-less service to have endpoints that are the specific IP address(es) of the external resource you want to add to the Kubernetes cluster. That way, when a Kubernetes pod performs a lookup for `your-database`, the built-in Kubernetes DNS server will translate that to a service IP address of your external service. Here is an example of a selector-less service for an external database:

```
apiVersion: v1
kind: Service
metadata:
  name: my-external-database
spec:
  ports:
  - protocol: TCP
    port: 3306
    targetPort: 3306
```

When the service exists, you need to update its endpoints to contain the database IP address serving at `24.1.2.3`:

```
apiVersion: v1
kind: Endpoints
metadata:
  # Important! This name has to match the Service.
```

```
      name: my-external-database
   subsets:
   - addresses:
      - ip: 24.1.2.3
     ports:
      - port: 3306
```

Figure 13-1 depicts how this integrates a service within Kubernetes. As you can see, the pod looks up the service in the cluster DNS server as it would for any other Kubernetes Service. But instead of being given the IP address of another pod in the Kubernetes cluster, it is instead given an IP address that corresponds to the resource outside of the Kubernetes cluster. In this way, the developer may not even know the service is implemented outside of the cluster.

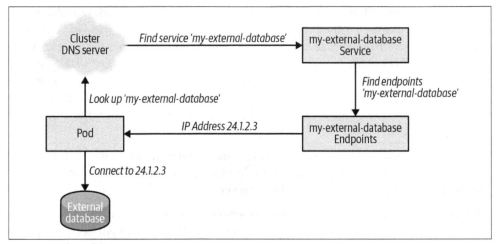

Figure 13-1. Service integration

CNAME-Based Services for Stable DNS Names

The previous example assumed that the external resource you were trying to integrate with your Kubernetes cluster had a stable IP address. Although this is often true of physical on-premises resources, depending on the network topology, it might not always be true. It is also significantly less likely to be true in a cloud environment where virtual machine (VM) IP addresses are more dynamic. Alternatively, the service might have multiple replicas sitting behind a single DNS-based load balancer. In these situations, the external service you are trying to bridge into your cluster doesn't have a stable IP address, but it does have a stable DNS name.

For these instances, you can define a CNAME-based Kubernetes Service. If you're not familiar with DNS records, a CNAME, or *Canonical Name*, record indicates that a particular DNS address should be translated to a different *Canonical* DNS name. For example, a CNAME record for *foo.com* that contains *bar.com* indicates that anyone looking up *foo.com* should perform a recursive lookup for *bar.com* to obtain the correct IP address. You can use Kubernetes Services to define CNAME records in the Kubernetes DNS server. For example, if you have an external database with a DNS name of *database.myco.com*, you might create a CNAME *Service* that is named `myco-database`. Such a Service looks like this:

```
kind: Service
apiVersion: v1
metadata:
  name: myco-database
spec:
  type: ExternalName
  externalName: database.myco.com
```

With a Service defined in this way, any pod that does a lookup for `myco-database` will be recursively resolved to *database.myco.com*. Of course, to make this work, the DNS name of your external resource *also* needs to be resolvable from the Kubernetes DNS servers. If the DNS name is globally accessible (e.g., from a well-known DNS service provider), this will automatically work. However, if the DNS of the external service is located in a company-local DNS server (e.g., a DNS server that services only internal traffic), the Kubernetes cluster might not know by default how to resolve queries to this corporate DNS server.

To set up the cluster's DNS server to communicate with an alternate DNS resolver, you need to adjust its configuration. You do this by updating a Kubernetes Config-Map with a configuration file for the DNS server.

CNAME records are a useful way to map external services with stable DNS names to names that are discoverable within your cluster. At first it might seem counter-intuitive to remap a well-known DNS address to a cluster-local DNS address, but the consistency of having all services look and feel the same is usually worth the small amount of added complexity. Additionally, because the CNAME Service, like all Kubernetes Services, is defined per namespace, you can use namespaces to map the same service name (e.g., `database`) to different external services (e.g., `canary` or `production`), depending on the Kubernetes namespace.

Active Controller-Based Approaches

In a limited set of circumstances, neither of the previous methods for exposing external services within Kubernetes is feasible. Generally, this is because there is neither a stable DNS address nor a single stable IP address for the service that you want to expose within the Kubernetes cluster. In such circumstances, exposing the external service within the Kubernetes cluster is significantly more complicated, but it isn't impossible.

To achieve this, you need some understanding of how Kubernetes Services work under the hood. Kubernetes Services are made up of two different resources: the Service resource, with which you are doubtless familiar, and the Endpoints resource that represents the IP addresses that make up the service. In normal operation, the Kubernetes controller manager populates the endpoints of a service based on the selector in the service. However, if you create a selector-less service, as in the first stable-IP approach, the Endpoints resource for the service will not be populated because no pods are selected. In this situation, you need to supply the control loop to create and populate the correct Endpoints resource. You need to dynamically query your infrastructure to obtain the IP addresses for the service external to Kubernetes that you want to integrate and then populate your service's endpoints with these IP addresses. After you do this, the mechanisms of Kubernetes take over and program both the DNS server and the `kube-proxy` correctly to load-balance traffic to your external service. Figure 13-2 presents a complete picture of how this works in practice.

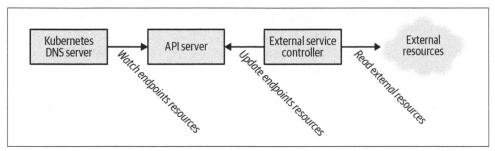

Figure 13-2. An external service

Exporting Services from Kubernetes

In the previous section, we explored how to import preexisting services to Kubernetes, but you might also need to export services from Kubernetes to the preexisting environments. This might occur because you have a legacy internal application for customer management that needs access to a new API you are developing in a cloud native infrastructure. Alternatively, you might be building new microservice-based APIs but you need to interface with a preexisting traditional web application firewall (WAF) because of internal policy or regulatory requirements. Regardless of the reason, being able to expose services from a Kubernetes cluster to other internal applications is a critical design requirement for many applications.

This can be challenging because in many Kubernetes installations, the pod IP addresses are not routable addresses from outside the cluster. Via tools like flannel, or other networking providers, routing is established within a Kubernetes cluster to facilitate communication between pods and also between nodes and pods, but the same routing is not generally extended to arbitrary machines in the same network. In many cases the IP ranges given to pods are distinct from the IP space of a corporate network and routing is not possible. Furthermore, in the case of cloud to on-premises connectivity, the IP addresses of the pods are not always advertised back across a VPN or network peering relationship into the on-premises network. Consequently, setting up routing between a traditional application and Kubernetes pods is the key task to enable the export of Kubernetes-based services.

Exporting Services by Using Internal Load Balancers

The easiest way to export from Kubernetes is by using the built-in `Service` object. If you have any previous experience with Kubernetes, no doubt you have seen how you can connect a cloud-based load balancer to bring external traffic to a collection of pods in the cluster. However, you might not have realized that most clouds also offer an *internal* load balancer. The internal load balancer provides the same capabilities to map a virtual IP address to a collection of pods, but that virtual IP address is drawn from an internal IP address space (e.g., `10.0.0.0/24`), so it is routable only from within that virtual network. You activate an internal load balancer by adding a cloud-specific annotation to your Service load balancer. For example, in Microsoft Azure, you add the `service.beta.kubernetes.io/azure-load-balancer-internal: "true"` annotation. On Amazon Web Services (AWS), the annotation is `service.beta.kubernetes.io/aws-load-balancer-internal: 0.0.0.0/0`. You place annotations in the `metadata` field in the Service resource as follows:

```
apiVersion: v1
kind: Service
metadata:
  name: my-service
  annotations:
    # Replace this as needed in other environments
    service.beta.kubernetes.io/azure-load-balancer-internal: "true"
...
```

When you export a Service via an internal load balancer, you receive a stable, routable IP address that is visible on the virtual network outside of the cluster. Then, you can either use that IP address directly or set up internal DNS resolution to provide discovery for your exported service.

Exporting Services on NodePorts

Unfortunately, in on-premises installations, cloud-based internal load balancers are unavailable. In this context using a NodePort-based service is often a good solution. A Service of type NodePort exports a listener on every node in the cluster that forwards traffic from the node's IP address and selected port into the Service that you defined, as shown in Figure 13-3.

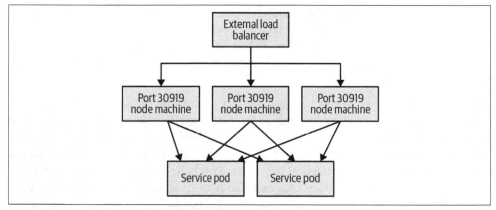

Figure 13-3. A NodePort-based service

Here's an example YAML file for a NodePort service:

```
apiVersion: v1
kind: Service
metadata:
  name: my-node-port-service
spec:
  type: NodePort
...
```

Following the creation of a Service of type NodePort, Kubernetes automatically selects a port for the Service; you can get that port from the Service by looking at the `spec.ports[*].nodePort` field. If you want to choose the port yourself, you can specify it when you create the Service, but the NodePort must be within the configured range for the cluster. The default for this range are ports between `30000` and `30999`.

Kubernetes' work is done when the Service is exposed on this port. To export it to an existing application outside of the cluster, you (or your network administrator) will need to make it discoverable. Depending on the way your application is configured, you might be able to give your application a list of `${node}:${port}` pairs, and the application will perform client-side load balancing. Alternatively, you might need to configure a physical or virtual load balancer within your network to direct traffic from a virtual IP address to this list of `${node}:${port}` backends. The specific details for this configuration will differ depending on your environment.

Integrating External Machines and Kubernetes

If neither of the previous solutions work well for you, perhaps because you want tighter integration for dynamic service discovery, the final choice for exposing Kubernetes Services to outside applications is to directly integrate the machine(s) running the application into the Kubernetes cluster's service discovery and networking mechanisms. This is significantly more invasive and complicated than either of the previous approaches, and you should use it only when necessary for your application (which should be infrequently). In some managed Kubernetes environments, it might not even be possible.

When integrating an external machine into the cluster for networking, you need to ensure that the pod network routing and DNS-based service discovery both work correctly. The easiest way to do this is to run the kubelet on the machine that you want to join to the cluster, but disable scheduling in the cluster. Joining a kubelet node to a cluster is beyond the scope of this book, but there are numerous other books or online resources that describe how to achieve this. When the node is joined, you need to immediately mark it as unschedulable using the `kubectl cordon ...` command to prevent any additional work being scheduled on it. This cordoning will not prevent DaemonSets from landing pods onto the node, and thus the pods for both the KubeProxy and network routing will land on the machine and make Kubernetes-based services discoverable from any application running on that machine.

The approach we just described is quite invasive to the node because it requires installing Docker or some other container runtime. As a result, it might not be feasible in many environments. A lighter weight but more complex approach is to just run the `kube-proxy` as a process on the machine and adjust the machine's DNS server. Assuming that you can set up pod routing to work correctly, running the `kube-proxy` will set up machine-level networking so that Kubernetes Service virtual IP addresses will be remapped to the pods that make up that Service. If you also change the machine's DNS to point to the Kubernetes cluster DNS server, you will have effectively enabled Kubernetes discovery on a machine that is not part of the Kubernetes cluster.

Both of these approaches are complicated and advanced, and you should not take them lightly. If you find yourself considering this level of service discovery integration, ask yourself whether it may be easier to actually bring the service you are connecting to the cluster into the cluster itself. We cover this in Chapter 16.

Sharing Services Between Kubernetes

The previous sections have described how to connect Kubernetes applications to outside services and how to connect outside services to Kubernetes applications, but another significant use case is connecting services *between* Kubernetes clusters. This may be to achieve East-West failover between different regional Kubernetes clusters, or it might be to link together services run by different teams. The process of achieving this interaction is actually a combination of the designs described in the previous sections.

First, you need to expose the Service within the first Kubernetes cluster to enable network traffic to flow. Let's assume that you're in a cloud environment that supports internal load balancers, and that you receive a virtual IP address for that internal load balancer of 10.1.10.1. Next, you need to integrate this virtual IP address into the second Kubernetes cluster to enable service discovery. You achieve this in the same manner as importing an external application into Kubernetes (we covered this in "Importing Services into Kubernetes" on page 179). You create a selector-less service and set its IP address to be 10.1.10.1. With these two steps you have integrated service discovery and connectivity between services within your two Kubernetes clusters.

These steps are fairly manual, and although this might be acceptable for a small, static set of services, if you want to enable tighter or automatic service integration between clusters, it makes sense to write a cluster daemon that runs in both clusters to perform the integration. This daemon would watch the first cluster for Services with a particular annotation, say something like `myco.com/exported-service`; all Services with this annotation would then be imported into the second cluster via selector-less services. Likewise, the same daemon would garbage-collect and delete any services that are exported into the second cluster but are no longer present in the first. If you set up such daemons in each of your regional clusters, you can enable dynamic, East-West connectivity between all clusters in your environment.

There has also been recent work within the Kubernetes project to define a Multi-Cluster Service API. This work is experimental and can be found within the Multi-Cluster Service (*https://oreil.ly/ZXZi4*) project on GitHub. At the time of writing, the experimental nature of this project means that it is probably not suitable for production use-cases, but it shows the future direction of multi-cluster service management in the Kubernetes ecosystem. As it moves from alpha to beta and eventually to general availability, this implementation of Service sharing will make it much easier to build cross-cluster microservice applications. Even today, tools such as the Fleet cluster manager in Microsoft Azure are starting to implement these Multi-Cluster Service APIs in response to user needs.

Third-Party Tools

So far, this chapter has described the various ways to import, export, and connect services that span Kubernetes clusters and some outside resource. If you have previous experience with service mesh technologies, these concepts might seem quite familiar. Indeed, there are a variety of third-party tools and projects that you can use to interconnect services both with Kubernetes and with arbitrary applications and machines. Generally, these tools provide a lot of functionality, but they are also significantly more complex operationally than the approaches described earlier. However, if you find yourself building more and more networking interconnectivity, you should explore the space of service meshes, which is rapidly iterating and evolving.

Nearly all these third-party tools have an open source component, but they also offer commercial support that can reduce the operational overhead of running additional infrastructure.

Connecting Cluster and External Services Best Practices

- Establish network connectivity between the cluster and on-premises. Networking can be varied between different sites, clouds, and cluster configurations, but first ensure that pods can talk to on-premises machines and vice versa.

- To access services outside of the cluster, you can use selector-less services and directly program in the IP address of the machine (e.g., the database) with which you want to communicate. If you don't have fixed IP addresses, you can instead use CNAME services to redirect to a DNS name. If you have neither a DNS name nor fixed services, you might need to write a dynamic operator that periodically synchronizes the external service IP addresses with the Kubernetes Service endpoints.

- To export services from Kubernetes, use internal load balancers or NodePort services. Internal load balancers are typically easier to use in public cloud environments where they can be bound to the Kubernetes Service itself. When such load balancers are unavailable, NodePort services can expose the service on all the machines in the cluster.

- You can achieve connections between Kubernetes clusters through a combination of these two approaches, exposing a service externally that is then consumed as a selector-less service in the other Kubernetes cluster.

Summary

In the real world, not every application is cloud native. Building production-ready applications often involves connecting preexisting systems with newer applications. This chapter described how you can integrate Kubernetes with legacy applications and also how to integrate different services running across multiple distinct Kubernetes clusters. Unless you have the luxury of building something brand new, cloud native development will always require legacy integration. The techniques described in this chapter will help you achieve that.

## CHAPTER 14

Running Machine Learning in Kubernetes

The age of microservices, distributed systems, and the cloud has provided the perfect environmental conditions for the democratization of machine learning models and tooling. Infrastructure at scale has now become commoditized, and the tooling around the machine learning ecosystem is maturing. Kubernetes is one of the platforms that has become increasingly popular among developers, data scientists, and the wider open source community as the perfect environment to enable the machine learning workflow and life cycle. Large machine learning models like GPT-4 (*https://oreil.ly/sGzRc*) and DALL·E (*https://oreil.ly/zTWNx*) have brought machine learning into the spotlight and organizations like OpenAI (*https://oreil.ly/bCXwF*) have been very public about their use of Kubernetes to support these models. In this chapter, we will cover why Kubernetes is a great platform for machine learning and provide best practices for both cluster administrators and data scientists alike on how to get the most out of Kubernetes when running machine learning workloads. Specifically, we focus on deep learning rather than traditional machine learning because deep learning has quickly become the area of innovation on platforms like Kubernetes.

Why Is Kubernetes Great for Machine Learning?

Kubernetes has quickly become the home for rapid innovation in deep learning. The confluence of tooling and libraries such as TensorFlow (*https://oreil.ly/nzHaG*) makes this technology more accessible to a large audience of data scientists. What makes Kubernetes such a great place to run your deep learning workloads? Let's cover what Kubernetes provides:

Ubiquitous

Kubernetes is everywhere. All the major public clouds support it, and there are distributions for private clouds and infrastructure. Basing ecosystem tooling on a platform like Kubernetes allows users to run their deep learning workloads anywhere.

Scalable

Deep learning workflows typically need access to large amounts of computing power to efficiently train machine learning models. Kubernetes ships with native autoscaling capabilities that make it easy for data scientists to achieve and fine-tune the level of scale they need to train their models.

Extensible

Efficiently training a machine learning model typically requires access to specialized hardware. Kubernetes allows cluster administrators to quickly and easily expose new types of hardware to the scheduler without having to change the Kubernetes source code. It also allows custom resources and controllers to be seamlessly integrated into the Kubernetes API to support specialized workflows, such as hyperparameter tuning.

Self-service

Data scientists can use Kubernetes to perform self-service machine learning workflows on demand, without needing specialized knowledge of Kubernetes itself.

Portable

Machine learning models can be run anywhere, provided that the tooling is based on the Kubernetes API. This allows machine learning workloads to be portable across Kubernetes providers.

Machine Learning Workflow

To effectively understand the needs of deep learning, you must understand the complete machine learning workflow. Figure 14-1 represents a simplified workflow.

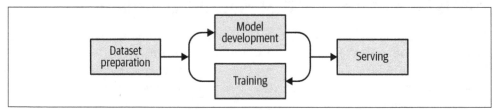

Figure 14-1. Machine learning development workflow

As you can see, the workflow has the following phases:

Dataset preparation
This phase includes the storage, indexing, cataloging, and metadata associated with the dataset used to train the model. For the purposes of this book, we consider only the storage aspect. Datasets vary in size, from hundreds of megabytes to hundreds of terabytes, and even petabytes, and need to be provided to the model in order for the model to be trained. You must consider storage that provides the appropriate properties to meet these needs. Typically, large-scale block and object stores are required and must be accessible via Kubernetes-native storage abstractions or directly accessible APIs.

Model development
In this phase, data scientists write, share, and collaborate on machine learning algorithms. Open source tools like JupyterHub are easy to install on Kubernetes because they typically function like any other workload.

Training
For a model to use the dataset to learn how to perform the tasks it's designed to perform, it must be trained. The resulting artifact of the training process is usually a checkpoint of the trained model state. The training process is the piece that takes advantage of all the capabilities of Kubernetes at the same time. Scheduling, access to specialized hardware, dataset volume management, scaling, and networking will all be exercised in unison to complete this task. We cover more of the specifics of the training phase in the next section.

Serving
This is the process of making the trained model accessible to service requests from clients so that it can make an inference based on the data supplied from the client. For example, if you have an image-recognition model that's been trained to detect dogs and cats, a client might submit a picture of a dog, and the model should be able to determine whether it is a dog, with a certain level of accuracy.

Machine Learning for Kubernetes Cluster Admins

There are a few topics to consider before running machine learning workloads on your Kubernetes cluster. This section is specifically targeted to cluster administrators. The largest challenge you will face as a cluster administrator responsible for a team of data scientists is understanding the terminology. There are myriad new terms that you must become familiar with over time, but rest assured, you can do it. Let's look at the main problem areas you'll need to address when preparing a cluster for machine learning workloads.

Model Training on Kubernetes

Training machine learning models on Kubernetes requires conventional CPUs and graphics processing units (GPUs). Typically, the more resources you apply, the faster the training will be completed. In most cases, model training can be achieved on a single machine that has the required resources. Many cloud providers offer multi-GPU virtual machine (VM) types, so we recommend scaling VMs vertically to four to eight GPUs before looking into distributed training. Data scientists use a technique known as *hyperparameter tuning* when training models. A hyperparameter is simply a parameter that has a set value before the training process begins. Hyperparameter tuning is the process of finding the optimal set of hyperparameters for model training. The technique involves running many of the same training jobs with a different set of hyperparameters.

Training your first model on Kubernetes

In this example, you are going to use the MNIST dataset to train an image-classification model. The MNIST dataset is publicly available and commonly used for image classification.

To train the model, you need GPUs. Let's confirm that your Kubernetes cluster has GPUs available. The following command shows how many GPUs are available in a Kubernetes cluster. From the output we can see that this cluster has four GPUs available:

```
$ kubectl get nodes -o yaml | grep -i nvidia.com/gpu
        nvidia.com/gpu: "1"
        nvidia.com/gpu: "1"
        nvidia.com/gpu: "1"
        nvidia.com/gpu: "1"
```

Given that training is a batch workload, to run your training you're going to use the Job kind in Kubernetes. You will run your training for 500 steps and use a single GPU. Create a file called *mnist-demo.yaml* using the following manifest, and save it to your filesystem:

```
apiVersion: batch/v1
kind: Job
metadata:
  labels:
    app: mnist-demo
  name: mnist-demo
spec:
  template:
    metadata:
      labels:
        app: mnist-demo
    spec:
      containers:
```

```
  - name: mnist-demo
    image: lachlanevenson/tf-mnist:gpu
    args: ["--max_steps", "500"]
    imagePullPolicy: IfNotPresent
    resources:
      limits:
        nvidia.com/gpu: 1
  restartPolicy: OnFailure
```

Now, create this resource on your Kubernetes cluster:

```
$ kubectl create -f mnist-demo.yaml
job.batch/mnist-demo created
```

Check the status of the job you just created:

```
$ kubectl get jobs
NAME         COMPLETIONS   DURATION   AGE
mnist-demo   1/1           31s        49s
```

If you look at the pods, you should see the training job running:

```
$ kubectl get pods
NAME               READY   STATUS    RESTARTS   AGE
mnist-demo-8lqrn   1/1     Running   0          63s
```

Looking at the pod logs, you can see the training happening:

```
$ $ kubectl logs mnist-demo-8lqrn
2023-02-10 23:14:42.007518: I
  tensorflow/core/platform/cpu_feature_guard.cc:137] Your CPU supports
    instructions that this TensorFlow binary was not compiled to
      use: SSE4.1 SSE4.2 AVX AVX2 FMA
2023-02-10 23:14:42.205555: I
  tensorflow/core/common_runtime/gpu/gpu_device.cc:1030] Found device 0 with
        properties:
name: Tesla K80 major: 3 minor: 7 memoryClockRate(GHz): 0.8235
pciBusID: 0001:00:00.0
totalMemory: 11.17GiB freeMemory: 11.12GiB
2023-02-10 23:14:42.205596: I
  tensorflow/core/common_runtime/gpu/gpu_device.cc:1120] Creating TensorFlow
        device (/device:GPU:0) -> (device: 0, name: Tesla K80, pci bus
          id: 0001:00:00.0, compute capability: 3.7)
2023-02-10 23:14:46.848342: I
  tensorflow/stream_executor/dso_loader.cc:139] successfully opened CUDA library
        libcupti.so.8.0 locally
Successfully downloaded train-images-idx3-ubyte.gz 9912422 bytes.
Extracting /tmp/tensorflow/input_data/train-images-idx3-ubyte.gz
Successfully downloaded train-labels-idx1-ubyte.gz 28881 bytes.
Extracting /tmp/tensorflow/input_data/train-labels-idx1-ubyte.gz
Successfully downloaded t10k-images-idx3-ubyte.gz 1648877 bytes.
Extracting /tmp/tensorflow/input_data/t10k-images-idx3-ubyte.gz
Successfully downloaded t10k-labels-idx1-ubyte.gz 4542 bytes.
Extracting /tmp/tensorflow/input_data/t10k-labels-idx1-ubyte.gz
Accuracy at step 0: 0.0886
```

```
Accuracy at step 10: 0.7094
Accuracy at step 20: 0.8354
Accuracy at step 30: 0.8667
Accuracy at step 40: 0.8833
Accuracy at step 50: 0.8902
Accuracy at step 60: 0.897
Accuracy at step 70: 0.9062
Accuracy at step 80: 0.9057
Accuracy at step 90: 0.906
Adding run metadata for 99
Accuracy at step 100: 0.9163
Accuracy at step 110: 0.9203
Accuracy at step 120: 0.9168
Accuracy at step 130: 0.9215
Accuracy at step 140: 0.9241
Accuracy at step 150: 0.9251
Accuracy at step 160: 0.9286
Accuracy at step 170: 0.9288
Accuracy at step 180: 0.9274
Accuracy at step 190: 0.9337
Adding run metadata for 199
Accuracy at step 200: 0.9361
Accuracy at step 210: 0.9369
Accuracy at step 220: 0.9365
Accuracy at step 230: 0.9328
Accuracy at step 240: 0.9409
Accuracy at step 250: 0.9428
Accuracy at step 260: 0.9408
Accuracy at step 270: 0.9432
Accuracy at step 280: 0.9438
Accuracy at step 290: 0.9433
Adding run metadata for 299
Accuracy at step 300: 0.9446
Accuracy at step 310: 0.9466
Accuracy at step 320: 0.9468
Accuracy at step 330: 0.9463
Accuracy at step 340: 0.9464
Accuracy at step 350: 0.9489
Accuracy at step 360: 0.9506
Accuracy at step 370: 0.9489
Accuracy at step 380: 0.9484
Accuracy at step 390: 0.9494
Adding run metadata for 399
Accuracy at step 400: 0.9513
Accuracy at step 410: 0.9474
Accuracy at step 420: 0.9499
Accuracy at step 430: 0.9462
Accuracy at step 440: 0.952
Accuracy at step 450: 0.952
Accuracy at step 460: 0.9487
Accuracy at step 470: 0.9569
Accuracy at step 480: 0.9547
```

```
Accuracy at step 490: 0.9516
Adding run metadata for 499
```

Finally, you can see that the training has completed by looking at the job status:

```
$ kubectl get jobs
NAME          COMPLETIONS   DURATION   AGE
mnist-demo    1/1           31s        2m19s
```

To clean up the training job, simply run the following command:

```
$ kubectl delete -f mnist-demo.yaml
job.batch "mnist-demo" deleted
```

Congratulations! You just ran your first model training job on Kubernetes.

Distributed Training on Kubernetes

Distributed training is still in its infancy and is difficult to optimize. Running a training job that requires eight GPUs will almost always be faster to train on a single eight-GPU machine compared to two machines with four GPUs each. The only time you should resort to using distributed training is when the model doesn't fit on the biggest machine available. If you are certain you must run distributed training, it is important to understand the architecture. Figure 14-2 depicts the distributed TensorFlow architecture, and you can see how the model and the parameters are distributed.

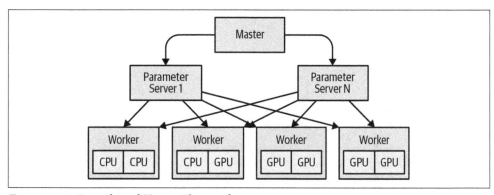

Figure 14-2. Distributed TensorFlow architecture

Resource Constraints

Machine learning workloads demand very specific configurations across all aspects of your cluster. The training phases are most certainly the most resource intensive. It's also important to note, as we mentioned a moment ago, that machine learning algorithm training is almost always a batch-style workload. Specifically, it will have a start time and a finish time. The finish time of a training run depends on how quickly you can meet the resource requirements of the model training. This means that scaling is almost certainly a quicker way to finish training jobs faster, but scaling has its own set of bottlenecks.

Specialized Hardware

Training and serving a model is almost always more efficient on specialized hardware. A typical example of such specialized hardware would be commodity GPUs. Kubernetes allows you to access GPUs via device plug-ins that make the GPU resource known to the Kubernetes scheduler and therefore able to be scheduled. A device plug-in framework facilitates this capability, which means that vendors do not need to modify the core Kubernetes code to implement their specific device. These device plug-ins typically run on each node as DaemonSets, which are processes that are responsible for advertising these specific resources to the Kubernetes API. Let's look at the NVIDIA device plug-in for Kubernetes (*https://oreil.ly/RgKuz*), which enables access to NVIDIA GPUs. After they're running, you can create a pod as follows, and Kubernetes will ensure that it is scheduled to a node that has these resources available:

```
apiVersion: v1
kind: Pod
metadata:
  name: gpu-pod
spec:
  containers:
    - name: digits-container
      image: nvidia/digits:6.0
      resources:
        limits:
          nvidia.com/gpu: 2 # requesting 2 GPUs
```

Device plug-ins are not limited to GPUs; you can use them wherever specialized hardware is needed—for example, Field Programmable Gate Arrays (FPGAs) or InfiniBand.

Scheduling idiosyncrasies

It's important to note that Kubernetes cannot make decisions about resources that it does not have knowledge about. One of the things you might notice is that the GPUs are not running at capacity when you are training. You are therefore not achieving the level of utilization you would like to see. Let's consider the previous example; it exposes only the number of GPU cores and omits the number of threads that can be run per core. It also doesn't expose which bus the GPU core is on, so that jobs that need access to one another or to the same memory might be colocated on the same Kubernetes nodes. All these considerations might be addressed by device plug-ins in the future but for now might leave you wondering why you cannot get 100% utilization on that beefy GPU you just purchased. It's also worth mentioning that you cannot request fractions of GPUs (for example, 0.1), which means that even if the specific GPU supports running multiple threads concurrently, you will not be able to utilize that capacity.

Libraries, Drivers, and Kernel Modules

To access specialized hardware, you typically need purpose-built libraries, drivers, and kernel modules. You will need to ensure that these are mounted into the container runtime so that they are available to the tooling running in the container. You might ask, "Why don't I just add these to the container image itself?" The answer is simple: the tools need to match the version on the underlying host and must be configured appropriately for that specific system. Container runtimes such as NVIDIA Docker (*https://oreil.ly/Re0Ef*) remove the burden of having to map host volumes into each container. In lieu of having a purpose-built container runtime, you might be able to build an admission webhook that provides the same functionality. It's also important to consider that you might need privileged containers to access some specialized hardware, which affects the cluster security profile. The installation of the associated libraries, drivers, and kernel modules might also be facilitated by Kubernetes device plug-ins. Many device plug-ins run checks on each machine to confirm that all installations have been completed before they advertise the schedulable GPU resources to the Kubernetes scheduler.

Storage

Storage is one of the most critical aspects of the machine learning workflow. You need to consider storage because it directly affects the following pieces of the machine learning workflow:

- Dataset storage and distribution among nodes during training
- Checkpoints and saving models

Dataset storage and distribution among nodes during training

During training, the dataset must be retrievable by every node. The storage needs are read-only, and, typically, the faster the disk, the better. The type of disk that's providing the storage is almost completely dependent on the size of the dataset. Datasets of hundreds of megabytes or gigabytes might be perfect for block storage, but datasets that are several or hundreds of terabytes in size might be better suited to object storage. Depending on the size and location of the disks that hold the datasets, there might be a performance hit on your networking.

Checkpoints and saving models

Checkpoints are created as a model is being trained, and saving models allows you to use them for serving. In both cases, you need storage attached to each of the nodes to store this data. The data is typically stored under a single directory, and each node is writing to a specific checkpoint or save file. Most tools expect the checkpoint and save data to be in a single location and require `ReadWriteMany`. `ReadWriteMany` simply means that the volume can be mounted as read-write by many nodes. When using Kubernetes PersistentVolumes, you will need to determine the best storage platform for your needs. The Kubernetes documentation keeps a list (*https://oreil.ly/aMjGd*) of volume plug-ins that support `ReadWriteMany`.

Networking

The training phase of the machine learning workflow has a large impact on the network (specifically, when running distributed training). If we consider TensorFlow's distributed architecture, two discrete phases create a lot of network traffic: variable distribution from each of the parameter servers to each of the nodes, and the application of gradients from each node back to the parameter server (refer back to Figure 14-2). The time it takes for this exchange to happen directly affects the time it takes to train a model. So, it's a simple game of the faster, the better (within reason, of course). With most public clouds and servers today supporting 1-Gbps, 10-Gbps, and sometimes 40-Gbps network interface cards, generally network bandwidth is a concern only at lower bandwidths. You might also consider InfiniBand if you need high network bandwidth.

While raw network bandwidth is more often than not a limiting factor, in some instances the problem is getting the data onto the wire from the kernel in the first place. Some open source projects take advantage of Remote Direct Memory Access (RDMA) to further accelerate network traffic without the need to modify your nodes or application code. RDMA allows computers in a network to exchange data in main memory without using the processor, cache, or operating system of either computer.

Specialized Protocols

Other specialized protocols you can consider when using machine learning on Kubernetes are often vendor specific, but they all seek to address distributed training scaling issues by removing areas of the architecture that quickly become bottlenecks. For example, parameter servers. These protocols often allow the direct exchange of information between GPUs on multiple nodes without the need to involve the node CPU and OS. Here are a couple you might want to look into to more efficiently scale your distributed training:

Message Passing Interface (MPI)
A standardized portable API for the transfer of data between distributed processes

NVIDIA Collective Communications Library (NCCL)
A library of topology-aware multi-GPU communication primitives

Data Scientist Concerns

Earlier in the chapter, we shared considerations you need to make in order to be able to run machine learning workloads on your Kubernetes cluster. But what about the data scientist? Here we cover some popular tools that make it easy for data scientists to utilize Kubernetes for machine learning without having to be a Kubernetes expert:

Kubeflow (https://oreil.ly/UVxjM)
A machine learning toolkit for Kubernetes, it is native to Kubernetes and ships with several tools necessary to complete the machine learning workflow. Tools such as Jupyter Notebooks, pipelines, and Kubernetes-native controllers make it simple and easy for data scientists to get the most out of Kubernetes as a platform for machine learning.

Polyaxon (https://oreil.ly/NZ7Nj)
A tool for managing machine learning workflows that supports many popular libraries and runs on any Kubernetes cluster. Polyaxon has both commercial and open source offerings.

Pachyderm (https://oreil.ly/CivM_)
An enterprise-ready data science platform with a rich suite of tools for dataset preparation, life cycle, and versioning, along with the ability to build machine learning pipelines. Pachyderm has a commercial offering you can deploy to any Kubernetes cluster.

Machine Learning on Kubernetes Best Practices

To achieve optimal performance for your machine learning workloads, consider the following best practices:

Smart scheduling and autoscaling
Given that most stages of the machine learning workflow are batch by nature, we recommend you utilize a Cluster Autoscaler. GPU-enabled hardware is costly, and you certainly do not want to be paying for it when it's not in use. We recommend batching jobs to run at specific times using either taints and tolerations or via a time-specific Cluster Autoscaler. That way, the cluster can scale to the needs of the machine learning workloads when needed, and not a moment sooner. Regarding taints and tolerations, upstream convention is to taint the node with

the extended resource as the key. For example, a node with NVIDIA GPUs should be tainted as follows: Key: nvidia.com/gpu, Effect: NoSchedule. Using this method means you can also utilize the ExtendedResourceToleration admission controller, which will automatically add the appropriate tolerations for such taints to pods requesting extended resources so that the users don't need to add them manually.

The truth is that model training is a delicate balance

Allowing things to move faster in one area often leads to bottlenecks in others. It's an endeavor of constant observation and tuning. As a general rule, we recommend you try to make the GPU become the bottleneck because it is the most costly resource. Keep your GPUs saturated. Be prepared to always be on the lookout for bottlenecks, and set up your monitoring to track the GPU, CPU, network, and storage utilization.

Mixed workload clusters

Clusters that are used to run the day-to-day business services might also be used for machine learning. Given the high performance requirements of machine learning workloads, we recommend using a separate node pool that's tainted to accept only machine learning workloads. This will help protect the rest of the cluster from any impact from the machine learning workloads running on the machine learning node pool. Furthermore, you should consider multiple GPU-enabled node pools, each with different performance characteristics to suit the workload types. We also recommend enabling node autoscaling on the machine learning node pool(s). Use mixed mode clusters only after you have a solid understanding of the performance impact that your machine learning workloads have on your cluster.

Achieving linear scaling with distributed training

This is the holy grail of distributed model training. Most libraries unfortunately don't scale linearly when distributed. A lot of work is being done to make scaling better, but it's important to understand the costs because this isn't as simple as throwing more hardware at the problem. In our experience, it's almost always the model itself and not the infrastructure supporting it that is the source of the bottleneck. It is, however, important to review the utilization of the GPU, CPU, network, and storage before pointing fingers at the model. Open source tools such as Horovod (*https://oreil.ly/3NMtg*) seek to improve distributed training frameworks and provide better model scaling.

Summary

We've covered a lot of ground in this chapter and hopefully have provided valuable insight into why Kubernetes is a great platform for machine learning, especially deep learning, and the considerations you need to be aware of before deploying your first machine learning workload. If you exercise the recommendations in this chapter, you will be well equipped to build and maintain a Kubernetes cluster for these specialized workloads.

## CHAPTER 15

Building Higher-Level Application Patterns on Top of Kubernetes

It's no secret that Kubernetes is a complex system. Although it simplifies the deployment and operations of distributed applications, it does little to make the development of such systems easy. In fact, when adding new concepts and artifacts for the developer to interact with, it adds a layer of complexity in the service of simplified operations. Consequently, in many environments, it makes sense to develop higher-level abstractions to provide more developer-friendly primitives on top of Kubernetes. Additionally, in many large companies, it makes sense to standardize the way in which applications are configured and deployed so that everyone adheres to the same operational best practices. This can also be achieved by developing higher-level abstractions so that developers automatically adhere to these principles. However, developing these abstractions can hide important details from the developer and might introduce a walled garden. This limits or complicates the development of certain applications or the integration of existing solutions. Throughout the development of the cloud, the tension between the flexibility of infrastructure and the power of the platform has been a constant. Designing the appropriate higher-level abstractions enables us to walk an ideal path through this divide.

Approaches to Developing Higher-Level Abstractions

When considering how to develop a higher-level primitive on top of Kubernetes, there are two basic approaches. The first is to wrap Kubernetes as an implementation detail. With this approach, developers who consume your platform should be largely unaware that they are running on top of Kubernetes; instead, they should think of themselves as consumers of the platform you supply, and thus Kubernetes is an implementation detail.

The second option is to use the extensibility capabilities built into Kubernetes itself. The Kubernetes Server API is quite flexible, and you can dynamically add arbitrary new resources to the Kubernetes API. With this approach, your new higher-level resources coexist alongside the built-in Kubernetes objects, and the users use the built-in tooling for interacting with all the Kubernetes resources, both built-in ones and extensions. This extension model results in an environment in which Kubernetes is still front and center for your developers but with additions that reduce complexity and make it easier to use.

How do you choose the approach that is appropriate? It depends on the goals for the abstraction layer that you are building. If you are constructing a fully isolated, integrated environment in which you have strong confidence that users will not need to "break glass" and escape, and where ease of use is an important characteristic, the first option is a great choice. A good example of this would be building a machine learning pipeline. The domain is relatively well understood. The data scientists who are your users are likely not familiar with Kubernetes. Enabling these data scientists to rapidly get their work done and focus on their domains rather than distributed systems is the primary goal. As a result, building a complete abstraction on top of Kubernetes makes the most sense.

On the other hand, when building a higher-level developer abstraction—for example, an easy way to deploy Java applications—it is a far better choice to extend Kubernetes rather than wrap it, for two reasons. First, the domain of application development is extraordinarily broad. It will be difficult for you to anticipate all the requirements and use cases for your developers, especially as the applications and business iterate and change over time. The other reason is to ensure that you can continue to take advantage of the Kubernetes ecosystem of tools. There are countless cloud native tools for monitoring, continuous delivery, and more. Extending rather than replacing the Kubernetes API ensures that you can continue to use these tools and new ones as they are developed. Additionally, when you choose to extend rather than obfuscate the Kubernetes API, it is relatively straightforward to find people with industry experience in Kubernetes. Experience building applications in a bespoke application platform that exists only in your environment is definitionally rare.

Extending Kubernetes

Because every layer that you might build over Kubernetes is unique, it is beyond the scope of this book to describe how you might build such a layer to extend Kubernetes. But the tools and techniques for extending Kubernetes are generic to any construction you might do on top of Kubernetes, so we'll spend time covering them.

Extending Kubernetes Clusters

A complete how-to for extending a Kubernetes cluster is a large topic and more completely covered in other books like *Managing Kubernetes* and *Kubernetes: Up and Running* (O'Reilly). Rather than going over the same material here, this section focuses on providing an understanding of how to use Kubernetes extensibility.

Extending the Kubernetes cluster involves understanding the touch points for resources in Kubernetes. There are three related technical solutions. The first is the *sidecar*. Sidecar containers (shown in Figure 15-1) have been popularized in the context of service meshes. These containers run alongside a main application container to provide additional capabilities that are decoupled from the main application and often maintained by a separate team. For example, in service meshes, a sidecar might provide transparent mutual Transport Layer Security (mTLS) authentication to a containerized application. You can use sidecars to add capabilities to your user-defined applications.

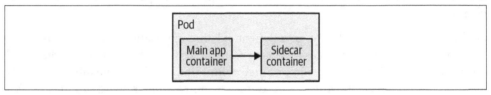

Figure 15-1. The sidecar design

Within the industry the sidecar approach has become increasingly popular, and many projects use it to deliver services alongside the developer's containers. A great example is the Dapr (*https://dapr.io*) (Distributed Application Runtime) project. Dapr is an open source project within the CNCF that implements a sidecar for applications that delivers many capabilities like encryption, key/value store, pub/sub queues, and much more with a very simple, consistent API. Sidecars like Dapr can be used as modular building blocks for a platform that you are developing on top of Kubernetes.

Of course, the entire goal of this effort was to make a developer's life easier, but if we require that they learn about and know how to use sidecars, we've actually made the problem worse. Fortunately, additional tools for extending Kubernetes simplify things. In particular, Kubernetes features *admission controllers*. Admission controllers are interceptors that read Kubernetes API requests prior to them being stored (or "admitted") into the cluster's backing store. You can use these admission controllers to validate or modify API objects. In the context of sidecars, you can use them to automatically add sidecars to all pods created in the cluster so that developers do not need to know about the sidecars to reap their benefits. Figure 15-2 illustrates how admission controllers interact with the Kubernetes API.

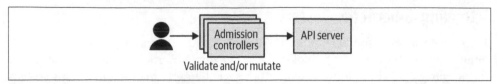

Figure 15-2. Admission controllers

The utility of admission controllers isn't limited to adding sidecars. You can also use them to validate objects submitted by developers to Kubernetes. For example, you could implement a *linter* (a tool that analyzes code) for Kubernetes that ensures developers submit pods and other resources that follow best practices for using Kubernetes. A common mistake for developers is to not reserve resources for their application. For those circumstances, an admission controller–based linter could intercept such requests and reject them. Of course, you should also leave an escape hatch (for example, a special annotation) so that advanced users can opt out of the lint rule, as appropriate. We discuss the importance of escape hatches later on in this chapter.

So far, we've only covered ways to augment existing applications and to ensure that developers follow best practices—we haven't really covered how to add higher-level abstractions. This is where custom resource definitions (CRDs) come into play. CRDs are a way to dynamically add new resources to an existing Kubernetes cluster. For example, using CRDs, you could add a new ReplicatedService resource to a Kubernetes cluster. When a developer creates an instance of a ReplicatedService, it turns around to Kubernetes and creates corresponding Deployment and Service resources. Thus, the ReplicatedService is a convenient developer abstraction for a common pattern. CRDs are generally implemented by a control loop that is deployed into the cluster itself to manage these new resource types.

Extending the Kubernetes User Experience

Adding new resources to your cluster is a great way to provide new capabilities, but to truly take advantage of them, it's often useful to extend the Kubernetes user experience (UX) as well. By default, the Kubernetes tooling is unaware of custom resources and other extensions and thus treats them in a very generic and not particularly user-friendly manner. Extending the Kubernetes command line can provide an enhanced user experience.

Generally, the tool used for accessing Kubernetes is the kubectl command-line tool. Fortunately, it too has been built for extensibility. kubectl plug-ins are binaries that have a name like kubectl-foo, where foo is the name of the plug-in. When you invoke kubectl foo ... on the command line, the invocation is in turn routed to an invocation of the plug-in binary. Using kubectl plug-ins, you can define new experiences that deeply understand the new resources that you have added to your cluster. You are free to implement whatever kind of experiences are suitable while at the same time taking advantage of the familiarity of the kubectl tooling. This is especially valuable because it means that you don't need to teach developers about a new tool set. Likewise, you can gradually introduce Kubernetes-native concepts as the developers advance their Kubernetes knowledge.

If you are looking to build graphical interfaces for your Kubernetes-based platform, several tools can help. In particular the open source Headlamp project (*https://oreil.ly/2-4fB*) is a library that enables easy construction of web-based, mobile, or desktop applications for interacting with Kubernetes infrastructure. Using a tool like Headlamp enables you to rapidly create a custom developer experience that perfectly fits your platform and its needs.

Making Containerized Development Easier

Before they can even deploy an application to Kubernetes, a developer must first containerize that application. Though building containers is second nature for those familiar with the cloud native ecosystem, for many it is a daunting task that prevents even getting started with modern application development.

Fortunately, several open source tools can help jump start your development. Tools like Draft (*https://draft.sh*) and Skaffold (*https://oreil.ly/H4DzY*) will automatically generate a Dockerfile for a particular language or development environment.

If developers are familiar with the buildpack idea from cloud foundry or other platforms, there are also tools like Paketo (*https://paketo.io*) that provide easy-to-use and vetted container images for building applications in popular languages as well as command-line tools to get started easily.

Developing a "Push-to-Deploy" Experience

One of the most popular features of many PaaS products is "push to deploy," meaning that a single push of code to a Git repository results in the application deploying to a cloud environment. Though this has previously been the domain of large-scale managed PaaS solutions, it is now very easy to build a similar experience using CI/CD solutions like GitHub Actions, Azure DevOps, or other continuous-build tooling.

With a properly designed pipeline, once a developer pushes code into their Git repository, it is automatically tested, built, packaged into a container image, and pushed to a container registry.

Once the new version of the container image is present in the container registry, it is a simple step to use another Git commit combined with GitOps to push that image out to a running application.

Combining GitHub actions and GitOps can enable your developers to achieve fast deployment while also staying true to the cloud native ecosystem and ideas like Infrastructure as Code (IaC).

Design Considerations When Building Platforms

Countless platforms have been built to enable developer productivity. Given the opportunity to observe all the places where these platforms have succeeded and failed, you can develop a common set of patterns and considerations to learn from the experience of others. Following these design guidelines can help to ensure that the platform you build is successful instead of a "legacy" dead end from which you must eventually move away.

Support Exporting to a Container Image

When you are building a platform, many designs provide simplicity by enabling the user to simply supply code (e.g., a function in Function as a Service [FaaS]) or a native package (e.g., a JAR file in Java) instead of a complete container image. This approach has a great deal of appeal because it lets the user stay within the confines of their well-understood tools and development experience. The platform handles the containerization of the application for them.

The problem with this approach, however, comes when the developer encounters the limitations of the programming environment that you have given them. Perhaps it's because they need a specific version of a language runtime to work around a bug. Or it might be that they need to package additional resources or executables that aren't part of the way you have structured the automatic containerization of the application.

No matter the reason, hitting this wall is an ugly moment for the developer, because it is a moment when they suddenly must learn a great deal more about how to package their application, when all they really wanted to do was to extend it slightly to fix a bug or deliver a new feature.

However, it doesn't need to be this way. If you support the exporting of your platform's programming environment into a generic container, the developer using your platform doesn't need to start from scratch and learn everything there is to know about containers. Instead, they have a complete working container image that represents their current application (i.e., the container image containing their function and the node runtime). Given this starting point, they can then make the small tweaks necessary to adapt the container image to their needs. This sort of gradual degradation and incremental learning dramatically smooths the path from higher-level platform down into lower-level infrastructure. It also increases the general utility of the platform because using it doesn't introduce steep cliffs for developers.

Support Existing Mechanisms for Service and Service Discovery

Another common story of platforms is that they evolve and interconnect with other systems. Many developers might be very happy and productive in your platform, but any real-world application will span both the platform that you build and lower-level Kubernetes applications as well as *other* platforms. Connections to legacy databases or open source applications built for Kubernetes will always be a part of a sufficiently large application.

Because of this need for interconnectivity, it's critically important that the core Kubernetes primitives for services and service discovery are used and exposed by any platform that you construct. Don't reinvent the wheel in the interest of improved platform experience, because in doing so you will be creating a walled garden incapable of interacting with the broader world.

If you expose the applications defined in your platform as Kubernetes Services, any application anywhere within your cluster will be able to consume your applications regardless of whether they are running in your higher-level platform. Likewise, if you use the Kubernetes DNS servers for service discovery, you will be able to connect from your higher-level application platform to other applications running in the cluster, even if they are not defined in your higher-level platform. It might be tempting to build something better or easier to use, but interconnectivity across different platforms is the common design pattern for any application of sufficient age and complexity. You will always regret the decision to build a walled garden.

Building Application Platforms Best Practices

Although Kubernetes provides powerful tools for operating software, it does considerably less to enable developers to build applications. It is often necessary to build platforms on top of Kubernetes to make developers more productive and/or Kubernetes easier. When building such platforms, you'll benefit from keeping the following best practices in mind:

- Use admission controllers to limit and modify API calls to the cluster. An admission controller can validate (and reject invalid) Kubernetes resources. A mutating admission controller can automatically modify API resources to add new sidecars or other changes that users might not even need to know about.

- Use kubectl plug-ins to extend the Kubernetes user experience by adding new tools to the existing command-line tool. In rare occasions, a purpose-built tool might be more appropriate.

- When building platforms on top of Kubernetes, think carefully about the platform's users and how their needs will evolve. Making things simple and easy to use is clearly a good goal, but if this also leads to users that are trapped and unable to be successful without rewriting everything outside of your platform, it will ultimately be a frustrating (and unsuccessful) experience.

Summary

Kubernetes is a fantastic tool for simplifying the deployment and operation of software; unfortunately, it is not always the most developer-friendly or productive environment. Because of this, a common task is to build a higher-level platform on top of Kubernetes to make it more approachable and usable by the average developer. This chapter described several approaches for designing such a higher-level system and provided a summary of the core extensibility infrastructure available in Kubernetes. It concluded with lessons and design principles drawn from our observation of other platforms that have been built on top of Kubernetes, with the hope that they can guide the design of your platform.

## CHAPTER 16

Managing State and Stateful Applications

In the early days of container orchestration, the targeted workloads were usually stateless applications that used external systems to store state when it was needed. The thought was that containers are very temporal, and orchestration of the backing storage needed to keep state consistently was difficult at best. Over time, the need for container-based workloads that kept state became a reality, and, in select cases, this need might be more performant. As more organizations looked to the cloud for computing power and Kubernetes became the de facto container runtime for applications, the impeding factor became the amount of data and performant access to the data, sometimes called "data gravity." Kubernetes adapted over many iterations. Now, not only does it allow for storage volumes mounted into the pod, but it also allows for those volumes to be managed by Kubernetes directly. This was an important component in orchestration of storage with the workloads that require it.

If the ability to mount an external volume to the container was enough, many more examples of stateful applications running at scale in Kubernetes would exist. The reality is that volume mounting is the easy component in the grand scheme of stateful applications. The majority of applications that require state to be maintained after node failure are complicated data-state engines such as relational database systems, distributed key/value stores, and complex document management systems. This class of applications requires more coordination among how members of the clustered application communicate with one another, how the members are identified, and the order in which members either appear or disappear in the system.

This chapter focuses on best practices for managing state, from simple patterns such as saving a file to a network share, to complex data management systems like MongoDB, MySQL, or Kafka. There is a small section on a new pattern for complex systems called Operators that brings not only Kubernetes primitives, but also allows for business or application logic to be added as custom controllers that can help make operating complex data management systems easier.

Volumes and Volume Mounts

Not every workload that requires a way to maintain state needs to be a complex database or high-throughput data queue service. Often, applications that are being moved to containerized workloads expect certain directories to exist and to be able to read and write pertinent information to those directories. The ability to inject data into a volume that can be read by containers in a pod is covered in Chapter 4; however, data mounted from ConfigMaps or secrets is usually read-only, and this section focuses on giving containers volumes that can be written to and will survive a container failure or, even better, a pod failure.

Every major container runtime, such as Docker, rkt, CRI-O, and even Singularity, allows for mounting volumes into a container that is mapped to an external storage system. At its simplest, external storage can be a memory location, a path on the container's host, or an external filesystem such as NFS, Glusterfs, CIFS, or Ceph. Why would this be needed? A useful example is that of a legacy application that was written to log application-specific information to a local filesystem. Many possible solutions, such as updating the application code to log out to a `stdout` or `stderr` of a sidecar container, can stream log data to an outside source via a shared pod volume. Some will take an infrastructure approach by using a host-based logging tool that can read a volume for both host logs and container application logs by using a volume mount in the container using a Kubernetes `hostPath` mount, as shown in the following:

```
apiVersion: apps/v1
kind: Deployment
metadata:
  name: nginx-webserver
spec:
  replicas: 3
  selector:
    matchLabels:
      app: nginx-webserver
  template:
    metadata:
      labels:
        app: nginx-webserver
    spec:
      containers:
      - name: nginx-webserver
        image: nginx:alpine
        ports:
        - containerPort: 80
        volumeMounts:
```

```
        - name: hostvol
          mountPath: /usr/share/nginx/html
    volumes:
      - name: hostvol
        hostPath:
          path: /home/webcontent
```

Volume Best Practices

- Try to limit the use of volumes to pods requiring multiple containers that need to share data, such as adapter or ambassador-type patterns. Use the `emptyDir` for those types of sharing patterns.

- Use `hostDir` when access to the data is required by node-based agents or services.

- Try to identify any services that write their critical application logs and events to local disk, and if possible change those to `stdout` or `stderr` and let a true Kubernetes-aware log aggregation system stream the logs instead of leveraging the volume map.

Kubernetes Storage

The examples we've walked through so far show basic volume mapping into a container in a pod, which is just a basic container engine capability. The real key is allowing Kubernetes to manage the storage backing the volume mounts. This allows for more dynamic scenarios where pods can live and die as needed, and the storage backing the pod will transition accordingly to wherever the pod may live. Kubernetes manages storage for pods using two distinct APIs, the PersistentVolume and PersistentVolumeClaim.

PersistentVolume

It is best to think of a PersistentVolume as a disk that will back any volumes that are mounted to a pod. A PersistentVolume will have a claim policy that will define the scope of life of the volume independent of the life cycle of the pod that uses the volume. Kubernetes can use either dynamic or statically defined volumes. To allow for dynamically created volumes, there must be a StorageClass defined in Kubernetes. PersistentVolumes of varying types and classes can be created in the cluster, and only when a PersistentVolumeClaim matches the PersistentVolume will it actually be assigned to a pod. The volume itself is backed by a volume plug-in. Numerous plug-ins are supported directly in Kubernetes, and each has different configuration parameters to adjust:

```
apiVersion: v1
kind: PersistentVolume
metadata:
name: pv001
labels:
  tier: "silver"
spec:
capacity:
  storage: 5Gi
accessModes:
- ReadWriteMany
persistentVolumeReclaimPolicy: Recycle
storageClassName: nfs
mountOptions:
  - hard
  - nfsvers=4.1
nfs:
  path: /tmp
  server: 172.17.0.2
```

PersistentVolumeClaims

PersistentVolumeClaims are a way to give Kubernetes a resource requirement definition for storage that a pod will use. Pods will reference the claim, and then if a persistentVolume that matches the claim request exists, it will allocate that volume to that specific pod. At minimum, a storage request size and access mode must be defined, but a specific StorageClass can also be defined. Selectors can also be used to ensure PersistentVolumes that meet a certain criteria will be allocated appropriately. In the following example, the label with key tier has a value of "silver":

```
apiVersion: v1
kind: PersistentVolumeClaim
metadata:
  name: my-pvc
spec:
  storageClass: nfs
    accessModes:
    - ReadWriteMany
  resources:
    requests:
      storage: 5Gi
  selector:
    matchLabels:
      tier: "silver"
```

The claim will match the PersistentVolume created earlier because the StorageClass name, the selector match, the size, and the access mode are all equal.

Kubernetes will match the PersistentVolume with the claim and bind them together. To use the volume, the pod.spec should reference the claim by name, as follows:

```
apiVersion: apps/v1
kind: Deployment
metadata:
  name: nginx-webserver
spec:
  replicas: 3
  selector:
    matchLabels:
      app: nginx-webserver
  template:
    metadata:
      labels:
        app: nginx-webserver
    spec:
      containers:
      - name: nginx-webserver
        image: nginx:alpine
        ports:
        - containerPort: 80
        volumeMounts:
          - name: hostvol
            mountPath: /usr/share/nginx/html
      volumes:
      - name: hostvol
        persistentVolumeClaim:
          claimName: my-pvc
```

StorageClasses

Instead of manually defining the PersistentVolumes ahead of time, administrators might elect to create StorageClass objects, which define the volume plug-in to use. They can also create any specific mount options and parameters that all PersistentVolumes of that class will use. This then allows the claim to be defined with the specific StorageClass to use, and Kubernetes will dynamically create the PersistentVolume based on the StorageClass parameters and options:

```
kind: StorageClass
apiVersion: storage.k8s.io/v1
metadata:
name: nfs
provisioner: cluster.local/nfs-client-provisioner
parameters:
  archiveOnDelete: True
```

Kubernetes also allows operators to create a default storage class using the DefaultStorageClass admission plug-in. If this has been enabled on the API server, then a default StorageClass can be defined, and any PersistentVolumeClaims that do not explicitly define a StorageClass will be assigned to the default class. Some cloud providers will include a default storage class to map to the cheapest storage allowed by their instances.

Container Storage Interface and FlexVolume

Most volume plug-ins today need to wait for direct code additions to the Kubernetes codebase. However, the Container Storage Interface (CSI) and FlexVolume, often referred to as "Out-of-Tree" volume plug-ins, enable storage vendors to create custom storage plug-ins without the need to wait for these direct code additions.

The CSI and FlexVolume plug-ins are deployed on Kubernetes clusters as extensions by operators and can be updated by the storage vendors when needed to expose new functionality.

The CSI states its objective on GitHub (*https://oreil.ly/AuMgE*) as:

> To define an industry standard Container Storage Interface that will enable storage vendors (SP) to develop a plug-in once and have it work across a number of container orchestration (CO) systems.

The FlexVolume interface has been the traditional method used to add additional features for a storage provider. It does require specific drivers to be installed on all the nodes of the cluster that will use it. This basically becomes an executable that is installed on the hosts of the cluster. This last component is the main detractor to using FlexVolumes, especially in managed service providers, because access to the nodes is frowned upon and accessing the control plane is practically impossible. The CSI plug-in solves this by exposing the same functionality and being as easy to use as deploying a pod into the cluster.

Kubernetes Storage Best Practices

Cloud native application design principles try to enforce stateless application design as much as possible; however, the growing footprint of container-based services has created the need for data storage persistence. These best practices around storage in Kubernetes will help to design an effective approach to providing the required storage implementations to the application design:

- If possible, enable the DefaultStorageClass admission plug-in and define a default storage class. Often, Helm charts for applications that require PersistentVolumes default to a `default` storage class for the chart, which allows the application to be installed without too much modification.

- When designing the architecture of the cluster, either on premises or in a cloud provider, take into consideration zone and connectivity between the compute and data layers. You will want to use the proper labels for both nodes and PersistentVolumes, and use affinity to keep the data and workload as close as possible. The last thing you want is a pod on a node in zone A trying to mount a volume that is attached to a node in zone B.

- Consider very carefully which workloads require state to be maintained on disk. Can that be handled by an outside service like a database system? Or, can your instance run in a cloud provider, by a hosted service that is API-consistent with currently used APIs, say a MongoDB or MySQL as a service?

- Determine how much effort would be involved in modifying the application code to be more stateless.

- While Kubernetes will track and mount the volumes as workloads are scheduled, it does not yet handle redundancy and backup of the data that is stored in those volumes. The CSI specification has added an API for vendors to plug in native snapshot technologies if the storage backend can support it.

- Verify the proper life cycle of the data that volumes will hold. By default the reclaim policy is set for dynamically provisioned PersistentVolumes, which will delete the volume from the backing storage provider when the pod is deleted. Sensitive data or data that can be used for forensic analysis should be set to reclaim.

Stateful Applications

Contrary to popular belief, Kubernetes has supported stateful applications since its infancy, from MySQL, Kafka, and Cassandra to other technologies. Those pioneering days, however, were fraught with complexities and were usually only for small workloads with lots of work required to get things like scaling and durability to function.

To fully grasp the critical differences, you must understand how a typical ReplicaSet schedules and manages pods, and how this could be detrimental to traditional stateful applications:

- Pods in a ReplicaSet are scaled out and assigned random names when scheduled.

- Pods in a ReplicaSet are scaled down arbitrarily.

- Pods in a ReplicaSet are never called directly through their name or IP address but through their association with a `Service`.

- Pods in a ReplicaSet can be restarted and moved to another node at any time.

- Pods in a ReplicaSet that have a PersistentVolume mapped are linked only by the claim, but any new pod with a new name can take over the claim if needed when rescheduled.

Those who have only cursory knowledge of cluster data management systems can immediately begin to see issues with these characteristics of ReplicaSet-based pods. Imagine a pod that has the current writable copy of the database just all of a sudden getting deleted! Pure pandemonium would ensue for sure.

Most neophytes to the Kubernetes world assume that StatefulSet applications are automatically database applications and therefore equate the two. This could not be farther from the truth. Kubernetes has no sense of what type of application it is deploying. It does not know that your database system requires leader election processes, that it can or cannot handle data replication between members of the set, or, for that matter, that it is a database system at all. This is where StatefulSets come into play.

StatefulSets

What StatefulSets do is make it easier to run application systems that expect more reliable node/pod behavior. If we look back at the list of typical pod characteristics in a ReplicaSet, StatefulSets offer almost the complete opposite. The original spec back in Kubernetes version 1.3 called `PetSets` was introduced to answer some of the critical scheduling and management needs for stateful-type applications such as complex data management systems:

- Pods in a StatefulSet are scaled out and assigned sequential names. As the set scales up, the pods get ordinal names, and by default a new pod must be fully online (pass its liveness and/or readiness probes) before the next pod is added.

- Pods in a StatefulSet are scaled down in reverse sequence.

- Pods in a StatefulSet can be addressed individually by name behind a headless Service.

- Pods in a StatefulSet that require a volume mount must use a defined Persistent-Volume template. Volumes claimed by pods in a StatefulSet are not deleted when the StatefulSet is deleted.

A StatefulSet specification looks very similar to a Deployment except for the Service declaration and the PersistentVolume template. The headless Service should be created first, which defines the Service that the pods will be addressed with individually. The headless Service is the same as a regular Service but does not do the normal load balancing:

```
apiVersion: v1
kind: Service
metadata:
  name: mongo
  labels:
    name: mongo
spec:
  ports:
  - port: 27017
    targetPort: 27017
  clusterIP: None #This creates the headless Service
```

```
  selector:
    role: mongo
```

The StatefulSet definition will also look exactly like a Deployment with a few changes:

```
apiVersion: apps/v1beta1
kind: StatefulSet
metadata:
  name: mongo
spec:
  serviceName: "mongo"
  replicas: 3
  template:
    metadata:
      labels:
        role: mongo
        environment: test
    spec:
      terminationGracePeriodSeconds: 10
      containers:
        - name: mongo
          image: mongo:3.4
          command:
            - mongod
            - "--replSet"
            - rs0
            - "--bind_ip"
            - 0.0.0.0
            - "--smallfiles"
            - "--noprealloc"
          ports:
            - containerPort: 27017
          volumeMounts:
            - name: mongo-persistent-storage
              mountPath: /data/db
        - name: mongo-sidecar
          image: cvallance/mongo-k8s-sidecar
          env:
            - name: MONGO_SIDECAR_POD_LABELS
              value: "role=mongo,environment=test"
  volumeClaimTemplates:
  - metadata:
      name: mongo-persistent-storage
      annotations:
        volume.beta.kubernetes.io/storage-class: "fast"
    spec:
      accessModes: [ "ReadWriteOnce" ]
      resources:
        requests:
          storage: 2Gi
```

Operators

StatefulSets have been a major factor in introducing complex stateful data systems as feasible workloads in Kubernetes. The only real issue, as stated earlier, is that Kubernetes does not really understand the workload that is running in the StatefulSet. All the other complex operations, like backups, failover, leader registration, new replica registration, and upgrades, are operations that need to happen regularly and will require some careful consideration when running as StatefulSets.

Early on in the growth of Kubernetes, CoreOS site reliability engineers (SREs) created a new class of cloud native software for Kubernetes called Operators. The original intent was to encapsulate domain-specific knowledge of running a specific application into a specific controller that extends Kubernetes. Imagine building up on the StatefulSet controller to be able to deploy, scale, upgrade, back up, and run general maintenance operations on Cassandra or Kafka. Some of the first Operators that were created were for etcd and Prometheus, which uses a time-series database to keep metrics over time. The proper creation, backup, and restore configuration of Prometheus or etcd instances can be handled by an Operator and are new Kubernetes-managed objects just like a pod or Deployment.

Until recently, Operators have been one-off tools created by SREs or by software vendors for their specific application. In mid-2018, Red Hat created the Operator Framework, a set of tools including an SDK life cycle manager and future modules that will enable features such as metering, marketplace, and registry type functions. Operators are not only for stateful applications, but because of their custom controller logic they are definitely more amenable to complex data services and stateful systems.

Operators have become a standard way not only of extending the Kubernetes API but also bringing in best practice and operational oversight to complex system processes in Kubernetes. A good place to discover existing Operators published for the Kubernetes ecosystem is OperatorHub (*http://operatorhub.io*). They maintain an updated list of curated Operators.

If you are interested in learning how Operators work, Chapter 21 is new to this edition and will give you a primer on the development of an Operator and best practices to use. Also check out *Kubernetes Operators* (O'Reilly) by Jason Dobies and Joshua Wood for a more in-depth run-through of building Operators.

StatefulSet and Operator Best Practices

Large distributed applications that require state and possibly complicated management and configuration operations benefit from Kubernetes StatefulSets and Operators. Operators are still evolving, but they have the backing of the community at large, so these best practices are based on current capabilities at the time of publication:

- The decision to use StatefulSets should be taken judiciously because stateful applications usually require much deeper management that the orchestrator cannot manage well yet (read "Operators" on page 220 for the possible future answer to this deficiency in Kubernetes).

- The headless Service for the StatefulSet is not automatically created and must be created at deployment time to properly address the pods as individual nodes.

- When an application requires ordinal naming and dependable scaling, this does not always mean it requires the assignment of PersistentVolumes.

- If a node in the cluster becomes unresponsive, any pods that are part of a StatefulSet are not automatically deleted; instead they will enter a `Terminating` or `Unknown` state after a grace period. The only ways to clear this pod are to remove the node object from the cluster, the kubelet beginning to work again and deleting the pod directly, or an Operator force deleting the pod. The force delete should be the last option, and great care should be taken that the node that had the deleted pod does not come back online, because there will now be two pods with the same name in the cluster. You can use `kubectl delete pod nginx-0 --grace-period=0 --force` to force delete the pod.

- Even after force deleting a pod, it might stay in an `Unknown` state, so a patch to the API server will delete the entry and cause the StatefulSet controller to create a new instance of the deleted pod: `kubectl patch pod nginx-0 -p '{"metadata":{"finalizers":null}}'`.

- If you're running a complex data system with some type of leader election or data replication confirmation processes, use `preStop` hook to properly close any connections, force leader election, or verify data synchronization before the pod is deleted using a graceful shutdown process.

- When the application that requires stateful data is a complex data management system, look to determine whether an Operator exists to help manage the more complicated life-cycle components of the application. If the application is built in-house, it might be worth investigating whether it would be useful to package the application as an Operator to add more manageability to the application. See the CoreOS Operator SDK (*https://oreil.ly/gRIej*) for an example.

Summary

Most organizations look to containerize their stateless applications and leave the stateful applications as is. As more cloud native applications run in cloud provider Kubernetes offerings, data gravity becomes an issue. Stateful applications require much more due diligence, but the reality of running them in clusters has been accelerated by the introduction of StatefulSets and Operators. Mapping volumes into containers allows Operators to abstract the storage subsystem specifics away from any application development. Managing stateful applications such as database systems in Kubernetes is still a complex distributed system and needs to be carefully orchestrated using the native Kubernetes primitives of pods, ReplicaSets, Deployments, and StatefulSets. Using Operators that have specific application knowledge built into them as Kubernetes-native APIs may help to elevate these systems into production-based clusters.

## CHAPTER 17

Admission Control and Authorization

Controlling access to the Kubernetes API is key to ensuring that your cluster is not only secured but also can be used as a means to impart policy and governance for all users, workloads, and components of your Kubernetes cluster. In this chapter, we share how you can use admission controllers and authorization modules to enable specific features and how you can customize them to suit your specific needs.

Before we jump into admission control and authorization let's review the API request flow through the API server. Figure 17-1 provides insight on how and where admission control and authorization take place in that flow. It depicts the end-to-end request flow through the Kubernetes API server until the object, if accepted, is saved to storage. Follow the API request from left to right through the API server, paying specific attention to the ordering of admission control and authorization. We will be covering best practices for those in this chapter.

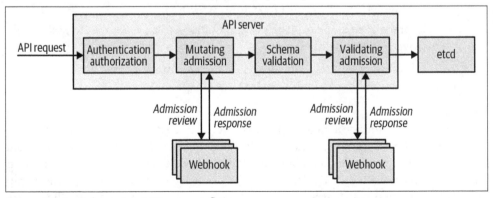

Figure 17-1. Kubernetes API request flow

Admission Control

Have you ever wondered how namespaces are automatically created when you define a resource in a namespace that doesn't already exist? Maybe you've wondered how a default storage class is selected? These changes are powered by a feature called *admission controllers*. In this section, we look at how you can use admission controllers to implement Kubernetes best practices server-side on behalf of the user and how you can utilize admission control to govern how a Kubernetes cluster is used.

What Are They?

Admission controllers sit in the path of the Kubernetes API server request flow and receive requests following the authentication and authorization phases. They are used to either validate or mutate (or both) the request object before saving it to storage. The difference between validating and mutating admission controllers is that mutating admission controllers can modify the request object they admit, whereas validating admission controllers cannot.

Why Are They Important?

Given that admission controllers sit in the path of all API server requests, you can use them in a variety of different ways. Most commonly, admission controller usage can be grouped into the following three categories:

Policy and governance
    Admission controllers allow policy to be enforced to meet business requirements; for example:

  - Only internal cloud load balancers can be used when in the dev namespace.

  - All containers in a pod must have resource limits.

  - Add predefined standard labels or annotations to all resources to make them discoverable to existing tools.

  - All Ingress resources only use HTTPS. For more details on how to use admission webhooks in this context, see Chapter 11.

Security
    You can use admission controllers to enforce a consistent security posture across your cluster. A canonical example is the Pod Security Admission controller, which determines whether a pod should be admitted based on the configuration of security-sensitive fields defined in the pod specification. For instance, it can deny privileged containers or usage of specific paths from the host filesystem. You can enforce more granular or custom security rules using admission webhooks.

Resource management

Admission controllers allow you to validate to provide best practices for your cluster users, for example:

- Ensure all ingress fully qualified domain names (FQDN) fall within a specific suffix.
- Ensure ingress FQDNs don't overlap.
- All containers in a pod must have resource limits.

Admission Controller Types

There are two classes of admission controllers: *standard* and *dynamic*. Standard admission controllers are compiled into the API server and are shipped as plug-ins with each Kubernetes release; they need to be configured when the API server is started. Dynamic controllers, on the other hand, are configurable at runtime and are developed outside the core Kubernetes codebase. The only type of dynamic admission control is admission webhooks, which receive admission requests via HTTP callbacks.

By default, the recommended admission controllers are enabled. You may enable additional admission controllers using the following flag on the Kubernetes API server:

```
--enable-admission-plugins
```

In the current version of Kubernetes, the following admission controllers are enabled by default:

```
CertificateApproval, CertificateSigning, CertificateSubjectRestriction,
DefaultIngressClass, DefaultStorageClass, DefaultTolerationSeconds,
LimitRanger, MutatingAdmissionWebhook, NamespaceLifecycle,
PersistentVolumeClaimResize, PodSecurity, Priority, ResourceQuota,
RuntimeClass, ServiceAccount, StorageObjectInUseProtection,
TaintNodesByCondition,
ValidatingAdmissionWebhook
```

You can find the list of Kubernetes admission controllers and their functionality in the Kubernetes documentation (*https://oreil.ly/APrUE*).

You might have noticed the following from the list of recommended admission controllers to enable: "MutatingAdmissionWebhook,ValidatingAdmissionWebhook." These standard admission controllers don't implement any admission logic themselves; rather, they are used to configure a webhook endpoint running in-cluster to forward the admission request object.

Configuring Admission Webhooks

As previously mentioned, one of the main advantages of admission webhooks is that they are dynamically configurable. It is important that you understand how to effectively configure admission webhooks because there are implications and trade-offs when it comes to consistency and failure modes.

The snippet that follows is a ValidatingWebhookConfiguration resource manifest. This manifest is used to define a validating admission webhook. The snippet provides detailed descriptions of the function of each field:

```
apiVersion: admissionregistration.k8s.io/v1
  kind: ValidatingWebhookConfiguration
  metadata:
    name: ## Resource name
  webhooks:
  - name: ## Admission webhook name, which will be shown to the user when
          ## any admission reviews are denied
    clientConfig:
      service:
        namespace: ## The namespace where the admission
                   ## webhook pod resides
        name: ## The service name that is used to connect to the admission
              ## webhook
        path: ## The webhook URL
      caBundle: ## The PEM encoded CA bundle which will be used to validate the
                ## webhook's server certificate
    rules: ## Describes what operations on what resources/subresources the API
           ## server must send to this webhook
    - operations:
      - ## The specific operation that triggers the API server to send to this
        ## webhook (e.g., create, update, delete, connect)
      apiGroups:
      - ""
      apiVersions:
      - "*"
      resources:
      - ## Specific resources by name (e.g., deployments, services, ingresses)
    failurePolicy: ## Defines how to handle access issues or unrecognized errors,
                   ## and must be Ignore or Fail
    admissionReviewVersions: ["v1"] ## Specify what versions of AdmissionReview
                                    ## objects are accepted
    sideEffects: ## Signal whether the webhook may out-of-band changes that need
                 ## to be handled
    timeoutSeconds: 5 ## How long the API server should wait for a response
                      ## before treating the request as a failure
```

For completeness, let's look at a MutatingWebhookConfiguration resource manifest. This manifest defines a mutating admission webhook. The snippet provides detailed descriptions on the function of each field:

```
apiVersion: admissionregistration.k8s.io/v1
  kind: MutatingWebhookConfiguration
  metadata:
    name: ## Resource name
  webhooks:
  - name: ## Admission webhook name, which will be shown to the user when any
          ## admission reviews are denied
    clientConfig:
      service:
        namespace: ## The namespace where the admission webhook pod resides
        name: ## The service name that is used to connect to the admission
              ## webhook
        path: ## The webhook URL
      caBundle: ## The PEM encoded CA bundle which will be used to validate the
              ## webhook's server certificate
    rules: ## Describes what operations on what resources/subresources the API
          ## server must send to this webhook
    - operations:
      - ## The specific operation that triggers the API server to send to this
        ## webhook (e.g., create, update, delete, connect)
      apiGroups:
      - ""
      apiVersions:
      - "*"
      resources:
      - ## Specific resources by name (e.g., deployments, services, ingresses)
    failurePolicy: ## Defines how to handle access issues or unrecognized errors,
                ## and must be Ignore or Fail
    admissionReviewVersions: ["v1"] ## Specify what versions of AdmissionReview
                ## objects are accepted
    sideEffects: ## Signal whether the webhook may out-of-band changes that need
                ## to be handled
    reinvocationPolicy: ## Control whether mutating webhooks are reinvoked if
                ## another mutation to an object occurs
    timeoutSeconds: 5 ## How long the API server should wait for a response
                ## before treating the request as a failure
```

You might have noticed that both resources are identical, with the exception of the kind and the reinvocationPolicy fields. There is one difference on the backend, however: MutatingWebhookConfiguration allows the admission webhook to return a modified request object, whereas ValidatingWebhookConfiguration does not. Still, it is acceptable to define a MutatingWebhookConfiguration and simply validate; there are security considerations that come into play, and you should consider following the *least-privilege rule*.

You have likely wondered, "What happens if I define a Validating-WebhookConfiguration or MutatingWebhookConfiguration with the resource field under the rule object to be either Validating-WebhookConfiguration or MutatingWebhookConfiguration?" The good news is that neither ValidatingAdmissionWebhooks or Muta-tingAdmissionWebhooks are ever called on admission requests for ValidatingWebhookConfiguration and MutatingWebhookConfiguration objects. This is for good reason: you don't want to accidentally put the cluster in an unrecoverable state.

Admission Control Best Practices

Now that we've covered the power of admission controllers, here are our best practices to help you make the most of using them.

Admission plug-in ordering doesn't matter

In earlier versions of Kubernetes, the ordering of the admission plug-ins was specific to the processing order; hence it mattered. In current supported Kubernetes versions, the ordering of the admission plug-ins as specified as API server flags via `--enable-admission-plugins` no longer matters. Ordering does, however, play a small role when it comes to admission webhooks, so it's important to understand the request flow in this case. Request admittance or rejection operates as a logical AND, meaning if any of the admission webhooks rejects a request, the entire request is rejected and an error is sent back to the user. It's also important to note that mutating admission controllers are always run prior to running validating admission controllers. If you think about it, this makes good sense: you probably don't want to validate objects that you are going to subsequently modify. Figure 17-2 illustrates a request flow via admission webhooks; you will see that the mutating admission controller is run before the validating admission controller.

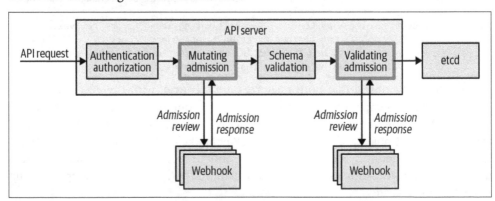

Figure 17-2. An API request flow via admission webhooks

Don't mutate the same fields

Configuring multiple mutating admission webhooks also presents challenges. There is no way to order the request flow through multiple mutating admission webhooks, so it's important to not have mutating admission controllers modify the same fields, because this can result in inconsistent behavior. In the case where you have multiple mutating admission webhooks, we generally recommend configuring validating admission webhooks to confirm that the final resource manifest is what you expect post-mutation because it's guaranteed to be run following mutating webhooks.

Mutating admission webhooks must be idempotent

This means that they must be able to process and admit an object that has already been processed and may have already been modified.

Fail open/fail closed

You might recall seeing the `failurePolicy` field as part of both the mutating and validating webhook configuration resources. This field defines how the API server should proceed in the case where the admission webhooks have access issues or encounter unrecognized errors. You can set this field to either `Ignore` or `Fail`. `Ignore` essentially fails to open, meaning that processing of the request will continue, whereas `Fail` denies the entire request. This might seem obvious, but the implications in both cases require consideration. Ignoring a critical admission webhook could result in policy that the business relies on not being applied to a resource without the user knowing.

One potential solution to protect against this would be to raise an alert when the API server logs that it cannot reach a given admission webhook. `Fail` can be even more devastating by denying all requests if the admission webhook is experiencing issues. To protect against this you can scope the rules to ensure that only specific resource requests are set to the admission webhook. As a tenet, you should never have any rules that apply to all resources in the cluster.

Admission webhooks must respond quickly

If you have written your own admission webhook, it's important to remember that user/system requests can be directly affected by the time it takes for your admission webhook to make a decision and respond. All admission webhook calls are configured with a 30-second timeout, after which time the `failurePolicy` takes effect. Even if it takes several seconds for your admission webhook to make an admit/deny decision, it can severely affect user experience when working with the cluster. Avoid having complex logic or relying on external systems such as databases to process the admit/deny logic.

Scoping admission webhooks

An optional field allows you to scope the namespaces in which the admission web-hooks operate on via the `NamespaceSelector` field. This field defaults to empty, which matches everything, but it can be used to match namespace labels via the use of the `matchLabels` field. We recommend that you always use this field because it allows for an explicit opt-in per namespace.

Always deploy in a separate namespace using NamespaceSelector

When self-hosting a webhook admission controller, deploy the webhook admission controller to a separate namespace and use the `NamespaceSelector` field to exclude resources deployed to that namespace from being processed.

Don't touch the kube-system namespace

The `kube-system` namespace is a reserved namespace that's common across all Kubernetes clusters. It's where all system-level services operate. We recommend never running admission webhooks against the resources in this namespace specifically, and you can achieve this by using the `NamespaceSelector` field and simply not matching the `kube-system` namespace. You should also consider doing this for any system-level namespaces that are required for cluster operation.

Lock down admission webhook configurations with RBAC

Now that you know about all the fields in the admission webhook configuration, you have probably thought of a really simple way to break access to a cluster. It goes without saying that the creation of both a MutatingWebhookConfiguration and ValidatingWebhookConfiguration is a root-level operation on the cluster and must be locked down appropriately using RBAC. Failure to do so can result in a broken cluster or, even worse, an injection attack on your application workloads.

Don't send sensitive data

Admission webhooks are essentially opaque boxes that accept AdmissionRequests and output AdmissionResponses. How they store and manipulate the request is opaque to the user. It's important to think about what request payloads you are send-ing to the admission webhook. In the case of Kubernetes secrets or ConfigMaps, they might contain sensitive information and require strong guarantees about how that information is stored and shared. Sharing these resources with an admission web-hook can leak sensitive information, which is why you should scope your resource rules to the minimum resource needed to validate and/or mutate.

Authorization

We often think about authorization in the context of answering the following question: "Is this user able to perform these actions on these resources?" In Kubernetes, the authorization of each request is performed after authentication but before admission. In this section, we explore how you can configure different authorization modules and better understand how you can create the appropriate policy to serve the needs of your cluster. Figure 17-3 illustrates where authorization sits in the request flow.

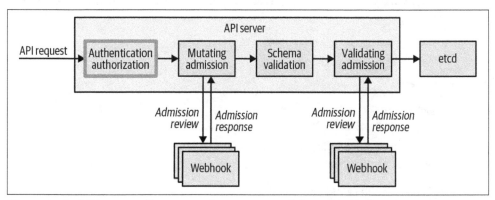

Figure 17-3. API request flow via authorization modules

Authorization Modules

Authorization modules are responsible for either granting or denying permission to access. They determine whether to grant access based on policy that must be explicitly defined; otherwise all requests will be implicitly denied.

Kubernetes ships with the following authorization modules out of the box:

Attribute-Based Access Control (ABAC)
Allows authorization policy to be configured via local files

RBAC
Allows authorization policy to be configured via the Kubernetes API (refer to Chapter 4 for more detail)

Webhook
Allows the authorization of a request to be handled via a remote REST endpoint

Node
Specialized authorization module that authorizes requests from kubelets

The modules are configured by the cluster administrator via the following flag on the API server: `--authorization-mode`. Multiple modules can be configured and are checked in order. Unlike admission controllers, if a single authorization module admits the request, the request can proceed. Only for the case in which all modules deny the request will an error be returned to the user.

ABAC

Let's look at a policy definition in the context of using the ABAC authorization module. The following grants user Mary read-only access to a pod in the `kube-system` namespace:

```
apiVersion: abac.authorization.kubernetes.io/v1beta1
kind: Policy
spec:
  user: mary
  resource: pods
  readonly: true
  namespace: kube-system
```

If Mary were to make the following request, it would be denied because Mary doesn't have access to get pods in the `demo-app` namespace:

```
apiVersion: authorization.k8s.io/v1
kind: SubjectAccessReview
spec:
  resourceAttributes:
    verb: get
    resource: pods
    namespace: demo-app
```

This example introduced a new API group, `authorization.k8s.io`. This set of APIs exposes API server authorization to external services and has the following APIs, which are great for debugging:

SelfSubjectAccessReview
    Access review for the current user

SubjectAccessReview
    Like SelfSubjectAccessReview but for any user

LocalSubjectAccessReview
    Like SubjectAccessReview but namespace specific

SelfSubjectRulesReview
    Returns a list of actions a user can perform in a given namespace

The cool part is that you can query these APIs by creating resources as you typically would. Let's take the previous example and test this using the SelfSubjectAccessReview. The status field in the output indicates that this request is allowed:

```
$ cat << EOF | kubectl create -f - -o yaml
apiVersion: authorization.k8s.io/v1
kind: SelfSubjectAccessReview
spec:
  resourceAttributes:
    verb: get
    resource: pods
    namespace: demo-app
EOF
apiVersion: authorization.k8s.io/v1
kind: SelfSubjectAccessReview
metadata:
  creationTimestamp: null
spec:
  resourceAttributes:
    namespace: kube-system
    resource: pods
    verb: get
status:
  allowed: true
```

In fact, Kubernetes ships with tooling built into kubectl to make this even easier. The kubectl auth can-i command operates by querying the same API as the previous example:

```
$ kubectl auth can-i get pods --namespace demo-app
yes
```

With administrator credentials, you can also run the same command to check actions as another user:

```
$ kubectl auth can-i get pods --namespace demo-app --as mary
yes
```

RBAC

Kubernetes role-based access control is covered in depth in Chapter 4.

Webhook

Using the webhook authorization module allows a cluster administrator to configure an external REST endpoint to delegate the authorization process to. This would run off-cluster and be reachable via URL. The configuration of the REST endpoint is found in a file on the control plane host filesystem and configured on the API server via --authorization-webhook-config-file=SOME_FILENAME. After you've configured it, the API server will send SubjectAccessReview objects as part of the request body to the authorization webhook application, which processes and returns the object with the status field complete.

Authorization Best Practices

Consider the following best practices before making changes to the authorization modules configured on your cluster:

Don't use ABAC on multiple control plane clusters

Given that the ABAC policies need to be placed on the filesystem of each control plane host and kept synchronized, we generally recommend *against* using ABAC in multiple control plane clusters. The same can be said for the webhook module because the configuration is based on a file and a corresponding flag being present. Furthermore, changes to these policies in the files require a restart of the API server to take effect, which is effectively a control plane outage in a single control plane cluster or inconsistent configuration in a multiple control plane cluster. Given these details, we recommend using the RBAC module only for user authorization because the rules are configured and stored in Kubernetes itself.

Don't use webhook modules

Webhook modules, although powerful, are potentially very dangerous. Given that every request is subject to the authorization process, a failure of a webhook service would be devastating for a cluster. Therefore, we generally recommend not using external authorization modules unless you completely vet and are comfortable with your cluster failure modes if the webhook service becomes unreachable or unavailable.

Summary

In this chapter, we covered the foundational topics of admission and authorization and covered best practices. Put these skills to use by determining the best admission and authorization configuration that allows you to customize the controls and policies needed for the life of your cluster.

## CHAPTER 18

GitOps and Deployment

In this chapter, we will discuss GitOps and how it can be used to deploy and manage applications on Kubernetes. We will deep dive into best practices of setting up a GitOps workflow and how to utilize the different tools available to achieve this.

GitOps is a way to do Kubernetes application deployment. It works by utilizing Git as a single source of truth for your Kubernetes resources. With Git at the center of your deployment pipelines, developers and operators can make pull requests to accelerate and simplify application deployments and operations tasks in Kubernetes. This allows you to utilize the same practices for managing Kubernetes resources as you do for managing application code. Developers will be very familiar with the workflow, as they can utilize the same tools they use to work with application code.

We cover the following topics in this chapter:

- What is GitOps?
- Why utilize GitOps?
- GitOps compared to other deployment methods
- Patterns and best practices
- GitOps tooling

We also go through an example GitOps workflow consisting of the following tasks:

- Setting up a GitOps agent with Flux
- Connecting Flux agent to a Git repository
- Syncing resources to a Kubernetes cluster
- Deploying an application to the cluster

What Is GitOps?

GitOps was popularized by the folks at Weaveworks, and the idea and fundamentals were based on their experience of running Kubernetes in production. GitOps takes the concepts of the software development life cycle and applies them to operations. With GitOps, your Git repository becomes your source of truth, and your cluster is synchronized to the configured Git repository. For example, if you update a Kubernetes Deployment manifest, those configuration changes are automatically reflected in the cluster state in Git.

By using this method, you can make it easier to maintain multiclusters that are consistent and avoid configuration drift across the fleet. GitOps allows you to declaratively describe your clusters for multiple environments and drives to maintain that state for the cluster. The practice of GitOps can apply to both application delivery and operations and provides developers with a common toolchain.

Weaveworks Flux was one of the first tools to enable the GitOps approach, and it's the tool we will use throughout the rest of the chapter. Many new tools that have been released into the cloud native ecosystem are worth a look, such as Argo CD, from the folks at Intuit, which has also been widely adopted for the GitOps approach. We will dive more into the tooling available for GitOps later in the chapter.

Figure 18-1 provides a representation of a GitOps workflow. We have a Git repository that contains the application code and Kubernetes manifests for our application. The Flux agent is configured to watch the repo for any changes. When a developer commits a code change, the Flux agent will sync any new changes to the Kubernetes clusters.

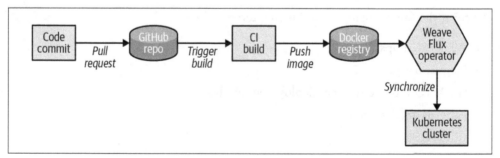

Figure 18-1. GitOps workflow

When building your GitOps workflow, you should consider the four core principals of GitOps defined by the OpenGitOps Project (*https://oreil.ly/3Rz55*):

Declarative configuration
    All configuration is stored in Git as declarative YAML files. This allows for a single source of truth for your cluster configuration.

Versioned configuration
> All configuration is stored in Git, and all changes are tracked and versioned. This allows for easy auditing of changes and rollbacks.

Immutable configuration
> All configuration is immutable. This means that once a change is made, it cannot be modified. This allows for a consistent state of the cluster.

Continuous state reconciliation
> The cluster state is continuously reconciled with the state defined in Git. This allows for the cluster to be in a consistent state.

Why GitOps?

GitOps is a excellent way to manage your Kubernetes clusters, and it can be used to deploy applications to your cluster as well as manage cluster and application configuration. Before we talk about all the benefits, let's first look at how we traditionally deployed and configured applications on Kubernetes.

Figure 18-2 shows a traditional deployment workflow. We have a developer who is working on a new feature for an application. The developer will make changes to the application code and then build a new container image. Next, the developer will push the new container image to a container registry. The developer will then update the Kubernetes manifest to use the new container image, and then apply the changes to the cluster. This is a very manual process, and it can be very time consuming. Some of these steps can be automated with tools, but this can become complex as the number of applications and clusters grow.

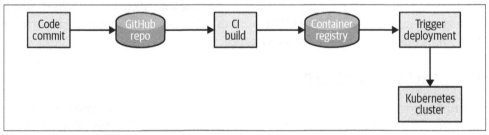

Figure 18-2. Traditional deployment workflow

This workflow can be very error prone, and it can be difficult to track down the source of the issue. It can also be difficult to roll back changes, as you will need to manually revert the changes to the Kubernetes manifest. It can also cause configuration drift, as users may make direct changes to the resources in Kubernetes. Controlling security access to the environment can also become complex with multiple pipelines and users needing access. Auditing of each interaction from change to deployment can also be difficult with multiple pipelines.

We can solve these problems with the following benefits GitOps provides:

Declarative configuration

> All configuration is stored in Git as declarative YAML files. This allows for a single source of truth. It also allows for easy auditing of changes using Git history. Developers will be accustomed to working with Git, so they will be familiar with the workflow.

Version controlled

> Git repository supports immutability and version history. For example, using Git for the previously mentioned configuration will give you a single source from which everything for your application is driven. This allows you to easily track any changes made at any time. It allows you to look at all changes found in Git history and compare those changes.

Continuous reconciliation

> The cluster state is continuously reconciled with the state defined in Git. It also allows for easy rollbacks, as you can simply revert the changes in Git. The system can automatically sync the same state in Git to your cluster. This allows for the cluster to be in a consistent state.

Security

> When you use Git to manage applications deployed to Kubernetes, you gain a complete audit log of all changes to the cluster. All changes are made to the Git repository, and the GitOps agent can automatically reconcile any changes made directly to a Kubernetes resource. This provides a full audit trail of who changed what. It enables consistent operations and enhances security of the environment.

While you may have a very automated CI/CD pipeline, you may still have some manual steps in your workflow. GitOps aims to solve these challenges by automating the workflow and providing a developer-centric workflow.

GitOps Repo Structure

One of the first questions about GitOps is how to structure your Git repository. There are many different ways to structure your Git repository, but all come with their own pros and cons.

Four common strategies for structuring your Git repository are:

Single monorepo

> All Kubernetes manifests and application code are stored in a single repository. This is the simple approach, but it becomes much more difficult as the company scales. This approach also does not allow for separation of concerns, as all teams' source code and Kubernetes manifests will live in a single repository. This can

work well for a smaller company, but you'll quickly outgrow this approach as your company grows. Following is a sample of this type of repo layout structure:

```
├── app-x
│   ├── common
│   └── deploy
│       └── manifest
├── app-y
│   ├── prod
│   └── staging
├── app-z
└── ops-team
    ├── flux
    ├── ingress
    └── prometheus
```

Repo per team

Each team has its own repository, and the Kubernetes manifests are stored in the same repository. This approach allows for better organization and separation of concerns but becomes more difficult to manage as your application portfolio grows over time. Following is a sample of this type of repo layout structure:

```
├── ops-team
│   ├── elk
│   ├── flux
│   └── prometheus
├── team-x
│   └── app-x
│       └── deploy
│           └── manifest
└── team-y
    ├── prod
    └── staging
```

Repo per application

Each application has its own repository, and the Kubernetes manifests are stored in the same repository. This approach allows for better organization and separation of concerns, as it can be locked down to read-only access for the team. The con of using this structure is not everything can be seen in one place. Following is a sample of this type of repo layout structure:

```
── ops-team-repo
│   ├── elk
│   ├── flux
│   └── prometheus

── team-x-repo
│   └── app-x
│       └── deploy
│           └── manifest
│
```

Branch per environment

Each environment has its own branch in the same repository. This approach allows you to promote environments with a simple Git merge. Promoting via a simple Git merge can lead to unwanted changes between environments and merge conflicts between environments. The downside to this is you will typically have a lot of branches, and it can be difficult to manage. This approach also doesn't fit with templating tools such as Kustomize and Helm. Following is a sample of this type of repo layout structure:

```
-- main
-- staging
-- QA
-- dev
```

Typically, you will want to assess your organization and team layout to decide which structure works best for you. Starting with a repo per team is a excellent starting point, as it's a good middle ground that provides clear separation of concerns and easy repo management.

Managing Secrets

Secrets management is a common challenge when implementing a GitOps workflow. There are many different ways to manage secrets, and the best approach will depend on your organization. Next we will dive into the five common approaches you can take with managing secrets in a GitOps way:

Store secrets directly in Git

This approach is the simplest, but it is not recommended. The problem with this approach is that you are storing plain text secrets in a repository that may be public. Even if your repository is internal and private, your are still storing the secrets in plain text. Multiple users may have access to this repo and will then have access to the secrets.

Bake secrets into container image

This approach is a little better than storing secrets in plain text in Git. The problem with this approach is baking secrets into the image will require you to rebuild the image each time secrets are rotated. It also doesn't address the security concerns as multiple users may be able to pull the image and run it. This approach is also not recommended due to security concerns.

Use Kubernetes Secrets

This approach is available directly in Kubernetes and provides an easy way to get started. The problem with this approach is that Kubernetes Secrets are not really secret. What we mean here is that Kubernetes Secrets look encrypted, but are actually just base64 encoded. This approach is also not recommended due to security concerns.

Use Sealed Secrets

Sealed Secrets is a project by Bitnami. It has two components: a cluster controller and a client-side tool call kubeseal. The kubeseal utility uses asymmetric crypto to encrypt secrets that only the controller can decrypt. These secrets can then be stored in Git encrypted and can only be decrypted by the controller in your cluster. This is a recommended approach for managing secrets in a GitOps way.

Store secrets in a secret management tool

This approach allows you to store secrets in a secure location and then access them from your cluster. These secrets can be stored in an external secret management solution like HashiCorp Vault, Azure Keyvault, Google KMS, etc. This approach allows you to use existing solutions you may already have in place and continue with the same workflow. This approach is also a recommended approach for managing secrets in a GitOps way.

While there are lot of different ways to manage secrets, the best approach will depend on your organization. As we discussed, Sealed Secrets and external secret management are the recommended approaches for managing secrets.

Setting Up Flux

Flux is a Kubernetes operator that watches your Git repository for changes and automatically applies those changes to your cluster. Flux is a mature tool for implementing GitOps in your cluster, and it is the tool we will use throughout the rest of the chapter.

First, we'll start by getting minikube set up to deploy Flux. You can install minikube from the minikube website (*https://oreil.ly/GMPMl*). We are using Macs so we'll use `brew` to install minikube:

```
brew install minikube
```

Now we'll install Flux and prepare our cluster to sync to a Git repository. We'll use the `flux` CLI to install Flux. You can install the `flux` CLI from the flux website (*https://oreil.ly/h2_hQ*).

Install Flux CLI:

```
brew install fluxcd/tap/flux
```

Export your GitHub token:

```
export GITHUB_TOKEN=<your-token>
export GITHUB_USER=<your-username>
```

Check that your cluster can install Flux:

```
flux check --pre
```

Bootstrap Flux:

```
flux bootstrap github \
  --owner=$GITHUB_USER \
  --repository=kbp-flux \
  --branch=main \
  --path=./clusters/prod \
  --personal
```

The preceding `bootstrap` command will create a Git repo called kbp-flux in your GitHub account. It will also create a `main` branch and a *clusters/prod* directory. The *clusters/prod* directory will contain the Flux components that will be deployed to your cluster. The *clusters/prod* directory will also contain a *gotk-components.yaml* file that will be used to deploy the Flux components to your cluster. This also installs the Flux components into the `flux-system` namespace.

Now let's check the `flux-system` namespace to see if the Flux components are deployed:

```
kubectl get pods -n flux-system
```

You should see the following output:

```
NAME                                       READY   STATUS    RESTARTS   AGE
helm-controller-8664d9dcfc-4gd2h           1/1     Running   0          6m30s
kustomize-controller-9888f965-ld5g6        1/1     Running   0          6m30s
notification-controller-b6d8458c7-vjb86    1/1     Running   0          6m30s
source-controller-5b68b64c65-pj2tn         1/1     Running   0          6m30s
```

Now let's clone the repo it created to our local machine:

```
git clone https://github.com/$GITHUB_USER/kbp-flux
```

Next we'll add a Flux configuration to our repo and use a public repository on GitHub. We'll use a sample application created by Stefan Prodan from Weaveworks.

Let's create a Git repository manifest pointing to the apps repository's main branch:

```
flux create source git podinfo \
  --url=https://github.com/stefanprodan/podinfo \
  --branch=master \
  --interval=30s \
  --export > ./clusters/prod/podinfo-source.yaml
```

Then we'll configure Flux to deploy the application and apply a Kustomize configuration to the application:

```
flux create kustomization podinfo \
  --target-namespace=default \
  --source=podinfo \
```

```
--path="./kustomize" \
--prune=true \
--interval=5m \
--export > ./clusters/prod/podinfo-kustomization.yaml
```

Now we'll push the changes to our repo:

```
git add -A && git commit -m "Add podinfo Kustomization"

git push
```

We can seeing this being applied by using the Flux CLI:

```
flux get kustomizations
```

You should see the following output:

```
flux get kustomizations --watch
NAME          REVISION                  SUSPENDED  READY  MESSAGE
flux-system   main@sha1:9c3fb6f1        False      True   Applied revision: main@sh...
podinfo       master@sha1:1abc44f0      False      True   Applied revision: master@...
```

We can see the resources have been deployed to our cluster:

```
kubectl get pods -n default
```

Any changes made to the podinfo Kubernetes manifests in the main branch are now reflected in your cluster automatically.

We have now set up Flux in our cluster, bootstrapped it to a Git repository, and configured Flux to deploy an application. We can now start to use Flux to manage our cluster.

This is a very basic example of how to get Flux set up, and if you want a deeper dive into Flux, you can check out the Flux documentation (*https://oreil.ly/F5D2p*).

GitOps Tooling

Many different tools can be used to implement GitOps in your cluster. In this section, we will go over some of the most popular.

When evaluating tools for GitOps, you should consider ease of use, enterprise features, and extensibility. Listed next are both open source and commercial tools that can be used to implement GitOps in your cluster:

Flux

Flux is a Kubernetes operator that watches your Git repository for changes and automatically applies those changes to your cluster. Flux is a mature tool for implementing GitOps in your cluster. Weaveworks also provides a hosted version of Flux. Flux is currently a CNCF graduated project.

ArgoCD

Argo CD is an open source GitOps continuous delivery tool. It monitors your cluster and your declaratively defined infrastructure stored in a Git repository and resolves differences between the two—effectively automating an application deployment. ArgoCD is currently a CNCF graduated project.

Codefresh

Codefresh is a CI/CD platform that can be used to implement GitOps in your cluster. Codefresh provides a hosted platform that provides ArgoCD as a service.

Harness

Harness is a CI/CD platform that can be used to implement GitOps in your cluster. Harness is a mature tool for implementing GitOps in your cluster and provides a hosted version. Harness is geared toward enterprise customers and provides a full suite of continuous delivery features.

GitOps Best Practices

Consider the following best practices when using GitOps with Kubernetes:

- Start with a small application and then scale your efforts for managing everything with a GitOps model. This will allow you to build confidence in your GitOps implementation.

- Evaluate tools that fit your requirements or start with proven OSS tools like Flux or ArgoCD.

- Avoid using branches for your repository layout, as this is the most complex and error-prone repository layout.

- Start with a folder per environment, as this provides flexibility and allows you to use tools like Kustomize or Helm for templating.

- Utilize Sealed Secrets or an external secrets provider to manage secrets in your cluster.

- Remember GitOps is a process and not a tool, and your existing tool set may fit your needs.

Summary

In this chapter, we went over what GitOps is and how it can be used to manage your Kubernetes cluster. We also went over some of the tools that can be used to implement GitOps in your cluster. When looking to see if GitOps is right for you, you should consider what problems you are trying to solve and what your requirements are. If GitOps help solves these problems for you, then looking at a tool like Flux or ArgoCD is a good place to start.

## CHAPTER 19

Security

Kubernetes is a powerful platform for orchestrating cloud native applications. However, under the veneer and polish of the APIs and tooling we know and love lies a large, complex distributed system that requires specific knowledge to secure. Securing Kubernetes is a complex topic that honestly requires its own book; however, there's so much at stake if you overlook taking the time to understand and implement security best practices that we cover it in brief here. The risk of not securing your Kubernetes clusters and workloads properly is the possibility of exposing your data and resources to hackers, malware, and unauthorized access. We would be remiss not to cover some of the main security areas and provide best practices to help along the way.

Given the complexity of Kubernetes, we recommend breaking the problem down into logical layers where you can focus on specific tooling at each layer. A great way to handle security is to follow the "defense in depth" strategy. This requires the use of multiple security measures at each layer to protect Kubernetes and your workloads. Additionally, keep the principle of least privilege in mind, which states that users and workloads should have access only to what they absolutely need to perform their functions. This all sounds great in theory, but what does it look like in practice? This chapter lays out an approach to bucketing security concerns into layers that will help you focus on the solutions and tooling available as well as cluster security, container security, and code security.

Many security best practices have been covered in detail in other chapters, including Chapters 4 through 11. We encourage you to review those chapters as we won't cover those specific topics in the same level of detail again here but rather focus on areas we haven't covered. In particular, this chapter will focus on layers; digging deeper into them, covering security areas, and providing best practices for each layer.

Cluster Security

Given that the Kubernetes control plane is exposed via a set of APIs, the first step in securing the cluster is to regulate and restrict who can access the cluster and what actions they can perform. Next, we will cover the different parts of the Kubernetes control plane and how to secure them.

etcd Access

The default storage system for Kubernetes is etcd. You must ensure that only the Kubernetes API server has access to etcd by using strong credentials that aren't shared. You must also make sure that only the API servers have network access to etcd by using network firewalls. Having direct access to etcd bypasses all the subsequent security measures you have in place, so this is an incredibly important layer to secure.

Authentication

Kubernetes provides several different authentication methods, from bearer tokens and certificates to OpenID Connect (OIDC) and Lightweight Directory Access Protocol (LDAP) integrations. It's important to choose the right authentication model that suits the needs of your business. Security challenges usually appear in the creation, distribution, and storage of Kubeconfig files that users require to authenticate to Kubernetes using tools like kubectl. Using authentication providers allows the retrieval of temporary dynamic tokens rather that using static tokens or certificates that can be easily retrieved by a malicious actor. Papers have been written about instances of malicious code stored in Kubeconfig files, so it's important to control their creation and distribution.

Authorization

We covered authorization in Chapter 17; however, in the context of Kubernetes security it's a powerful tool to enforce who can perform what actions on what resources. The primary tool at your disposal is role-based access control (RBAC). Thankfully, Kubernetes ships with sane defaults; however, you will want to consider incorporating attributes such as team membership as well as namespaces as a way of scaling the number of RBAC resources that need to be created to support a growing number of workloads and users. It's also very important to lock down service accounts using RBAC to confirm that workloads that need access to the Kubernetes API can access only the minimum actions required to perform their function.

TLS

By default, Kubernetes ships with TLS-secured API endpoints enabled. However, different tools and platforms may enable HTTP plaintext communications, which opens up an attack vector as the traffic will be unsecure. It's important to safely store and control access to any certificates and keys in use by Kubernetes and create a plan to rotate them if they are lost or compromised. Having short lifetimes on certificates helps decrease the security risk.

Kubelet and Cloud Metadata Access

Kubelets are the component that run on each node and are responsible for managing the node and the pods that run on it. Unfortunately, Kubelet ships with unauthenticated API enabled. The Kubelet API is extremely powerful and hence should have authentication and authorization enabled. It is likely that your Kubernetes provider has taken care of this for you; however, you should double check if rolling your own Kubernetes cluster. In addition to the Kubelet API, if running on a cloud provider it's likely that the node has access to a cloud metadata API that could be used to expose Kubernetes provisioning credentials. It's recommended that you lock down access to the metadata endpoint using network policies.

Secrets

It's no secret that Kubernetes secrets are not encrypted by default. This means that malicious actors may be able to read these secrets at rest from other vectors. Thankfully, there are several different solutions to help with this. The Kubernetes API server provides the ability to configure an encryption provider that is used in partnership with a configuration file to encrypt specific Kubernetes resources prior to storage in etcd. Encryption providers are typically cloud secret storage services. The only challenge with the current encryption provider implementation is that there is no way to encrypt everything, and the configuration is cumbersome and error prone. Another solution that the Kubernetes community has built is csi secret store (*https://oreil.ly/cbiYT*), which enables secrets to be mounted directly into pods via a temporary RAMDISK filesystem. Using `csi-secret-store` enables you to bypass the need to use Kubernetes secrets and instead directly access them from another trusted secret store.

Logging and Auditing

Kubernetes ships with rich logging configured out of the box. In addition, it's important to also enable audit logging on the API server, which will enable a chronological log of all security-specific events and is configurable via an audit policy. Enabling auditing is only part of the solution; you also must make sure that the audit logs are shipped to a point of aggregation and configure triggers that, if detected, fire an alert to the security team that a suspicious event has occurred.

Cluster Security Posture Tooling

Getting Kubernetes security implemented can be challenging. The great news is that there are open source tools that can scan your Kubernetes clusters, detect security risks, and flag common misconfigurations. Additionally, they can scan all the resources on a cluster and provide best practices. Tools like Kubescape (*https://oreil.ly/qPoHQ*) are quick to run and provide outputs based on severity. It's recommended that you run these tools periodically on all clusters to determine the security posture of your cluster and the resources deployed to it.

Cluster Security Best Practices

Now that we've covered the biggest security areas at the cluster layer, here is a handy list of security best practices for you to check off:

- Lock down etcd access and store access credentials and certificates in secure locations.
- Disable insecure and unauthenticated API endpoints.
- Use authentication providers that provide temporary dynamic tokens rather than static configured tokens in Kubeconfig.
- Ensure users and services follow least privilege.
- Rotate infrastructure credentials regularly.
- Encrypt sensitive data at rest and in transit using keys and certificates.
- Scan container images for vulnerabilities and malware before deploying them to the cluster.
- Enable audit logging and monitoring to detect and respond to suspicious activities.
- Use security scanning tools such as Kubescape to baseline the security posture of your Kubernetes cluster and workloads.

Workload Container Security

Now that we've covered the core components of cluster security we'll look at the security mechanisms at the workload layer. Kubernetes offers many security-focused APIs, which makes configuration simple via the same tooling that you use to deploy your workloads.

Pod Security Admission

Pod Security Admission is a critical piece of your workload security story that allows you to configure and manage all the security-sensitive components of your pod configuration and apply out-of-the-box best practices either to a namespace or at the cluster level. Chapter 10 is dedicated to container and pod security, and we encourage you to review it for further detail.

Seccomp, AppArmor, and SELinux

Linux offers several different security mechanisms that can be utilized in concert with Kubernetes to increase the security posture of your workloads running on Kubernetes. Seccomp allows the creation of syscall filtering profiles that can be used to restrict syscalls coming from a container. Unfortunately, Seccomp profiles aren't talked about enough in the Kubernetes community and have not been configured at all or are misconfigured, allowing containers access to syscalls that could be used for malicious purposes. The Kubernetes community has created a great tool called the security profile operator (*https://oreil.ly/g0tNJ*) that simplifies the management overhead in the configuration of Seccomp profiles. Seccomp is low-hanging fruit to configure from a security perspective, so you are strongly encouraged to enable the Seccomp default profile at a minimum.

AppArmor and SELinux are Linux kernel security modules that allow the granular configuration of per-container mandatory access control. These allow a cluster administrator fine-grained control over what action a container can perform. Using both Pod Security Admission and these Linux security mechanisms, you can control the level of access a container should have to the operating system.

Admission Controllers

Admission controllers are a critical piece in securing your workloads. Kubernetes ships with a set of integrated admission controllers, and all security-related admission controllers are enabled by default. For example, the NodeRestriction admission controller restricts Kubelet's permissions to only be able to modify pods assigned to that specific node. Admission controllers are a big topic, and we suggest you look at Chapter 17 for more details.

Operators

Operators are controllers that use the Kubernetes APIs to provide custom resources to support specific workloads that require application-specific knowledge. If you would like to learn more about the Operator pattern, refer to Chapter 21 where we cover how to implement an operator in detail. In the context of security, unfortunately, many operators ship with very permissive RBAC configuration, for ease of use. Many grant cluster-admin or equivalent privileges, which may serve as an attack vector. Additionally, though less common, these operators may expose other APIs directly, which could provide a pathway to privilege escalation.

Network Policy

Kubernetes ships with a network policy resource; however, you need to double check that your networking provider implements the resource at runtime. For more details on network security, refer to Chapter 9. Kubernetes network policy provides fine-grained control over what network traffic is allowed to enter or exit a service or namespace for resources both internal and external to your cluster. Network policy also allows cluster administrators to create cluster-wide or namespace-specific policies and delegate application-specific network policy to application developers. Network policy covers only IP addresses and TCP/UDP ports and not specific HTTP traffic or endpoint routing access control. If you require application-specific access policies, service meshes include higher-level access policies that aren't part of the integrated APIs of Kubernetes.

Runtime Security

Most Kubernetes clusters utilize container runtimes such as containerd (*https:// oreil.ly/Vyq_N*) or CRI-O (*https://oreil.ly/OiXpP*) by default, which leverage Linux cgroups under the hood to provide a lightweight sandbox for the container runtime. For some security-sensitive workloads, these security guarantees may not be sufficient. There is an ecosystem of different container runtimes, including Kata containers (*https://oreil.ly/ANDje*) and gvisor (*https://oreil.ly/fuNPn*), that provide different security profiles to suit the needs of the workload. Kubernetes supports the use of multiple container runtimes on the same cluster using the `RuntimeClass` field in the pod specification. Please refer to Chapter 10 for more detail on `RuntimeClass`. If you still require a higher level of security then Confidential Containers (*https://oreil.ly/ v66K0*) may also be something to consider. Confidential Containers leverage trusted execution environments (*https://oreil.ly/eSJfX*), which are secure areas on the CPU to run the workload.

Like audit logs at the Kubernetes control plane, you should also invest in audit logging inside the container runtime. Tooling like Falco (*https://oreil.ly/9KOeg*) provides a way to enable audit logging and policy on what the application can do inside the container runtime. Having visibility into the container runtime allows you to monitor and catch malicious behavior as close to the source as possible.

Workload Container Security Best Practices

Kubernetes provides a rich set of security tooling for you to use that can almost be overwhelming to grok. Here is a shortlist of best practices you can focus on to quickly improve the security posture of the workloads running on your cluster:

- Use the Node and RBAC authorizers together, in combination with the NodeRestriction admission plug-in.
- Secure the cluster control plane with strong authentication and authorization mechanisms.
- Review operator API permissions and make sure that they follow least privilege.
- Apply the principle of least privilege to limit the access and permissions of users, pods, and service accounts.
- Implement network policies to restrict the traffic between pods and namespaces.
- Ensure the recommended set of security-based admission controllers are enabled.
- Use Seccomp, AppArmor, and SELinux to minimize the Linux kernel attack surface area the container runtime has access to.
- Ensure dynamic webhook admission controllers are securely configured, scoped to only the resources they need to validate/mutate, and follow least privilege RBAC.
- Provide different container runtime sandboxes on your cluster and use `Runtime Class` to allow application developers to select the runtime to match the security requirements.
- Use admission controllers to validate security best practices on application workloads.

Code Security

Good security starts before the code even reaches Kubernetes. We'll cover some different tools and techniques that you can introduce to further improve your security posture.

Non-Root and Distroless Containers

There are two quick wins when it comes to building containers with an improved security posture. Configure the application process to not run as the root user by specifying a non-root user as part of the container build file. Kubernetes allows for this also to be set as part of the `securityContext` section of the pod specification via the `runAsUser`. This can be used as a fail-safe; however, configuring it in the container build file is preferred. Additionally, many base containers provide commonly used packages preinstalled in the container. These packages may not be used and can introduce vulnerabilities. Tools like distroless (*https://oreil.ly/tpSEA*) and scratch containers provide the smallest possible base container image, which again decreases the attack surface area.

Container Vulnerability Scanning

Many open source tools provide vulnerability scanning of container images. These tools, like Trivy (*https://oreil.ly/pFbNN*), are easy to use and can provide a baseline of the vulnerabilities in a container image. You can then decide whether or not to deploy the container based on these results. However, these tools can be very noisy and provide inconsistent results. Many container repository providers offer integrated vulnerability scanning, and some admission controllers will either admit or deny a workload being deployed based on the vulnerabilities present in the image.

Code Repository Security

Source code repositories are another great place to improve security, and thankfully there is tooling and guidance to help improve the security posture at this layer.

Supply-Chain Levels for Software Artifacts (*https://oreil.ly/CWXWD*), or SLSA, is a framework that provides a checklist of controls based on incremental levels that you can adopt to help improve software security and integrity. Many open source projects are adopting SLSA in an effort to improve software security. The levels are well-defined and when implemented raise the security posture of your source code.

OpenSSF Scorecard (*https://oreil.ly/q-NI3*) gives an automated set of tools that provide a 0–10 score on the security posture of an open source repository that you might be using or considering to use as a dependency. The aggregate score provides an at-a-glance view that can be used to evaluate how trustworthy an open source project is. Many prominent open source projects are adopting this scorecard.

Code Security Best Practices

Good security starts well before a container is deployed to a Kubernetes cluster. The code repository is a great place to also implement security measures to build your in-depth security strategy. Here are some best practices to help guide you to some quick wins on your code security front:

- Review operator API permissions and make sure that they follow least privilege.
- Configure the container build file to run application processes as a non-root user.
- Use container base images like scratch and distroless.

- Perform vulnerability scanning on your containers, and implement policy on whether to allow a container to be deployed based on these vulnerabilities.

- Review OpenSSF scorecards on open source projects that you depend on.

- Implement SLSA level 1 to provide baseline-level transparency and integrity for your software.

Summary

We've covered a lot of ground in this chapter. It's important to understand the full breadth of what it takes to secure Kubernetes so that you can start to break down the problem into smaller pieces that you can implement. Security is a journey and not a destination. It will always be a moving target, and by following these best practices, you can improve the security posture of your Kubernetes cluster and reduce the risk of data breaches or compromises.

## CHAPTER 20

Chaos Testing, Load Testing, and Experiments

This chapter covers three different methods of testing applications in your Kubernetes cluster: chaos testing, load testing, and experiments. All these tools can be used to help you build more useful, more resilient, and more performant applications. They can also provide insight into your application and help you better understand your users and anticipate the impact of changes before you roll them out broadly. This insight enables you to make better decisions and identify areas for future improvements. The following sections will describe the details of each type of test, their goals, and the prerequisites necessary before starting each test.

Chaos Testing

Chaos testing, as its name indicates, is testing your application's ability to respond to chaos in the world, But what exactly does chaos mean? Broadly speaking, for an application chaos means introducing unusual, but not wholly unexpected, edge conditions to your application and seeing how it responds. This enables you to understand if your application is resilient to these edge conditions that may not have previously occurred during development of the application but may occur at some point during the operation of your application. Often our application development occurs during idealized conditions. Unfortunately, when exposed to the real world for long enough, these idealized conditions are challenged by errors and failures that were not present during initial development. These errors can include communication errors, network disconnections, storage problems, and application crashes and failures. Chaos testing is the art of artificially introducing these errors into your test environments and observing how well your application copes with them.

Goals for Chaos Testing

The goals for chaos testing are to introduce extreme conditions into your application's environment and to observe how your application behaves in these conditions, especially, how it fails. It may seem unusual to test in such a way that failures are expected and desirable. While application failures in general are something that we try to avoid, it is far better to observe those failures in a test environment where customers or users are not impacted. We hope to observe failures when chaos testing because they offer an opportunity to fix those problems before they affect our users or customers.

Of course the goal is to introduce a *realistic* level of error into our applications to see how they behave. Introducing a level of error that is not expected to ever occur in practice, while interesting, isn't a great use of time or resources. Excessive levels of error can help us harden our applications for extreme environments, but if such extremes never occur, the effort to harden the application is wasted. Of course each application has a different level of both variability and resilience that is desired. The level of resiliency expected of a mobile game is dramatically less than the level of resilience expected of an aircraft or automobile. Understanding both the resilience requirements and expected environment for your application is a critical prerequisite for high-quality chaos testing.

Prerequisites for Chaos Testing

To build a useful chaos test it is critical to understand the environmental conditions that your application may encounter. This includes both the expected frequency of errors and also the types of errors that may occur. For example, is your storage already resilient? If you are building a stateless application that uses cloud-backed storage as a service, you may not need to test your application for disk failures, but you will likely want to introduce chaos in the communication with the cloud storage solution.

Before beginning chaos testing think about the risks in your application, and identify places where you want to introduce error and at what frequency. When thinking about frequency, remember that we're not trying to test for the average case. The average case is already well represented in your existing integration tests. Instead we are looking to simulate the kind of environment that may occur only once a year or once in a decade. You need to understand your application well enough to describe what is plausible.

In terms of understanding your application, the other important prerequisite for chaos testing is high-quality monitoring for the correctness and behavior of your application. It is one thing to introduce chaos into your environment, but to make this chaos useful you also need to be able to observe the operation of your application with sufficient detail to determine the impact of the chaos and to identify the areas where your application needs hardening to be able to deal with the chaos. In general, this monitoring is necessary for any production application. In addition to its core contributions around resiliency, chaos testing can also be a good test to see if your monitoring and logging are sufficient to handle a real outage.

Chaos Testing Your Application's Communication

One of the easiest ways to inject chaos into your application's communication is to place a proxy between each client and your service. This proxy handles all the network traffic between your client and the server and injects random faults like extra latency, disconnects, or other errors. There are several different open source options for such a proxy, but one of the most popular is ToxiProxy (*https://oreil.ly/N8QNF*), which was created by Shopify. The easiest way to add ToxiProxy to your system is to effectively run a ToxiProxy layer in front of each actual service in your cluster.

To achieve this, you first need to rename each service to which you want to add chaos. To see this in more detail, suppose you have a service named backend that serves traffic on port 8080. You can update a Kubernetes Service named backend to be called backend-real. Then you can create new Deployment of ToxiProxy Pods that are configured using the ToxiProxy command-line tool as follows:

```
toxiproxy-cli create -l 0.0.0.0:8080 -u backend-real:8080 backend
```

When you build the Pod definition for this Deployment of ToxiProxy, you can run this command as a PostStart life-cycle hook. This command configures ToxiProxy to listen on port 8080 within the pod and then forward traffic to your actual backend service, which has the DNS name backend-real.

Next you create a new service named backend to replace the one that you renamed, and you point this service at the Deployment of ToxiProxy Pods that you just created. In this way, any client in your application that communicates with backend will automatically start communicating with the chaos proxy instead.

Finally, you can start adding chaos to your application using the ToxiProxy command-line tool by issuing commands like:

```
kubectl exec $SomeToxiProxyPod -- toxiproxy-cli toxic add -t latency
  -a latency=2000 backend
```

This will add 2,000 milliseconds of latency to all traffic through this proxy. If you create multiple pods in your proxy Deployment, you will need to run this command for each pod, or automate it using scripts or code.

Chaos Testing Your Application's Operation

In addition to testing the operation of your application when communication is flaky, it is also a good idea to test your application in situations where the infrastructure it is running on is flaky or overloaded.

The easiest way to start with infrastructure failures is to simply delete pods. Starting with a single Deployment, you can delete random pods within the Deployment based on its label selector using a simple bash script:

```
NAMESPACE="some-namespace"
LABEL=k8s-app=my-app
PODS=$(kubectl get pods --selector=${LABEL} -n ${NAMESPACE} --no-headers | awk
    '{print $1}')
for x in $PODS; do
    if [ $[ $RANDOM % 10 ] == 0 ]; then
        kubectl delete pods -n $NAMESPACE $x;
    fi;
done
```

Of course if you'd rather have something more complete you can write code using the various Kubernetes clients (*https://oreil.ly/Ib1kp*) out there or even an existing open source tool like Chaos Mesh (*https://chaos-mesh.org*).

Once you have moved through all the microservice Deployments in your application, you can move on to deleting pods within the different services at once. This simulates a more broad outage. You can extend the previous script to randomly delete pods within a particular namespace as follows:

```
NAMESPACE="some-namespace"
PODS=$(kubectl get pods -n ${NAMESPACE} --no-headers | awk '{print $1}')
for x in $PODS; do
    if [ $[ $RANDOM % 10 ] == 0 ]; then
        kubectl delete pods -n $NAMESPACE $x;
    fi;
done
```

Finally, you can simulate complete failures in your infrastructure by causing entire nodes in your cluster to fail. There are a variety of ways to accomplish this. If you are running in a cloud-based Kubernetes, you can use cloud VM APIs to shut down or reboot a machine in your cluster. If you are running on physical infrastructure, you can literally pull the power plug on a particular machine, or reboot it by logging in and running commands. On both physical and virtual hardware you can also cause your kernel to panic by running `sudo sh -c 'echo c > /proc/sysrq-trigger'`.

Here is a simple script that will randomly panic approximately 10% of the machines in a Kubernetes cluster:

```
NODES=$(kubectl get nodes -o jsonpath='{.items[*].status.addresses[0].address}')
for x in $NODES; do
```

```
    if [ $[ $RANDOM % 10 ] == 0 ]; then
      ssh $x sudo sh -c 'echo c > /proc/sysrq-trigger'
    fi
done
```

Fuzz Testing Your Application for Security and Resiliency

One final type of testing in the same spirit as chaos testing is fuzz testing. Fuzz testing is like chaos testing in that it introduces randomness and chaos into your application, but instead of introducing failures, fuzz testing focuses on introducing inputs that are technically legal but extreme in one way or another. For example, you might send an endpoint a legal JSON request but include duplicate fields or data that is especially long or contains random values. The goal of fuzz testing is to test the resiliency of your application to random extreme or malicious inputs. Fuzz testing is most often used in the context of security testing because random inputs can cause unexpected code paths to be executed and to introduce vulnerabilities or crashes. Fuzz testing can help you ensure that your application is resilient to chaos from malicious or erroneous input in addition to failures in the environment. Fuzz testing can be added at both the cluster service level as well as the unit test level.

Summary

Chaos testing is the art of introducing unexpected but not impossible conditions into the runtime of your application and observing what happens. Introducing potential errors and failures into an environment before any failures can impact actual usage of your application helps you identify problem areas before they become critical.

Load Testing

Load testing is used to determine how your application behaves under load. A load-testing tool is used to generate realistic application traffic that is equivalent to real production usage of your application. This traffic can either be artificially generated or recorded traffic from actual production traffic that is replayed. Load testing can be used to either identify areas that may become problems in the future or to ensure that new code and features do not cause regressions.

Goals for Load Testing

The core goal for load testing is to understand how your application behaves under load. When you are building an application, it is generally exposed to occasional traffic from only a few users. This traffic is sufficient for understanding the correctness of the application, but it doesn't help us understand how the application behaves under realistic load. Thus, to understand how your application works when deployed in production, load testing is necessary.

Two fundamental uses of load testing are estimating current capacity and regression prevention. Regression prevention is the use of load testing to ensure that a new release of software can sustain the same load as the previous version of the software. Whenever we roll out a new version of our software there is new code and configuration in the release (if there wasn't, then what is the point of the release?). While these code changes introduce new features and fix bugs, they can also introduce performance regressions: the new version cannot serve the same level of load as the previous version. Of course sometimes these performance regressions are known and expected; for example, a new feature may have made a computation more complex and thus slower, but even in such cases, load testing is necessary to determine how the infrastructure (e.g., the number of pods, the resources they require) needs to be scaled up to sustain production traffic.

In contrast to regression prevention, which is used to catch problems newly introduced into your application, predictive load testing is used to anticipate problems before they occur. For many services, there is a steady growth in the use of the service. Each month there are more users and more requests to your service. In general this is a good thing, but keeping those users happy means continuing to improve your infrastructure to keep up with the new load. Predictive load testing takes the historical growth trends from your application and uses them to test your application as if it were operating in the future. For example, if your application's traffic is growing 10% each month, you might run a predictive load test at 110% of the current peak traffic to simulate how your application will work in the next month. While scaling up your application can be as easy as adding more replicas and more resources, often fundamental bottlenecks in your application require rearchitecting. Predictive load testing allows you to anticipate the future and perform these changes without the emergency of a user-facing outage due to increased load.

Predictive load testing can also be used to anticipate how an application will behave prior to launch. Rather than using historical information, you can use your predictions about usage at launch to ensure that such a launch is successful and not a disaster.

Prerequisites for Load Testing

Load testing is used to ensure that your application can perform while operating under significant load. Further, like chaos testing, load testing can also introduce failure conditions in your application due to that load. Consequently, load testing shares the same prerequisites as chaos testing around application observability. To successfully use a load test, you need to be able to verify that your application is operating correctly and have enough information to gain insight into where and why failures occur if they do.

In addition to the core observability of your application, another critical prerequisite for load testing is the ability to generate realistic load for your test. If your load test doesn't closely mimic real-world user behaviors, then it is of little use. As a concrete example, imagine if your load test continuously makes repeated requests for a single user. In many applications, such traffic will produce an unrealistic cache hit rate, and your load test will seem to show an ability to handle large amounts of load that is not possible under more realistic traffic.

Generating Realistic Traffic

Methods for generating real-world traffic patterns for your application vary depending on your application. For certain types of more read-only sites, for example, a news site, it may be sufficient to repeatedly access each of the different pages using some sort of probability distribution. But for many applications, especially those that involve both reading and writing operations, the only way to generate a realistic load test is to record real-world traffic and play it back. One of the easiest ways to do this is to write the complete details of each HTTP request to a file, and then resend those requests back to the server at a later time.

Unfortunately, such an approach can have complications. The first and foremost consequence of recording all the requests to your application is user privacy and security. In many cases requests to an application contain both private information as well as security tokens. If you record all this information to a file for playback, you must be very, very careful in handling these files to ensure that user privacy and security are respected.

Another challenge with recording and playing back actual user requests has to do with the timeliness of the requests themselves. If there is a time component to the requests, for example, search queries about the latest news events, these requests will have a very different behavior several weeks (or months) after those events have occurred. There will be many fewer messages related to old news. Timeliness also affects the correct behavior of your application. Requests often contain security tokens and if you are doing security properly, those tokens are short lived. This means that recorded tokens will likely not work correctly when verified.

Finally, when requests write data to backend storage systems, replaying requests that modify storage must be performed in a copy or snapshot of the production storage infrastructure. If you are not careful about how you set this up, you can cause significant problems with customer data.

For all these reasons, simply recording and playing back requests, though easy, is not a best practice. Instead the more useful way to use requests is to build up a model of the ways in which your service is used. How many read requests? For what resources? How many writes? Using this model you can generate synthetic load that has realistic characteristics.

Load Testing Your Application

Once you have generated the requests to power your load test, it is simply a matter of applying that load to your service. Unfortunately, it is rarely that simple. In most real-world applications there are databases and other storage systems involved. To correctly simulate your application under load, you also need to write into storage systems, but not to the production data store since this is artificial load. Thus, to correctly load test your application, you need to be able to turn up a true copy of your application with all its dependencies.

Once your application clone is up and running, it is a matter of sending all the requests. It turns out large-scale load testing is also a distributed systems problem. You will want to use a large number of different pods to send load onto your application. This is to ensure an even distribution of requests through the load balancers and to make it feasible to send more load than a single pod's network can support. One of the choices you will need to make is whether to run these load testing pods within the same cluster as your application or in a separate cluster. Running the pods within the same cluster maximizes the load that you can send to your application, but it does exercise the edge load balancers that bring traffic from the internet onto your application. Depending on which parts of your application you wish to test, you may want to run the load within the cluster, outside of the cluster, or both.

Two popular tools for running distributed load tests in Kubernetes are JMeter (*https://oreil.ly/MXBgj*) and Locust (*https://locust.io*). Both provide ways to describe the load that you want to send to your service and allow you to deploy distributed load test bots to Kubernetes.

Tuning Your Application Using Load Tests

In addition to using load tests to prevent performance regressions and to anticipate future performance problems, load testing can also be used to optimize the resource utilization of your application. For any given service multiple variables can be tuned and can impact system performance. For the purposes of this discussion we consider three: number of pods, number of cores, and memory.

At first it might seem that an application would perform the same given the same number of replicas times cores. That is, an application with five pods, each with three cores, would perform the same as an application with three pods, each with five cores. In some cases this is true, but in many cases it is not; the specific details of the service and location of its bottlenecks often cause differences in behavior that are hard to anticipate. For example, an application built in a language like Java, dotnet, or Go that provides garbage collection: with one or two cores, the application is going to tune the garbage collector significantly differently than if it has many cores.

The same thing is true of memory. More memory means that more things can be kept in cache, and this often leads to more performance, but this benefit has an asymptotic limit. You cannot simply throw more memory at a service and expect it to continue to improve in performance.

Often times the only way to understand how your application will behave under different configurations is to actually do the experimentation. To do this properly you can set up an experimental set of configurations with different values for pods, cores, and memory and run each configuration through a load test. Using the data from these experiments you often can identify patterns of behavior that can drive insight into the particular details of your system's performance, and you can use the results to select the most efficient configuration for your service.

Summary

Performance is a critical part of building an application that delights users. Load testing ensures that you do not introduce regressions that impact performance and lead to poor user experiences. Load testing can also serve as a time machine, enabling you to imagine your application's behavior in the future and make changes to your architecture to support additional growth. Load testing can also help you understand and optimize your resource usage, lowering costs and improving efficiency.

Experiments

In contrast to chaos testing and load testing, experiments are used not to discover problems in your service's architecture and operation but to identify ways to improve how your users use your service. An experiment is a long-running change to your service, generally in the user experience, in which a small percentage of users (for example, 1% of all traffic) receive a slightly different experience. From examining the difference between the control (the group with no changes) and the experiment (the group that had a different experience) you can understand the impact of the changes and decide whether to continue to experiment or to roll out the changes more broadly.

Goals for Experiments

When we build a service, we build it with a goal in mind. That goal more often than not is to provide something that is useful, easy to use, and pleasing to our customers or users. But how can we know if we have achieved that goal? It's relatively easy to see that our site breaks in the presence of chaos or that it can only handle a small amount of load before failing, but understanding how a user experiences our services can be tricky to determine.

Several traditional methods for understanding user experience include surveys, in which you ask users how they feel about the current service. While this can be useful in understanding the current performance of our service, it is much harder to use surveys to predict the impact of future changes. Much like performance regressions, it is far better to know the impact *before* the change is rolled out everywhere. That is the main goal of any experiment: to learn with minimal impact on our users' experience.

Prerequisites for an Experiment

Just like when we were kids in a science fair, every good experiment starts with a good hypothesis, and that is a natural prerequisite for our service experiments also. There is some change that we are thinking about making, and we need to have a guess as to what impact it will have on user experience.

Of course to understand the impact on user experience, we also need to be able to measure the user experience. This data can come in the form of the surveys mentioned previously, through which you can gather metrics like satisfaction ("please rate us one through five") or net promoter score ("how likely are you to recommend this to a friend?"). Or it can come from passive metrics associated with user behavior ("how long did they spend on our site?" or "how many pages did they click on?" etc.).

Once you have a hypothesis and a way to measure user experience, you're ready to begin the experiment.

Setting Up an Experiment

There are two different ways to set up an experiment. The approach you take depends on the specific things being tested. You can include multiple possible experiences in a single service, or you can deploy two copies of your service and use a service mesh to direct traffic between them.

The first approach is to check both versions of the code into your release binary and switch between the experiment and control using some property of the requests that your service is receiving. You can use HTTP headers, cookies, or query parameters to enable users to explicitly opt in to the experiment. Alternatively you can use characteristics of the requests, such as the source IP, to randomly select users for your experiments. For example, you could choose people for the experiments whose IP addresses ended in one.

A common way to implement experiments is to use explicit feature flagging where a user decides to opt in to an experiment by supplying the query parameter or cookie that turns on the experiment. This is a good way to allow specific customers to try new functionality or to demonstrate a new feature without releasing it broadly. Feature flags can also be used to rapidly turn features on or off in the case of instability. Numerous open source projects, for example Flagger (*https://flagger.app*), can be used to implement feature flagging.

The benefit of placing the experiment in the same binary as your control code is that it is simplest to roll it out into production, but this simplicity also leads to two drawbacks. The first is that if the experimental code is unstable and crashes, it can also impact your production traffic. The other is that because any changes are tied to a complete release of your service it is much slower to make changes to update the experiment or to roll out new experiments.

The second approach to experiments is to deploy two (or more) different versions of your service. In this approach, you have the control production service that receives the bulk of the traffic and a separate experimental deployment of your service that receives only a fraction of the traffic. You can use a service mesh (described in Chapter 9) to route a small percentage of traffic to this experimental deployment instead of the production deployment. Though this approach is more complex to implement, it is significantly more agile and robust than including experimental code in your production binary. Because it requires a completely new deployment of code the upfront cost of setting up an experiment is increased, but because it has no impact on anything except the experimental traffic, you can easily deploy new versions of the experiment (or even multiple versions of the experiment) at any time without impacting the bulk of your traffic.

Additionally, because the service mesh can measure whether requests are successful, if the experimental code starts failing it can quickly be removed from use and user impact is minimized. Of course detecting these failures can be a challenge. You need to make sure that the experimental infrastructure is monitored independently from the standard production monitoring; otherwise the experimental failures may be lost in successful requests that are processed by the current production infrastructure. Ideally the name of the pod or the deployment provides sufficient context to determine if the monitoring signals are from production or an experiment.

In general, using separate deployments and some sort of traffic router like a service mesh is the best practice for experiments, but it is a lot of infrastructure to set up. For your initial experiments, or if you are a small team that is already fairly agile, it may be that checking in experimental code is the easiest path to experimentation and iteration.

Summary

Experiments enable you to understand the impact of changes on your users' experience before those changes are rolled out to the broad user base. Experiments play a critical role in helping us quickly understand what changes are possible and how we can update our services to better serve our users. Experiments make the improvement of our services easier, quicker, and safer.

Chaos Testing, Load Testing, and Experiments Summary

In this chapter we've covered a variety of different ways to learn more about your service to make it more resilient, more performant, and more useful. Just as testing your code with unit tests is a critical part of the software development process, testing your service with chaos, load, and experiments is a critical part of service design and operation.

## CHAPTER 21

Implementing an Operator

A key tenet of Kubernetes is its ability to be extended beyond the core API by the operators of the system. Many (these authors included) believe this extensibility was a driving factor in the dominance of Kubernetes in the marketplace. As developers began to create applications that would run on Kubernetes, operators developed helper applications that knew how to call the Kubernetes API and automate much of the routine work they would need to do to keep the applications stable. Many of these applications were bash scripts or helper containers running in a cluster.

In 2016, a key group of Kubernetes contributors, led by CoreOS (now Red Hat), positioned an Operator pattern to allow for easier development and implementation of Kubernetes applications. The Operator pattern outlined a way to package, deploy, and maintain an application that is integrated with the Kubernetes API and client tooling such as kubectl. Using an Operator, an application developer could natively create an application that could run in Kubernetes, be integrated with the existing Kubernetes process, and embed institutional knowledge. This knowledge wasn't limited to deploying the application but also allowed for smooth upgrades, reconciliation across disparate services, custom scaling processes, and embedding observability into the complex system, which drove the acceptance of the framework into the Kubernetes ecosystem.

The goal of this chapter is not to teach you how to write an Operator. Numerous resources are available on this topic and have much more in-depth coverage than what can be covered in a single chapter. The goal here is to introduce the concept and explain when and why to implement an Operator into your environment while sharing some of the key considerations you will need to plan.

Operator Key Components

The Operator Framework (*https://oreil.ly/YG0gU*) itself is an open source toolkit with a well-defined software development kit (SDK), life-cycle management, and publication tooling. A few projects out there have been built around the concept of the Operator pattern and making it easier for the community to develop. The members of the API Machinery SIG in the Kubernetes community sponsored the development of kubebuilder to offer a base SDK for working with the two main components of an Operator: Custom Resource Definitions (CRDs) and controllers. Sponsored by Google as part of the community, kubebuilder is being positioned as the base SDK for all operators and other projects such as KUDO, KubeOps, and Kopf. Examples in this chapter will be based on kubebuilder syntax where specific code is discussed; however, the concepts are very similar in many of the Operator SDKs out there.

Custom Resource Definitions

Often the need to define complex application dependencies and resources using only native Kubernetes resources becomes challenging in actual practice. The platform engineers usually have to build complex yaml templates, with rendering pipelines and additional resources like jobs and init containers to manage much of the customization needed to run a large application. However, the Custom Resource Definition allows developers to extend the Kubernetes API to provide new resource types that can then better represent declaratively the resource needs of an application.

Kubernetes allows for the dynamic registration of new resources using the `Custom ResourceDefinition` interface and will automatically register a new RESTful resource path for the versions you specify. Unlike many of the resources that are built into Kubernetes natively, CRDs can be maintained independently and updated when needed. CRDs will define a specification of the resource under the `spec` field and will have a `spec.scope` defining if the custom resources that are created from the CRD will be namespaced or cluster-wide resources. Before we see a CRD and its custom resource implementation, a small diversion into nomenclature of the Kubernetes API is important.

Kubernetes API objects, resources, version, group, and kind

Objects in Kubernetes are the actual entities that are persisted in the system to represent the state of the cluster. The object itself is what the typical CRUD operations act on within a cluster. In essence an object will be the entire resource definition in state such as a pod or PersistentVolume.

A Kubernetes resource is an endpoint in the API that represents a collection of objects of a specific kind. So a pod resource will contain a collection of Pod objects. One can see this in the cluster easily with:

```
kubectl api-versions
NAME               SHORTNAMES  APIVERSION                NAMESPACED  KIND
bindings                       v1                        true        Binding
componentstatu... cs           v1                        false       ComponentS...
configmaps        cm           v1                        true        ConfigMap
edited for space
mutatingwebhoo...              admissionregistration...  false       MutatingWe...
validatingwebh...              admissionregistration...  false       Validating...
customresource... crd,crds     apiextensions.k8s.io/...  false       CustomReso...
apiservices                    apiregistration.k8s.i...  false       APIService
controllerrevi...              apps/v1                   true        Controller...
daemonsets        ds           apps/v1                   true        DaemonSet
deployments       deploy       apps/v1                   true        Deployment
replicasets       rs           apps/v1                   true        ReplicaSet
statefulsets      sts          apps/v1                   true        StatefulSet
```

Groups bring objects of similar concern together. This grouping combined with versioning allows for objects within the same group to be managed individually and updated as needed. The group is represented in the RESTful path in the apiVersion field of the object. In Kubernetes the core group (also described as legacy) will fall under the */api/REST* path. Often seen in a Pod spec or Deployment yaml in the apiVersion field with the base path removed as such:

```
kind: Deployment
apiVersion: apps/v1
metadata:
  name: sample
spec:
  selector:
    matchLabels:
```

As with any good API, Kubernetes APIs are versioned and support multiple versions using different API paths. There are guidelines for Kubernetes versioning and the same guidelines should be used when versioning Custom Resources. APIs can also fall into different levels based on support or stability of the API, so often you will see Alpha, Beta, or Stable APIs. In a cluster, for example, you may have v1 and v1beta1 for the same group:

```
kubectl api-versions
---- excerpt
autoscaling/v1
autoscaling/v2
autoscaling/v2beta1
autoscaling/v2beta2
```

Often, Kind and Resource are used as the same context; however, a resource is a concrete implementation of a Kind. Often there is a direct Kind to Resource relationship such as when defining a `kind: Pod` specification that will create a pod resource in the cluster. On occasion there is a one to many relationship such as the `Scale` kind, which can be returned by different resources such as `Deployment` or `ReplicaSet`. This is known as a subresource.

Putting these principles together we can begin to model our API for our customer resource. For the rest of this chapter, kubebuilder-generated snippets will be used, but the actual code is not important and will be only a partial representation. The concept discussed is what the focus will be and how it relates to best practices when implementing an Operator.

Creating Our API

A Customer Resource Definition can be created in yaml by hand; however, kubebuilder and other Operator SDKs will automatically generate the API definition for you based on the code provided. In kubebuilder you can create a scaffold of the API and the required Go code after your project is initialized. To initialize a project, once kubebuilder and its prerequisites are met, you can simply run an `init` command from a new directory that will contain your project files:

```
$ kubebuilder init --domain platform.evillgenius.com
    --repo platform.evillgenius.com/platformapp --project-name=pe-app
Writing kustomize manifests for you to edit...
Writing scaffold for you to edit...
Get controller runtime:
$ go get sigs.k8s.io/controller-runtime@v0.14.1
go: downloading sigs.k8s.io/controller-runtime v0.14.1
go: downloading k8s.io/apimachinery v0.26.0
.................................................. removed for brevity ...
Update dependencies:
$ go mod tidy
go: downloading github.com/go-logr/zapr v1.2.3
go: downloading go.uber.org/zap v1.24.0
go: downloading github.com/onsi/ginkgo/v2 v2.6.0
go: downloading github.com/onsi/gomega v1.24.1
go: downloading gopkg.in/check.v1 v1.0.0-20200227125254-8fa46927fb4f
go: downloading github.com/niemeyer/pretty v0.0.0-20200227124842-a10e7caefd8e
Next: define a resource with:
$ kubebuilder create api
```

This will create some basic files and placeholder boilerplate code:

```
$ tree
.
├── config
│   ├── default
│   │   ├── kustomization.yaml
```

```
│   │   ├── manager_auth_proxy_patch.yaml
│   │   └── manager_config_patch.yaml
│   ├── manager
│   │   ├── kustomization.yaml
│   │   └── manager.yaml
│   ├── prometheus
│   │   ├── kustomization.yaml
│   │   └── monitor.yaml
│   └── rbac
│       ├── auth_proxy_client_clusterrole.yaml
│       ├── auth_proxy_role_binding.yaml
│       ├── auth_proxy_role.yaml
│       ├── auth_proxy_service.yaml
│       ├── kustomization.yaml
│       ├── leader_election_role_binding.yaml
│       ├── leader_election_role.yaml
│       ├── role_binding.yaml
│       └── service_account.yaml
├── Dockerfile
├── go.mod
├── go.sum
├── hack
│   └── boilerplate.go.txt
├── main.go
├── Makefile
├── PROJECT
└── README.md
```

Once that is completed you can create the scaffold for the API definition by running the following:

```
$ kubebuilder create api --group egplatform --version v1alpha1 --kind EGApp
Create Resource [y/n]
y
Create Controller [y/n]
y
Writing kustomize manifests for you to edit...
Writing scaffold for you to edit...
api/v1alpha1/egapp_types.go
controllers/egapp_controller.go
Update dependencies:
$ go mod tidy
Running make:
$ make generate
mkdir -p /home/eddiejv/dev/projects/operators/platformapp/bin
test -s /home/eddiejv/dev/projects/operators/platformapp/bin/controller-gen
  && /home/eddiejv/dev/projects/operators/platformapp/bin/controller-gen
  --version | grep -q v0.11.1 || \
GOBIN=/home/eddiejv/dev/projects/operators/platformapp/bin
  go install sigs.k8s.io/controller-tools/cmd/controller-gen@v0.11.1
go: downloading sigs.k8s.io/controller-tools v0.11.1
go: downloading github.com/spf13/cobra v1.6.1
go: downloading github.com/gobuffalo/flect v0.3.0
```

```
go: downloading golang.org/x/tools v0.4.0
go: downloading k8s.io/utils v0.0.0-20221107191617-1a15be271d1d
go: downloading github.com/mattn/go-colorable v0.1.9
/home/eddiejv/dev/projects/operators/platformapp/bin/controller-gen
  object:headerFile="hack/boilerplate.go.txt" paths="./..."
Next: implement your new API and generate the manifests (e.g. CRDs,CRs) with:
$ make manifests
```

This will add an API, bin, and controllers directories and update other directories with more boilerplate code. The two main files to work with are the *api/<version>/<kind>_types.go* and *controllers/<kind>_controller.go* files.

To start modifying your API to map to the resources you want expressed in your CRD, you will add new fields to the struct created for your new object in the *api/<version>/<kind>_types.go* file. So for our example here we add the following:

```
type EGAppSpec struct {
    // INSERT ADDITIONAL SPEC FIELDS - desired state of cluster
    // Important: Run "make" to regenerate code after modifying this file

    // Foo is an example field of EGApp. Edit egapp_types.go to remove/update
    Foo string `json:"foo,omitempty"`

}

// EGAppStatus defines the observed state of EGApp
// +kubebuilder:subresource:status
type EGAppStatus struct {
    // INSERT ADDITIONAL STATUS FIELD - define observed state of cluster
    // Important: Run "make" to regenerate code after modifying this file

}
```

If you are not a Go programmer do not worry as there are other projects such as Java Operator SDK and Kopf that can help you build Operators in either Java or Python as well. The Operator Framework SDK also has support to create Operators from Ansible or Helm.

To continue with the example, we want to add specific fields to the spec and also have a status. To update specification the information can be added as such:

```
type EGAppSpec struct {
    // INSERT ADDITIONAL SPEC FIELDS - desired state of cluster
    // Important: Run "make" to regenerate code after modifying this file

    // AppId is the unique AppId match to internal catalog systems
    AppId string `json:"appId,omitempty"`

    // +kubebuilder:validation:Enum=java;python;go
    Framework string `json:"framework"`
```

```
    // +kubebuilder:validation:Optional
    // +kubebuilder:validation:Enum=lowMem;highMem;highCPU;balanced
    // +kubebuilder:default="lowMem"
    InstanceType string `json:"instanceType"`

    // +kubebuilder:validation:Enum=dev;stage;prod
    Environment string `json:"environment"`

    // +kubebuilder:validation:Optional
    // +kubebuilder:default:=1
    ReplicaCount int32 `json:"replicaCount"`
}

// EGAppStatus defines the observed state of EGApp
// +kubebuilder:subresource:status
type EGAppStatus struct {
    // INSERT ADDITIONAL STATUS FIELD - define observed state of cluster
    // Important: Run "make" to regenerate code after modifying this file

    Pods []string `json:"pods"`
}
```

What is of importance here is we mapped the information we need in the spec that defines the application into data types and gave them a JSON representation. The `// +kubebuilder:` lines that look like they are in comments are marker comments that kubebuilder uses to generate code based on the information provided. As an example, we are declaring to kubebuilder to generate all the needed code to ensure that the `Framework` field is validated against three possible strings of Java, Python, or Go. That is why it was noted at the end of the kubebuilder `create api` command that any changes made to the API require a `make generate` to update all the other generated code required and the `make manifests` to update all the yaml manifests' boilerplate. This will then give you a starting CRD that looks something like this:

```
apiVersion: apiextensions.k8s.io/v1
kind: CustomResourceDefinition
metadata:
  annotations:
    controller-gen.kubebuilder.io/version: v0.11.1
  creationTimestamp: null
  name: egapps.egplatform.platform.evillgenius.com
spec:
  group: egplatform.platform.evillgenius.com
  names:
    kind: EGApp
    listKind: EGAppList
    plural: egapps
    singular: egapp
  scope: Namespaced
  versions:
  - name: v1alpha1
```

```yaml
    schema:
      openAPIV3Schema:
        description: EGApp is the Schema for the egapps API
        properties:
          apiVersion:
            description: 'APIVersion defines the versioned schema of this
              representation of an object. Servers should convert recognized
              schemas to the latest internal value, and may reject unrecognized
              values. More info: https://git.k8s.io/community/contributors/
              devel/sig-architecture/api-conventions.md#resources'
            type: string
          kind:
            description: 'Kind is a string value representing the REST resource
              this object represents. Servers may infer this from the endpoint
              the client submits requests to. Cannot be updated. In CamelCase.
              More info: https://git.k8s.io/community/contributors/devel/
              sig-architecture/api-conventions.md#types-kinds'
            type: string
          metadata:
            type: object
          spec:
            description: EGAppSpec defines the desired state of EGApp
            properties:
              appId:
                description: Foo is an example field of EGApp. Edit
                  egapp_types.go to remove/update
                type: string
              environment:
                enum:
                - dev
                - stage
                - prod
                type: string
              framework:
                enum:
                - java
                - python
                - go
                type: string
              instanceType:
                default: lowMem
                enum:
                - lowMem
                - highMem
                - highCPU
                - balanced
                type: string
              replicaCount:
                default: 1
                format: int32
                type: integer
              required:
```

```
        - environment
        - framework
       type: object
     status:
       description: EGAppStatus defines the observed state of EGApp
       properties:
         pods:
           items:
             type: string
           type: array
       required:
       - pods
       type: object
   type: object
 served: true
 storage: true
 subresources:
   status: {}
```

You will notice that kubebuilder also added the OpenAPI validation information so the CR can be validated against the requirements of the CRD. Kubebuilder also allows for the creation of additional validators using logic via a webhook. To add admission webhooks for your CRD, by implementing the Defaulter and/or the Validator interface, kubebuilder provides code generation to create the webhook server and registers it with the controller manager. Using the kubebuilder CLI this can easily be generated in a scaffold again with:

```
$ kubebuilder create webhook --group egplatform --version v1alpha1 --kind EGApp
    --defaulting --programmatic-validation
```

We can deploy this custom resource easily with kubebuilder:

```
$ make install
test -s /home/eddiejv/dev/projects/operators/platformapp/bin/controller-gen &&
/home/eddiejv/dev/projects/operators/platformapp/bin/controller-gen --version |
grep -q v0.11.1 || \
GOBIN=/home/eddiejv/dev/projects/operators/platformapp/bin go install
sigs.k8s.io/controller-tools/cmd/controller-gen@v0.11.1/home/eddiejv/dev/
projects/operators/platformapp/bin/controller-gen rbac:roleName=manager-role
crd webhook paths="./..." output:crd:artifacts:config=config/crd/bases
/home/eddiejv/dev/projects/operators/platformapp/bin/kustomize build config/crd
| kubectl apply -f -
customresourcedefinition.apiextensions.k8s.io/
egapps.egplatform.platform.evillgenius.com created
```

We can then see from the kubectl command that the egapp resource is now installed in the cluster, and we can see the structure of the resource itself:

```
$ kubectl explain egapp --recursive
KIND:      EGApp
VERSION:   egplatform.platform.evillgenius.com/v1alpha1
```

```
DESCRIPTION:
     EGApp is the Schema for the egapps API

FIELDS:
   apiVersion   <string>
   kind <string>
   metadata     <Object>
      annotations        <map[string]string>
      creationTimestamp <string>
      deletionGracePeriodSeconds      <integer>
      deletionTimestamp <string>
      finalizers        <[]string>
      generateName      <string>
      generation        <integer>
      labels   <map[string]string>
      managedFields     <[]Object>
         apiVersion     <string>
         fieldsType     <string>
         fieldsV1       <map[string]>
         manager        <string>
         operation      <string>
         subresource    <string>
         time   <string>
      name     <string>
      namespace <string>
      ownerReferences   <[]Object>
         apiVersion     <string>
         blockOwnerDeletion     <boolean>
         controller     <boolean>
         kind   <string>
         name   <string>
         uid    <string>
      resourceVersion   <string>
      selfLink <string>
      uid      <string>
   spec <Object>
      appId    <string>
      environment       <string>
      framework <string>
      instanceType      <string>
      replicaCount      <integer>
   status       <Object>
      pods     <[]string>
```

Now that the API has been created and installed in the cluster, it can't really do anything. At this stage if we create a yaml and deploy it to the cluster in a namespace it will create an entry in etcd with the information stated in the yaml, but until we create the controller, nothing will happen. Now let's explore how the controller works.

Controller Reconciliation

The controller code was created when the API was created and will have much of the boilerplate needed to start building the reconciliation logic needed. Note that the code is not important here, but the understanding of what is happening behind the scenes is key to understanding what an Operator can do. The controller code is located in the *controllers/<kind>_controller.go* file. The Reconcile method is where the logic should be added. Before we dive into that, a plan for reconciliation and understanding the phases is required. This is shown in Figure 21-1.

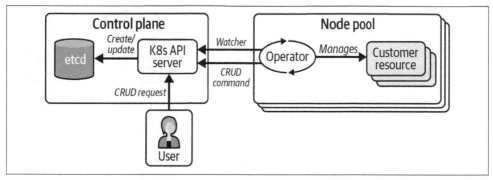

Figure 21-1. Operator overview

Operators are services that watch for events related to the resource types the operator cares about. When an event occurs that meets the criteria, called a predicate in the Operator pattern, the Operator begins the process of reconciling the desired state to the running state. During the reconciliation process, any logic to determine how to handle the state change is implemented; regardless of what exactly changed, the reconcile cycle handles it all. This is known as level-based triggering, and while less efficient, it is well-suited for complex distributed system like Kubernetes.

In the Operator, developers will code into the Reconcile method the logic represented in Figure 21-2:

1. Is there an instance of the Custom Resource?

2. If so, do some validation.

3. If valid, check to see if state needs to be changed and change it.

If the resource is being deleted, the logic to handle cleanup is also implemented here.

If your CR implements other resources that it does not directly own, you should implement a Finalizer to handle the cleanup of those sources and block the deletion of the CR until the finalizer completes its process. This is often used for CRs that will create resources on a cloud provider, for example, or PersistentVolumes as they may have some reclaim policy defined that needs to be honored before the PV is considered deleted.

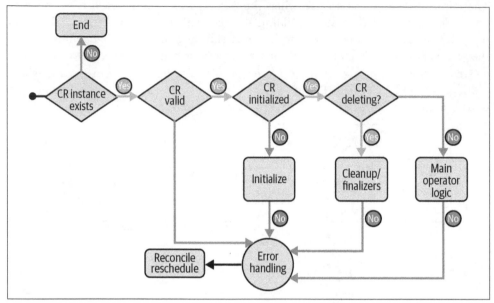

Figure 21-2. Reconciliation logic

Resource Validation

An important aspect of designing an efficient Operator is the validation of the resources being requested. As mentioned there are a few ways to validate the resource against the API specification; however, it is important to build redundancies into the process to ensure consistent behavior. The first layer of validation should be the OpenAPI validation defined in the CRD specification. This validation will prevent the CR from ever making it to the etcd server as a resource and causing detrimental aftereffects. The second layer of validation should be a validating admission controller implementation that will check the resource against the API specification through a webhook request. This again prevents the resource from ever making it into the API server. Adding some validation logic in the reconciliation loop code is also a valid strategy, but it is important to understand that it will be validation against an already existing resource in the cluster state, and therefore proper error handling needs to take place. Often this is implemented as an `IsValid` method that calls the same validation logic that the Validating Webhook implementation has.

Controller Implementation

If we continue with the example used so far, the logic for our controller will be in the following code:

```
// +kubebuilder:rbac:groups=egplatform.platform.evillgenius.com,
  resources=egapps,verbs=get;list;watch;create;update;patch;delete
// +kubebuilder:rbac:groups=egplatform.platform.evillgenius.com,
  resources=egapps/status,verbs=get;update;patch
// +kubebuilder:rbac:groups=egplatform.platform.evillgenius.com,
  resources=egapps/finalizers,verbs=update

// Reconcile is part of the main Kubernetes reconciliation loop which aims to
// move the current state of the cluster closer to the desired state.
// TODO(user): Modify the Reconcile function to compare the state specified by
// the EGApp object against the actual cluster state, and then
// perform operations to make the cluster state reflect the state specified by
// the user.
//
// For more details, check Reconcile and its Result here:
// - https://pkg.go.dev/sigs.k8s.io/controller-runtime@v0.14.1/pkg/reconcile
func (r *EGAppReconciler) Reconcile(ctx context.Context, req ctrl.Request)
  (ctrl.Result, error) {
    _ = log.FromContext(ctx)

    // TODO(user): your logic here
    logger := log.Log.WithValues("EGApp", req.NamespacedName)
    logger.Info("EGApp Reconcile started...")

    // fetch the EGApp CR instance
    egApp := &egplatformv1alpha1.EGApp{}

    err := r.Get(ctx, req.NamespacedName, egApp)
    if err != nil {
        if errors.IsNotFound(err) {
            logger.Info("EGApp resource not found. Object must be deleted")
            return ctrl.Result{}, nil
        }
        logger.Error(err, "Failed to get EGApp")
        return ctrl.Result{}, nil
    }
    // check if the deployment already exists, if not create a new one
    found := &appsv1.Deployment{}
    err = r.Get(ctx, types.NamespacedName{Name: egApp.Name, Namespace:
      egApp.Namespace}, found)
    if err != nil {
        dep := r.deploymentForEGApp(egApp)
        logger.Info("Creating a  new deployment", "Deployment.Namespace",
          dep.Namespace, "Deployment.Name", dep.Name)
        err = r.Create(ctx, dep)
        if err != nil {
            logger.Error(err, "Failed to create new deployment",
```

```
                        "Deployment.Namespace", dep.Namespace, "Deployment.Name", dep.Name)
            return ctrl.Result{}, err
        }
        return ctrl.Result{}, nil
    } else if err != nil {
        logger.Error(err, "Failed to get deployment")
        return ctrl.Result{}, nil
    }
    // This point, we have the deployment object created
    // Ensure the deployment size is same as the spec
    replicas := egApp.Spec.ReplicaCount
    if *found.Spec.Replicas != replicas {
        found.Spec.Replicas = &replicas
        err = r.Update(ctx, found)
        if err != nil {
            logger.Error(err, "Failed to update Deployment",
              "Deployment.Namespace", found.Namespace, "Deployment.Name",
              found.Name)
            return ctrl.Result{}, err
        }
        // Spec updated return and requeue
        // Requeue for any reason other than an error
        return ctrl.Result{Requeue: true}, nil
    }

    // Update the egApp status with pod names
    // List the pods for this egApp's deployment
    podList := &corev1.PodList{}
    listOpts := []client.ListOption{
        client.InNamespace(egApp.Namespace),
        client.MatchingLabels(egApp.GetLabels()),
    }

    if err = r.List(ctx, podList, listOpts...); err != nil {
        logger.Error(err, "Failed to list pods", "egApp.Namespace",
          egApp.Namespace, "egApp.Name", egApp.Name)
        return ctrl.Result{}, err
    }
    podNames := getPodNames(podList.Items)

    // Update status.Pods if needed
    if !reflect.DeepEqual(podNames, egApp.Status.Pods) {
        egApp.Status.Pods = podNames
        err := r.Status().Update(ctx, egApp)
        if err != nil {
            logger.Error(err, "Failed to update egApp status")
            return ctrl.Result{}, err
        }
    }

    return ctrl.Result{}, nil
}
```

```go
func (r *EGAppReconciler) deploymentForEGApp(m *egplatformv1alpha1.EGApp)
  *appsv1.Deployment {
    ls := m.GetLabels()
    replicas := m.Spec.ReplicaCount

    deploy := &appsv1.Deployment{
        ObjectMeta: metav1.ObjectMeta{
            Name:      m.Name,
            Namespace: m.Namespace,
        },
        Spec: appsv1.DeploymentSpec{
            Replicas: &replicas,
            Selector: &metav1.LabelSelector{
                MatchLabels: ls,
            },
            Template: corev1.PodTemplateSpec{
                ObjectMeta: metav1.ObjectMeta{
                    Labels: ls,
                },
                Spec: corev1.PodSpec{
                    Containers: []corev1.Container{{
                        Image: "gcr.io/kuar-demo/kuard-amd64:1",  // hard-coded
                          here, make this dynamic
                        Name:  m.Spec.AppId,
                        Ports: []corev1.ContainerPort{{
                            ContainerPort: 8080,
                            Name:          "http",
                        }},
                    }},
                },
            },
        },
    }
    ctrl.SetControllerReference(m, deploy, r.Scheme)
    return deploy
}

// Utility function to iterate over pods and return the names slice
func getPodNames(pods []corev1.Pod) []string {
    var podNames []string
    for _, pod := range pods {
        podNames = append(podNames, pod.Name)
    }
    return podNames
}

// SetupWithManager sets up the controller with the Manager.
func (r *EGAppReconciler) SetupWithManager(mgr ctrl.Manager) error {
    return ctrl.NewControllerManagedBy(mgr).
        For(&egplatformv1alpha1.EGApp{}).
```

```
    Complete(r)
}
```

The main steps are implemented here through the reconcile process. Two important points to reference are:

- The Custom Resource actually creates deployments. If the specific instance is not found, a deployment is created using values from the CR spec to fill in the required data. The line `ctrl.SetControllerReference(m, deploy, r.scheme)` is where ownership of the deployment is obtained by the CR. This allows for the resource to also clean up any deployments it owns when deleted.

- The status is updated on the resource with a list of pods associated with the deployment. This update is done to the `status.pods` property of the CR, which was created as a subresource on the line `err := r.Status().Update(ctx, egApp)`. This is important because it will not update the status of our resource without increasing the `ResourceGeneration` metadata field. By implementing a predicate on the watch to not trigger a reconciliation on events that did not increase the `ResourceGeneration` metadata field, we can ensure the entire loop is not repeated for a noop scenario.

Once the controller logic is implemented, to test it against the CR spec deployed earlier to the cluster, kubebuilder can run the code locally to verify all is working and then also package it as a container and deploy to the cluster when ready to operationalize.

Here is what that looks like:

```
$ make run
test -s /home/eddiejv/dev/projects/operators/platformapp/bin/controller-gen &&
/home/eddiejv/dev/projects/operators/platformapp/bin/controller-gen --version
| grep -q v0.11.1 || \
GOBIN=/home/eddiejv/dev/projects/operators/platformapp/bin go install
sigs.k8s.io/controller-tools/cmd/controller-gen@v0.11.1
/home/eddiejv/dev/projects/operators/platformapp/bin/controller-gen
rbac:roleName=manager-role crd webhook paths="./..."
output:crd:artifacts:config=config/crd/bases
/home/eddiejv/dev/projects/operators/platformapp/bin/controller-gen
object:headerFile="hack/boilerplate.go.txt" paths="./..."
go fmt ./...
go vet ./...
go run ./main.go
2023-02-24T11:07:21-06:00 INFO controller-runtime.metrics Metrics server is
  starting to listen {"addr": ":8080"}
2023-02-24T11:07:21-06:00 INFO setup starting manager
2023-02-24T11:07:21-06:00 INFO Starting server {"path": "/metrics", "kind":
  "metrics", "addr": "[::]:8080"}
2023-02-24T11:07:21-06:00 INFO Starting server {"kind": "health probe",
  "addr": "[::]:8081"}
```

```
2023-02-24T11:07:21-06:00 INFO Starting EventSource {"controller": "egapp",
  "controllerGroup": "egplatform.platform.evillgenius.com", "controllerKind":
  "EGApp", "source": "kind source: *v1alpha1.EGApp"}
2023-02-24T11:07:21-06:00 INFO Starting Controller {"controller": "egapp",
  "controllerGroup": "egplatform.platform.evillgenius.com", "controllerKind":
  "EGApp"}
2023-02-24T11:07:21-06:00 INFO Starting workers {"controller": "egapp",
  "controllerGroup": "egplatform.platform.evillgenius.com", "controllerKind":
  "EGApp", "worker count": 1}
```

The logs show that the controller is up and listening for events. Then a CR was deployed to the cluster using:

```
apiVersion: egplatform.platform.evillgenius.com/v1alpha1
kind: EGApp
metadata:
  labels:
    app.Kubernetes.io/name: egapp
    app.Kubernetes.io/instance: egapp-sample
    app.Kubernetes.io/part-of: pe-app
    app.Kubernetes.io/managed-by: kustomize
    app.Kubernetes.io/created-by: pe-app
  name: egapp-sample
spec:
  appId: egapp-sample
  framework: go
  instanceType: lowMem
  environment: dev
  replicaCount: 2
```

The controller log shows the reconciliation loop starting, and because a deployment did not exist it created the deployment:

```
2023-02-24T11:12:46-06:00 INFO EGApp Reconcile started... {"EGApp":
  "default/egapp-sample"}
2023-02-24T11:12:46-06:00 INFO Creating a  new deployment {"EGApp":
  "default/egapp-sample", "Deployment.Namespace": "default", "Deployment.Name":
  "egapp-sample"}
```

Then a `kubectl delete` was called on the instance and the controller began another reconciliation loop and deleted the object:

```
2023-02-24T11:21:39-06:00 INFO EGApp Reconcile started... {"EGApp":
  "default/egapp-sample"}
2023-02-24T11:21:39-06:00 INFO EGApp resource not found. Object must
  be deleted {"EGApp": "default/egapp-sample"}
```

Much more can be done within the context of the controller and API itself, for example, implementing complex logic around cleanup, such as calling backups, rebalancing workloads across nodes, scaling with custom logic, etc. This is where an engineer's deep knowledge of how a system should behave, how it should be deployed, and how to react in case of a problem is codified. The whole premise of the benefits of the Operator pattern is encapsulated in this code example.

Operator Life Cycle

The development of an Operator is not an easy undertaking, but it does not have to answer all the operational problems of the application. Development should focus on the big hurdles and then iterate through versions to enhance the Operator's capabilities over time. The team at CoreOS and RedHat put together a solid spectrum of capabilities they call Operator Capability Levels (*https://oreil.ly/X_Lun*) that outline some of the main concerns the Operator should tackle when maturing through the levels. These are:

Basic install
Automated application provisioning and configuration management

Seamless upgrades
Patch and minor version upgrades are supported

Full life cycle
App life cycle, storage life cycle (backup, failure recovery)

Deep insights
Metrics, alerts, log processing and workload analysis

Auto pilot
Horizontal/vertical scaling, auto config tuning, abnormal detection, scheduling tuning

This is a solid framework for planning the life of an Operator that will progress over time. The focus is that the Operator should be treated like any piece of software with defined life cycle, product management, deprecation policies, and clear and consistent versioning.

Version Upgrades

In our example we started with `v1alphav1` as our stated version supported in the CRD. Through the life cycle of the Operator there may be a need to support multiple versions depending on the stage and stability of the API.

When a new version is introduced, a process should be followed carefully to ensure that issues will not arise with existing resources. A Custom Resource object will need the ability to be served by all defined versions of the CRD. That means there could be a mismatch between the version being served and the one stored in state. A conversion process should be implemented on the Custom Resource object to be converted between the version stored and the version that is served. When the conversion involves schema changes or custom logic, a conversion webhook can be used to make the required updates. The default None conversion strategy is used when there are no schema or custom logic is needed as only the apiVersion field will be changed.

You will add a conversion strategy field to the CRD and point it to the webhook listening for the specific resource. This would look like:

```
apiVersion: apiextensions.k8s.io/v1
kind: CustomResourceDefinition
...
spec:
  ...
  conversion:
    strategy: Webhook
    webhook:
      clientConfig:
        service:
          namespace: egapp-conversion
          name: egapp
          path: /egapp-conversion
          port: 8081
        caBundle: "Hf8j0Kw...<base64-encoded PEM bundle>...tLS0K"
...
```

Operator Best Practices

The development and ongoing upkeep of an Operator is no small endeavor and should be thought about and planned very carefully. Many times it is easier to package an application using simpler paradigms such as Helm charts, Kustomize repositories, or Terraform modules. When it becomes important to include special reconciliation logic to maintain the application or ease the burden for the users of the application, then an Operator pattern may make sense. If you decide to build an Operator then best practice guidelines are:

- Do not overload an Operator to manage more than a single application, and own each CRD it controls.
- If your Operator manages multiple CRDs then the Operator should also have multiple controllers. Keep it simple: one controller for each CRD.
- Operators should not be specific to the namespace they are watching resources in and also should not be specific to the namespace they will be deployed in.
- Operators should be versioned using semantic versioning (*https://semver.org*), and as extensions of the Kubernetes API, they should also follow the Kubernetes API versioning guidelines (*https://oreil.ly/O-5lH*) as they relate to version changes.

- CRDs should follow the OpenAPI spec to allow for a known schema. Most Operator SDK-based tooling will provide a method to create boilerplate CRDs based on the OpenAPI spec to make them easier to develop.

- As with any Kubernetes service the Operator itself should follow sound security guidelines such as run as non-root, least privilege RBAC, and observability. Metrics and logs should be external to the system. The Operator should be instrumented to allow for visibility into the Operator's health and any known Service Level Indicators (SLIs). Metric exports such as Prometheus, DataDog, Cloud Operations, and OpenTelemetry can all be leveraged.

- Operators do not install other Operators and should not register their own CRDs as those resources are global to the cluster and would require escalated privileges for the Operator.

- Check all CRDs for validity before accepting the request. The CRDs could be validated against a known schema such as an OpenAPI validation schema or through an admission controller that can validate the CRD. These methods will prevent the resource from wasting space on etcd as it will not be submitted to the API. There should also be some validation logic within the reconciliation cycle as a last effort to validate and clean up the resource.

- The Operator should be self-cleaning when no longer needed. Proper resource clean up after deletion is important, not only for direct resources created by the Operator but also for any external resources that may have been created in support of the application requirements of the Operator (e.g., PVs for storage attached to pods as needed by the application, external resources to the cluster, etc.).

- Think carefully about the life cycle of the Operator and when breaking changes are introduced to the upgrade path for existing users of the prior versions. Implement conversion webhooks to allow the conversion to and from a specific version to ensure there is no loss of information converting a resource from a vX to a vY and back to vX.

- Be thoughtful on the status information written to the resources managed by the Operator. The customer resource is the only interface to the user to understand the state of the resource. By having a status that is clear and concise written to the resource by the controller the user can easily use the existing Kubernetes client tooling to query and act on the status as desired. Status should be implemented as a subresource, and a predicate should be used so as not to trigger a reconciliation loop after an update that did not increase the `ResourceGeneration` metadata field of the main resource.

Summary

The promise of fully automated deployment and "day 2" operations for an application has driven the Operator market beyond just experimental to become a key feature in the Kubernetes ecosystem. Operators should be used when complex applications are needed to support an organization's business, but be careful in creating them when easier mechanisms exist. Leverage existing Operators created by software vendors that help support and maintain them, many of which can be found on operatorhub.io (*https://oreil.ly/wMLSA*). While the Operator pattern can be a very powerful tool, it requires commitment to ensure that it doesn't create more problems than it can solve. All warnings aside, if you are building a large application platform based on Kubernetes the Operator pattern should be front and center in reducing operator toil.

## CHAPTER 22

Conclusion

The primary strength of Kubernetes is its modularity and generality. Nearly every kind of application that you might want to deploy you can fit within Kubernetes, and no matter what kind of adjustments or tuning you need to make to your system, they're generally possible.

Of course, this modularity and generality come at a cost, and that cost is a reasonable amount of complexity. Understanding how the APIs and components of Kubernetes work is critical to successfully unlocking the power of Kubernetes to make your application development, management, and deployment easier and more reliable.

Likewise, understanding how to connect Kubernetes to a wide variety of external systems like on-premise databases and continuous delivery systems is critical to efficiently using Kubernetes in the real world.

Throughout this book we have worked to provide insights from concrete, real-world experience on specific topics that you will likely encounter whether you are a newcomer to Kubernetes or an experienced administrator. Regardless of whether you are facing a new area where you're working to become an expert, or you simply want a refresher about how others have addressed a familiar problem, our goal is that the chapters in this book have enabled you to learn from our experience. It is our hope that you can consult this book throughout your Kubernetes journey and quickly flick to a chapter and have a handful of best practices accessible at your fingertips.

By following these best practices, you can leverage our combined experience to help avoid common pitfalls, optimize performance and security, and quickly grow in confidence to get the most out of Kubernetes. Thank you, and we look forward to seeing you out in the real world!

Index

A

ABAC (Attribute-Based Access Control), 232-233
access control, 10
    RBAC (see RBAC)
activating Pod Security, 149-150
active controller-based services, 182-183
admission controllers, 153, 205-206
    best practices, 228-230
    configuring admission webhooks, 226-228
    purpose of, 224-225
    types of, 225
    workload security, 249
admission webhooks
    best practices, 229-230
    configuring, 226-228
alert thresholds, 53
alerting
    best practices, 55
    when to alert, 53-54
algorithm development phase (machine learning), 191
anti-affinity rules, 109-110
API request flow, 223, 231
APIs (application programming interfaces), creating, 270-276
AppArmor, 249
application container logs, 49
application example
    authentication management, 9-12
    CI/CD workflow, 81-85
    configuration file management, 2-3
    configuring with ConfigMaps, 8-9
    external ingress setup, 6-8
    list of components, 1
    parameterization with Helm, 19-20
    replicated service creation, 3-6
    stateful database deployment, 12-16
    static file server setup, 17-19
    TCP load balancer creation, 16-17
application scaling, 121
ArgoCD, 244
assigning namespaces, 30-31
audit logs, 49, 247, 250
authentication
    cluster security, 246
    with secrets, 9-12
authorization
    in API request flow, 231
    best practices, 234
    cluster security, 246
    modules
        ABAC, 232-233
        list of, 231-232
        webhook, 233
autoscaling, 120-121, 199
AWS Container Insights, 44
Azure Monitor, 43

B

best practices
    admission controllers, 228-230
    alerting, 55
    authorization, 234
    CI/CD workflow, 85-86
    cluster security, 248
    CNI plug-in, 130
    code security, 252

ConfigMaps, 9, 59-64
connecting services, 188
deployments, 21
development clusters, 34-35
GitOps, 244
global distribution, 105
higher-level abstractions, 209
image management, 4
Kubenet, 129
logging, 55
machine learning, 199-200
monitoring, 54
multiple cluster management, 176-177
network security policies, 142-143
Operators, 285-286
policy and governance, 164
RBAC (Role Based Access Control), 68-69
resource management, 124
secrets, 59-65
service meshes, 145
services/ingress controllers, 139
stateful applications, 221
stateful services, 13
storage, 216-217
version control, 6
versioning/releases/rollouts, 93-94
volumes, 213
workload container security, 251-251
workload isolation/RuntimeClass, 152
binding
    secrets, 10
    users to namespaces, 29-30
blue/green deployments, 78
bounded time to live (TTL) namespaces, 30
burstable QoS, 114

C

cAdvisor, 39
canary deployments, 79-80
canary regions, 102
CD (continuous delivery)
    multiple clusters, 171
    setting up, 84
    testing, importance of, 75
certificates for shared development clusters,
    26-28
chaos engineering, 80, 85
chaos testing
    application operation, 258

communication, 257
    goals of, 256
    prerequisites, 256-257
    purpose of, 255
Chaos Toolkit, 85
checkpoints, 198
CI (continuous integration), 72, 81-84
CI/CD (continuous integration/continuous
    delivery), 6
    application example, 81-85
    best practices, 85-86
    continuous deployment in, 75
    continuous integration in, 72
    deployment strategies, 75-80
    image size optimization, 73-74
    image tagging, 74-75
    purpose of, 71
    testing in, 73
    version control, 72
closed-box monitoring, 37
cloud metadata access, 247
cloud native policy engine, 156
cloud provider monitoring tools, 43
CloudWatch Container Insights, 44
Cluster API, 171
cluster daemons, 187
cluster-level services, 31
ClusterIP service type, 131-132
clusters
    components of, 39
    development (see development clusters)
    extending, 205-206
    mixed workload, 200
    multiple (see multiple clusters)
    scaling, 120-121
    security, 246-248
CNAME-based services, 181-182
CNI (Container Network Interface) plug-in,
    129-130
code review, 3
code security, 251-253
Codefresh, 244
comments, 5
communication, chaos testing of, 257
compliance with multiple clusters, 168
ConfigMaps resource, 8-9, 58, 59-64
configuration drift, 75
configuration files, managing, 2-3
configurations, passwords as, 10

configuring
    admission webhooks, 226-228
    with ConfigMaps, 8-9, 58
    Flux, 241-243
    with secrets, 58-59
constraint templates, 156, 157-159
constraints
    defining, 159-160
    in machine learning, 195
    purpose of, 157
container runtime security, 150-152
container-to-container communication, 126
containerized development, 207
containers
    exporting to, 208
    image size optimization, 73-74
    image tagging, 74-75
controller implementation, 279-284
controller reconciliation, 277-278
CRDs (custom resource definitions)
    allocating namespaces, 31
    definition of, 172
    dynamically adding resources, 206
    Operators and, 268
CSI (Container Storage Interface) drivers, 11, 216
custom controllers, 172
Custom Metrics API, 40

D

Dapr (Distributed Application Runtime), 205
data replication, 160, 170
data scientist tools, 199
databases, stateful deployment, 12-16
Datadog, 43
dataset preparation phase (machine learning), 191
datasets for machine learning, 197
debugging development clusters, 34
declarative approach, 2
deep learning (see machine learning)
dependencies, installing, 32-33
deploying
    best practices, 21
    parameterization with Helm, 19-20
    stateful databases, 12-16
Deployment resource, 4-6
    adding Volumes to, 10
    rolling out, 33

    static file server setup, 17
    versioning/releases/rollouts example, 90-93
deployment strategies, 75-80
deployments
    multiple clusters, managing, 171-173
    parameterizing, 97-98
    replicated service creation, 3-6
    traditional workflow, 237
designing
    higher-level abstractions, 208-209
    multiple clusters, 169-171
developer workflows (see development clusters)
developing phase (development clusters), 24
development clusters
    best practices, 34-35
    dependencies, installing, 32-33
    Deployment resource, rolling out, 33
    goals of, 23-24
    purpose of, 23
    shared
        multiple clusters versus, 24-25
        setting up, 25-31
    testing/debugging, 34
directory organization, 3
distributed training, 195, 200
distribution, global (see global distribution)
distroless images, 73, 251
DNS names, 181-182
docker-registry secrets, 58
drivers for machine learning, 197
Drone, 81
dynamic admission controllers, 225

E

enabling Pod Security Admission controller, 148
encryption, 11
enforcement actions, 161-163
environment variables with Config-Maps/secrets, 61-64
etcd access, 246
evicting pods, 115-116
experiments
    goals of, 263-264
    prerequisites, 264
    purpose of, 263
    setting up, 264-265
exporting
    to container images, 208

services, 183-184
  best practices, 188
  integration with external machines,
    185-186
  with internal load balancers, 184
  with NodePorts, 184-185
exposing services, 209
extending
  clusters, 205-206
  user experience, 206-207
external ingress setup for HTTP traffic, 6-8
external services, importing, 179-180
  active controller-based services, 182-183
  best practices, 188
  CNAME-based services, 181-182
  selector-less services, 180-181
ExternalName service type, 134

F

Falco, 153
feature flags, 99, 264
Federation, 176
filesystems, directory organization, 3
flaky tests, 24
FlexVolume plug-in, 216
Flux
  configuring, 241-243
  purpose of, 243
Four Golden Signals (Google), 39
fuzz testing, 259

G

Gardener, 175
Gatekeeper, 156
  constraint templates, 158-159
  constraints, 159-160
  data replication, 160
  demonstration, 163
  enforcement actions/audit, 161-163
  example policies, 157
  mutation policies, 163
  terminology, 157
  testing policies, 163
  violation feedback, 161
Gateway API for Kubernetes, 7, 137-139
GCP Stackdriver, 43
generic secrets, 58
geo-replication, 96
GeoDNS, 97

Git, 3, 72
GitHub, 3
GitOps, 6
  benefits of, 237-238
  best practices, 244
  Flux configuration, 241-243
  multiple cluster management, 173-175
  purpose of, 235-236
  repo structure, 238-240
  secrets management, 240-241
  tools for, 243
  workflow, 236-237
global distribution
  best practices, 105
  image distribution stage, 96-97
  load balancing, 98
  parameterizing deployments, 97-98
  reasons for, 95
  rollouts, 98-99
    canary regions, 102
    planning, 103-104
    pre-rollout validation, 99-102
    region types, 103
    troubleshooting, 104-105
governance (see policy and governance)
Grafana, 46-47
Gremlin, 85
groups, 269
guaranteed QoS, 114

H

hard multitenancy, 168
hardware for machine learning, 196-197
Harness, 244
Headlamp project, 207
headless Services, 16
Helm, 19-20
higher-level abstractions
  best practices, 209
  designing, 208-209
  development approaches, 203-204
  extending Kubernetes
    clusters, 205-206
    containerized development, 207
    "push to deploy" experience, 207
    user experience, 206-207
HPA (Horizontal Pod Autoscaler), 122
HTTP requests, external ingress setup, 6-8
hyperparameter tuning, 192

I

IaC (Infrastructure as Code) tools, 170
identity management for shared development
    clusters, 26-28
image management
    best practices, 4
    exporting to container images, 208
    global distribution, 96-97
    size optimization, 73-74
    tagging, 74-75
    vulnerability scanning, 252
imperative approach, 2
importing services, 179-180
    active controller-based services, 182-183
    best practices, 188
    CNAME-based services, 181-182
    selector-less services, 180-181
indentation in YAML, 2
InfluxDB, 43
Infrastructure as Code (IaC) tools, 170
infrastructure as Software, 171
Ingress API, 136
    challenges with, 137
    HTTP load balancing, 6-8
    static file server setup, 17-19
ingress controllers, 136, 139
installing
    dependencies, 32-33
    kube-prometheus-stack chart, 46
    minikube, 46, 241
    Prometheus, 45
integrating external machines with Kubernetes,
    185-186
integration testing, 99-100
internal load balancers, 184
internal services, exporting, 183-184
    best practices, 188
    integration with external machines, 185-186
    with internal load balancers, 184
    with NodePorts, 184-185
intrusion and anomaly detection, 153
involuntary evictions, 115
IP addresses for selector-less services, 180-181

J

journal service example (see application exam-
    ple)
JSON, syntax support, 2

K

kernel modules for machine learning, 197
Kinds, 270
kube-prometheus-stack chart, installing, 46
kube-state-metrics, 40-41
kube-system namespace, 230
kubeconfig files, 26
kubectl command, 34
Kubeflow, 199
Kubelet, 247
KubeMonkey, 85
Kubenet, 129
Kubernetes control plane logs, 49
Kubernetes Secrets, 240

L

labels, 89
    activating Pod Security, 149-150
    for deployments, 5
libraries for machine learning, 197
life cycle of Operators, 284
LimitRanges, 119
limits (resource management), 113
linear scaling, 200
linters, 206
load balancers
    creating with Services, 16-17
    internal, 184
load balancing, 6-8, 98
load testing, 100-102, 262
    application tuning with, 262-263
    goals of, 259-260
    prerequisites, 260-261
    purpose of, 259
    traffic generation, 261
LoadBalancer service type, 134
logging, 247, 250
    best practices, 55
    defined, 37
    with Loki-Stack, 50-52
    retention/archival process, 48
    tools for, 49
    what to log, 48-49
Logging as a Service (LaaS), 31
Loki-Stack, 50-52

M

machine learning

advantages of Kubernetes, 189-190
best practices, 199-200
data scientist tools, 199
distributed training, 195
libraries/drivers/kernel modules, 197
model training, 192-195
networking, 198
resource constraints, 195
specialized hardware for, 196-197
specialized protocols for, 198
storage, 197
workflow, 190-191
Message Passing Interface (MPI), 199
metrics
    with cAdvisor, 39
    defined, 37
    with kube-state-metrics, 40-41
    in load testing, 101-102
    with metrics server, 40
    scaling with, 123
    what to monitor, 41-42
Metrics Server API, 40
Microsoft Azure Monitor, 43
minikube, installing, 46, 241
mixed workload clusters, 200
model training, 192-195
monitoring
    best practices, 54
    with cAdvisor, 39
    closed-box monitoring, 37
    with kube-state-metrics, 40-41
    with metrics server, 40
    open-box monitoring, 38
    patterns of, 38-39
    with Prometheus, 44-48
    tools for, 42-44
    what to monitor, 41-42
mounting volumes as ConfigMaps/secrets,
    59-61
Multi-Cluster Service API, 187
multicast IP addresses, 97
multiple clusters
    designing, 169-171
    Federation, 176
    managing
        best practices, 176-177
        deployments, 171-173
        GitOps, 173-175
        tools for, 175-176
    reasons for using, 167-169
    shared clusters versus, 24-25
multistage builds, 73
multitenancy, hard, 168
mutation policies, 163

N
namespaces
    activating Pod Security, 149-150
    creating/securing, 29-30
    managing, 30-31
    purpose of, 25
    resource management with, 116-117
network policies, workload security, 250
networking
    container-to-container communication, 126
    for machine learning, 198
    plug-ins, 128-130
    pod-to-pod communication, 126
    security policies, 140-143
    service meshes, 143-145, 187
    service-to-pod communication, 127
    services
        best practices, 139
        best practices for connecting, 188
        ClusterIP, 131-132
        exporting, 183-186
        ExternalName, 134
        Gateway API, 137-139
        importing, 179-183
        Ingress API/ingress controllers, 136
        LoadBalancer, 134
        NodePort, 132
        purpose of, 130-131
NetworkPolicy API, 140-143
node logs, 48
NodePort service type, 132, 184-185
nodeSelectors, 110
non-root containers, 251
NVIDIA Collective Communications Library
    (NCCL), 199

O
objects (Kubernetes), 268
OCM (Open Cluster Management), 175
onboarding phase (development clusters), 23,
    26-28
OPA (Open Policy Agent), 156
open-box monitoring, 38

OpenSSF Scorecard, 252
operational management of multiple clusters, 170
Operator pattern, 172-173
Operators, 220-221
    API creation, 270-276
    best practices, 285-286
    components of, 268-270
    controller implementation, 279-284
    controller reconciliation, 277-278
    life cycle of, 284
    purpose of, 267
    resource validation, 278
    version upgrades, 284
    workload security, 249
optimized base images, 74
optimizing images, 73-74

P

Pachyderm, 199
parameterization, 10
    for global distributions, 97-98
    with Helm, 19-20
passwords, as configurations, 10
PersistentVolumeClaims resource, 214
PersistentVolumes resource, 12-16, 213
planning global distribution rollouts, 103-104
platforms (see higher-level abstractions)
plug-ins for networking, 128-130
pod affinity rules, 109-110
pod eviction, 115-116
Pod Security Admission controller, 147-150, 249
    activating with namespace labels, 149-150
    enabling, 148
    security levels, 148-149
pod-to-pod communication, 126
PodDisruptionBudgets, 115-116
PodSecurityPolicy API, 147
policy and governance
    admission controllers, 224
    best practices, 164
    cloud native policy engine, 156
    Gatekeeper, 156
        constraint templates, 158-159
        constraints, 159-160
        data replication, 160
        demonstration, 163
        enforcement actions/audit, 161-163

example policies, 157
        mutation policies, 163
        terminology, 157
        testing policies, 163
        violation feedback, 161
    importance of, 155
    network policies, 250
    network security, 140-143
    purpose of, 155
Polyaxon, 199
PowerfulSeal, 85
predicates, 107
predictive load testing, 260
prerequisites
    chaos testing, 256-257
    experiments, 264
    load testing, 260-261
preStop life-cycle hooks, 76
priorities (in scheduling), 108
production, testing in, 80-81
Prometheus, 42, 44-48
"push to deploy" experience, 207

Q

QoS (Quality of Service), 114

R

Rancher, 175
RBAC (Role Based Access Control)
    best practices, 68-69
    components of, 66-67
readiness probes, 76
reconciliation, 277-278
RED method (monitoring), 38
Redis database
    authentication management, 9-12
    stateful deployment, 12-16
regional distribution, 169
Rego, 157
regression prevention, 260
releases, 88-89
    best practices, 93-94
    example, 90-93
ReplicaSet resource, 4, 217
replicated services, creating with deployments, 3-6
repositories
    GitOps structure, 238-240
    security, 252

request flow, 223, 231
requests (for resources), 112-113
resource constraints in machine learning, 195
resource management
    admission controllers, 225
    best practices, 124
    importance of, 112
    LimitRanges, 119
    limits, 5-6, 113
    namespaces, 116-117
    PodDisruptionBudgets, 115-116
    QoS (Quality of Service), 114
    requests, 112-113
    ResourceQuotas, 117-119
    scaling
        application scaling, 121
        cluster scaling, 120-121
        with custom metrics, 123
        with HPA, 122
        with VPA, 123
    scheduling
        nodeSelectors, 110
        pod affinity/anti-affinity, 109-110
        predicates, 107
        priorities, 108
        taints/tolerations, 110-112
ResourceQuotas, 117-119
resources
    Kinds versus, 270
    purpose of, 269
    validating, 278
retention/archival process for logging, 48
RoleBinding objects, 29, 67
roles (RBAC), 67
rolling updates, 75-78, 84
rollouts
    best practices, 93-94
    Deployment resource, 33
    example, 90-93
    global, 98-99
        canary regions, 102
        planning, 103-104
        pre-rollout validation, 99-102
        region types, 103
rules (RBAC), 67
runtime security, 250
RuntimeClass, 150-152

S

saving machine learning models, 198
scaling
    applications, 121
    clusters, 120-121
    with custom metrics, 123
    with HPA, 122
    linear, 200
    with VPA, 123
scheduling
    machine learning, 196
    nodeSelectors, 110
    pod affinity/anti-affinity, 109-110
    predicates, 107
    priorities, 108
    taints/tolerations, 110-112
Sealed Secrets, 241
Seccomp, 249
Secret resource, 10
secrets
    authentication management with, 9-12
    best practices, 59-65
    binding, 10
    configuring with, 58-59
    encryption, 11
secrets management
    cluster security, 247
    in GitOps, 240-241
security
    admission controllers, 153, 224
    clusters, 246-248
    code security, 251-253
    intrusion and anomaly detection, 153
    multiple clusters, 168
    namespaces, 29-30
    network policies, 140-143
    Pod Security Admission controller, 147-150
        activating with namespace labels,
            149-150
        enabling, 148
        security levels, 148-149
    strategies for, 245
    workload containers, 248-251
    workload isolation/RuntimeClass, 150-152
selector-less services, 180-181
self-testing, 102
SELinux, 249
semantic versioning, 88
service accounts, 67

service discovery, 170, 209
Service Mesh Interface (SMI), 144
service meshes, 143-145, 187, 265
Service resource, 7
  static file server setup, 18
  TCP load balancer creation, 16-17
Service-Level Objectives (SLOs), 53
services
  best practices, 139
  ClusterIP, 131-132
  exporting, 183-184
    best practices, 188
    integration with external machines, 185-186
    with internal load balancers, 184
    with NodePorts, 184-185
  exposing, 209
  ExternalName, 134
  Gateway API, 137-139
  importing, 179-180
    active controller-based services, 182-183
    best, 188
    CNAME-based services, 181-182
    selector-less services, 180-181
  Ingress API/ingress controllers, 136
  LoadBalancer, 134
  NodePort, 132
  purpose of, 130-131
  sharing, 186-187
    best practices, 188
serving phase (machine learning), 191
shared development clusters
  multiple clusters versus, 24-25
  setting up
    cluster-level services, 31
    creating/securing namespaces, 29-30
    managing namespaces, 30-31
    onboarding users, 26-28
sharing services, 186-187
  best practices, 188
sidecar proxies, 144, 205
SLOs (Service-Level Objectives), 53
SLSA (Supply-Chain Levels for Software Artifacts), 252
SMI (Service Mesh Interface), 144
source control (see version control)
specialized hardware (machine learning), 196-197
specialized protocols (machine learning), 198

specialized workloads, 169
Stackdriver Kubernetes Engine Monitoring, 43
staging, testing in, 81
standard admission controllers, 225
state management
  importance of, 211
  stateful applications
    best practices, 221
    Operators, 220
    ReplicaSets, 217
    StatefulSets, 218-219
  storage
    best practices, 216-217
    CSI (Container Storage Interface) plug-in, 216
    FlexVolume plug-in, 216
    PersistentVolumeClaims resource, 214
    PersistentVolumes resource, 213
    StorageClasses resource, 215
  volumes, 212-213
stateful applications
  best practices, 221
  Operators, 220
  ReplicaSets, 217
  StatefulSets, 218-219
stateful deployment, 12-16
StatefulSet resource, 13, 218-219, 221
stateless, 4
static file server setup, 17-19
storage
  best practices, 216-217
  CSI (Container Storage Interface) plug-in, 216
  FlexVolume plug-in, 216
  for machine learning, 197
  PersistentVolumeClaims resource, 214
  PersistentVolumes resource, 213
  StorageClasses resource, 215
StorageClasses resource, 215
subjects (RBAC), 66
supply-chain attacks, 4
Supply-Chain Levels for Software Artifacts (SLSA), 252
Sysdig Monitor, 43

T

tagging images, 74-75
taint-based eviction, 112
taints, 110-112

TCP load balancers, creating with Services, 16-17
templating systems, 19
test flakiness, 24
testing
    chaos testing
        application operation, 258
        communication, 257
        goals of, 256
        prerequisites, 256-257
        purpose of, 255
    in CI/CD pipeline, 73
    development clusters, 34
    experiments
        goals of, 263-264
        prerequisites, 264
        purpose of, 263
        setting up, 264-265
    fuzz testing, 259
    load testing, 262
        application tuning with, 262-263
        goals of, 259-260
        prerequisites, 260-261
        purpose of, 259
        traffic generation, 261
    policies, 163
    pre-rollout validation, 99-102
    in production, 80-81
    in staging, 81
testing phase (development clusters), 24
tls secrets, 59
TLS security, 247
tolerations, 110-112
ToxiProxy, 257
traditional deployment workflow, 237
traffic generation for load testing, 261
training phase (machine learning), 191-195
troubleshooting global distributions, 104-105
tuning with load testing, 262-263

U
USE method (monitoring), 38
user experience, extending, 206-207
users
    assigning namespaces, 30-31
    binding to namespaces, 29-30
    onboarding, 26-28

V
validating resources, 278
version control
    best practices, 6
    CI/CD, 72
    declarative state, 3
version upgrades, 284
versioning, 269
    best practices, 93-94
    example, 90-93
    semantic, 88
Virtual Clusters, 169
Visual Studio (VS) Code for Kubernetes, 34
volumes
    adding to Deployments, 10
    mounting ConfigMaps/secrets as, 59-61
    state management, 212-213
voluntary evictions, 115
VPA (Vertical Pod Autoscaler), 123
vulnerability scanning, 252

W
webhook authorization module, 233
workload isolation, 150-152
workload security, 248-251
worldwide distribution (see global distribution)

Y
YAML, syntax support, 2

About the Authors

Brendan Burns is a distinguished engineer at Microsoft Azure and cofounder of the Kubernetes open source project. He's been building cloud applications for more than a decade.

Eddie Villalba is the engineering manager and application platform practice lead for North America at Google Cloud. He leads a team of engineers that focus on helping customers build container-optimized platforms for scalable, reliable distributed applications.

Dave Strebel is a global cloud native architect at Microsoft Azure focusing on open source cloud and Kubernetes. He's deeply involved in the Kubernetes open source project, helping with the Kubernetes release team and leading SIG-Azure.

Lachlan Evenson is a principal program manager on the container compute team at Microsoft Azure. He's helped numerous people onboard to Kubernetes through both hands-on teaching and conference talks.

Colophon

The animal on the cover of *Kubernetes Best Practices* is an Old World mallard duck (*Anas platyrhynchos*), a kind of dabbling duck that feeds on the surface of water rather than diving for food. Species of *Anas* are typically separated by their ranges and behavioral cues; however, mallards frequently interbreed with other species, which has introduced some fully fertile hybrids.

Mallard ducklings are precocial and capable of swimming as soon as they hatch. Juveniles begin flying between three and four months of age. They reach full maturity at 14 months and have an average life expectancy of 3 years.

The mallard is a medium-sized duck that is just slightly heavier than most dabbling ducks. Adults average 23 inches long with a wingspan of 36 inches, and weigh 2.5 pounds. Ducklings have yellow and black plumage. At around six months of age, males and females can be distinguished visually as their coloring changes. Males have green head feathers, a white collar, purple-brown breast, gray-brown wings, and a yellowish-orange bill. Females are mottled brown, which is the color of most female dabbling ducks.

Mallards have a wide range of habitats across both northern and southern hemispheres. They are found in fresh- and salt-water wetlands, from lakes to rivers to seashores. Northern mallards are migratory and winter father south. The mallard diet is highly variable and includes plants, seeds, roots, gastropods, invertebrates, and crustaceans.

Brood parasites will target mallard nests. These are species of other birds who may lay their eggs in the mallard nest. If the eggs resemble those of the mallard, the mallard will accept them and raise the hatchlings with their own.

Mallards must contend with a wide variety of predators, most notably foxes and birds of prey such as falcons and eagles. They have also been preyed upon by catfish and pike. Crows, swans, and geese have all been known to attack the ducks over territorial disputes. Unihemispheric sleep (or sleeping with one eye open), which allows one hemisphere of the brain to sleep while the other is awake, was first noted in mallards. It is common among aquatic birds as a predation-avoidance behavior.

Many of the animals on O'Reilly covers are endangered; all of them are important to the world.

The cover illustration is by Jose Marzan, based on a black and white engraving from *The Animal World*. The cover fonts are Gilroy Semibold and Guardian Sans. The text font is Adobe Minion Pro; the heading font is Adobe Myriad Condensed; and the code font is Dalton Maag's Ubuntu Mono.

Printed in the USA
CPSIA information can be obtained
at www.ICGtesting.com
JSHW051512111223
53613JS00013B/135